Industrial Drawing

[redacted]

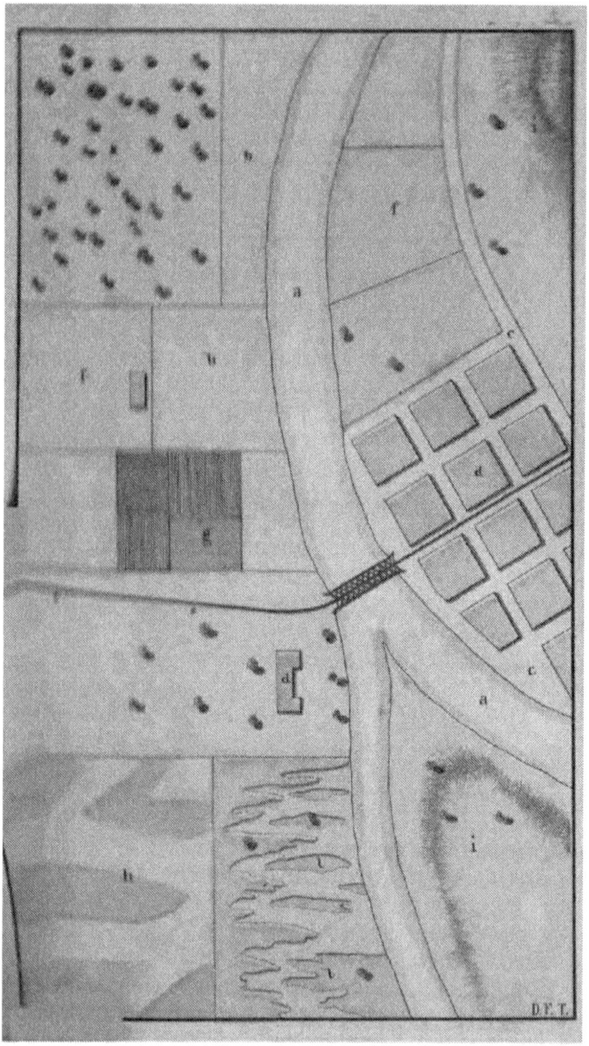
D.F.T.

INDUSTRIAL DRAWING:

COMPRISING

THE DESCRIPTION AND USES

OF

DRAWING INSTRUMENTS,

THE CONSTRUCTION OF PLANE FIGURES,

TINTING,

THE PROJECTIONS AND SECTIONS OF GEOMETRICAL SOLIDS, SHADOWS,
SHADING, ISOMETRICAL DRAWING, OBLIQUE PROJECTION,
PERSPECTIVE, ARCHITECTURAL ELEMENTS,

MECHANICAL AND TOPOGRAPHICAL DRAWING.

FOR THE USE OF HIGH SCHOOLS, ACADEMIES, AND SCIENTIFIC SCHOOLS.

By D. H. MAHAN, LL.D.,
LATE PROFESSOR OF CIVIL ENGINEERING, ETC., IN THE UNITED STATES
MILITARY ACADEMY.

REVISED AND ENLARGED

BY

DWINEL F. THOMPSON, B.S.,
PROFESSOR OF DESCRIPTIVE GEOMETRY, STEREOTOMY, AND DRAWING IN THE
RENSSELAER POLYTECHNIC INSTITUTE, TROY, N. Y.

FIFTH THOUSAND.

NEW YORK
JOHN WILEY & SONS
LONDON
CHAPMAN & HALL, LTD
1911

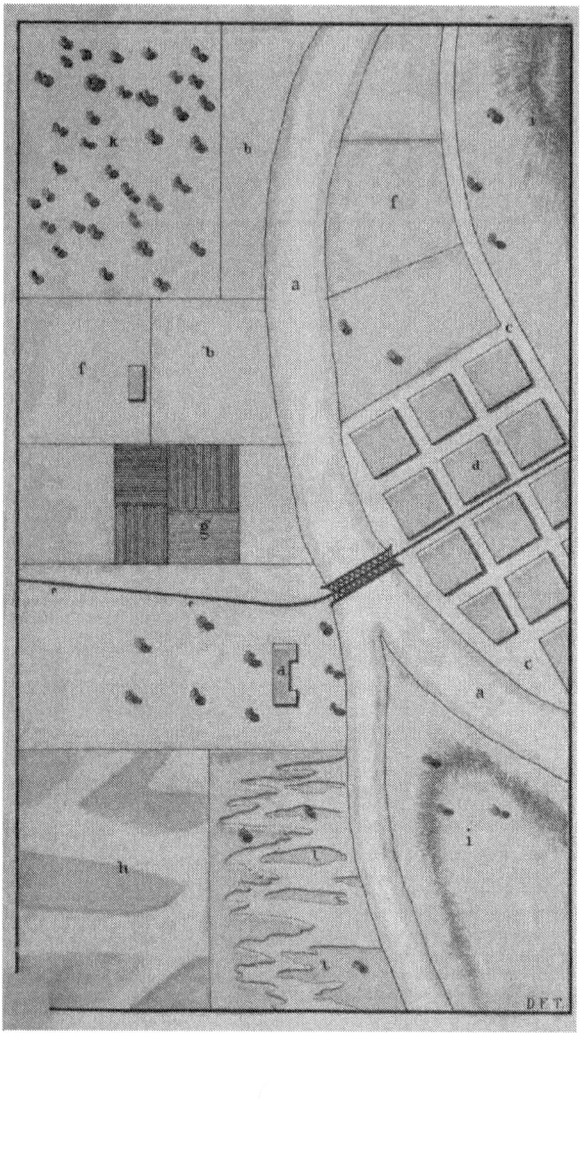
k
b
f
b
a
c
d
g
d
c
a
h
i
D.F.T.

INDUSTRIAL DRAWING:

COMPRISING

THE DESCRIPTION AND USES

OF

DRAWING INSTRUMENTS,

THE CONSTRUCTION OF PLANE FIGURES,

TINTING,

THE PROJECTIONS AND SECTIONS OF GEOMETRICAL SOLIDS, SHADOWS, SHADING, ISOMETRICAL DRAWING, OBLIQUE PROJECTION, PERSPECTIVE, ARCHITECTURAL ELEMENTS,

MECHANICAL AND TOPOGRAPHICAL DRAWING.

FOR THE USE OF HIGH SCHOOLS, ACADEMIES, AND SCIENTIFIC SCHOOLS.

BY D. H. MAHAN, LL.D.,

LATE PROFESSOR OF CIVIL ENGINEERING, ETC., IN THE UNITED STATES MILITARY ACADEMY.

REVISED AND ENLARGED

BY

DWINEL F. THOMPSON, B.S.,

PROFESSOR OF DESCRIPTIVE GEOMETRY, STEREOTOMY, AND DRAWING IN THE RENSSELAER POLYTECHNIC INSTITUTE, TROY, N. Y.

FIFTH THOUSAND.

NEW YORK

JOHN WILEY & SONS

LONDON

CHAPMAN & HALL, LTD

1911

PREFACE.

This revised edition has been enlarged by the addition of the chapters on Tinting, Shadows, Shading, Isometrical Drawing, Oblique Projection, and Perspective. The chapters on Drawing Instruments and their Uses have been rewritten and much new matter added; while some changes and additions have been made in the chapters on Projections and Topography.

It is hoped that by these changes the book will prove more useful in the class-room, or as a guide for self-instruction.

The cuts of Drawing Instruments used in this work, marked *K. & E.* in the table of contents, have been kindly furnished by Keuffel & Esser, No. 111 Fulton St., New York.

D. F. T.

CONTENTS.

CHAPTER I.

DRAWING INSTRUMENTS AND MATERIALS.

CHAPTER II.

USE AND CARE OF INSTRUMENTS.

CHAPTER III.

CONSTRUCTION OF PROBLEMS OF POINTS AND STRAIGHT LINES.

Construction of Arcs of Circles, Straight Lines and Points.

Construction of Problems of Circles and Rectilineal Figures.

Construction of Proportional Lines and Figures.

Construction of Equivalent Figures.

Construction of Curved Lines by Points.

CHAPTER IV.

TINTING AND SHADING.

CHAPTER V.

CONVENTIONAL MODES OF REPRESENTING DIFFERENT MATERIALS

CHAPTER VI.

CONSTRUCTION OF REGULAR FIGURES.

CHAPTER VII.

PROJECTIONS.

CHAPTER XIII.

ARCHITECTURAL ELEMENTS.

CHAPTER XIV.

MECHANISM.

CHAPTER XV.

TOPOGRAPHICAL DRAWING.

CHAPTER I.

DRAWING INSTRUMENTS AND MATERIALS.

1. Good instruments are necessary for good work, and the beginner who desires to excel should procure the best. These can be purchased by the case, or by the piece. The latter being the best way, as there are sometimes pieces in the case which are seldom, if ever, used. After selecting the pieces a case can be made for them, or, if one does not wish to incur that expense, roll them up in a piece of chamois skin, arranging so that they do not touch each other. By folding over one edge of the skin, and stitching together, little pockets may be formed for each piece.

The following instruments will be necessary: a compass with pen, pencil and needle points, and lengthening bar; hair-spring dividers; bow compass with pen and pencil points; and one or two drawing pens. These with a drawing board, T square, triangles, etc., will make a sufficient outfit.

2. *Compasses.* These instruments are so well known as hardly to require description here. They consist of two legs, which are connected by a joint or hinge. The extremities of the legs are finished with fine steel points, the upper portions are of brass, German silver, or some other metal that does not readily rust. The joint is generally made partly of steel, as the wear will be more equal. The joint should be accurate and firm, but admit of easy play without any sudden jerks in opening and closing the legs. If by use the joint becomes loose, it can be tightened with the small screw-driver which accompanies the instruments. The points should come accurately together when the legs are closed.

3. *Compass with movable parts.* Fig. 1. represents a good form of this instrument, with its furniture, the pen, pencil

and needle points, and lengthening bar. This form of needle point is much the best; the shoulder of the needle should be large enough to prevent making a hole in the paper when used. This style of pencil point is also very convenient, being made for the use of leads. The lengthening bar is used in describing larger circles than the compasses would otherwise admit of. With some of these instruments there is a dotting pen, but this is not recommended as it cannot be depended upon. In selecting, see that the parts all fit well together.

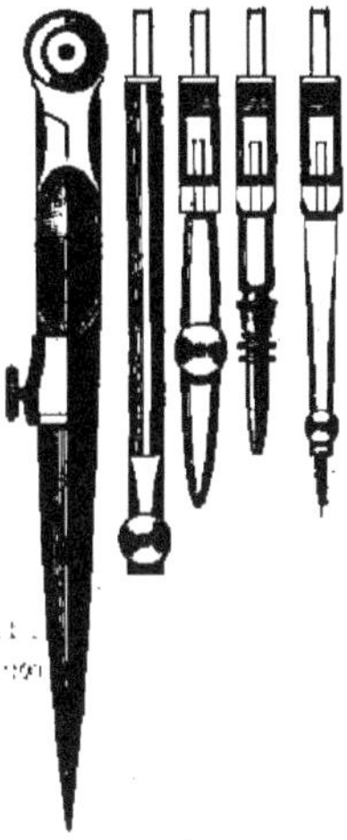

FIG. 1.

FIG. 2.

4. *Hair-spring dividers.* These are so constructed, that by means of a spring and screw, the distance between the points may be changed without any motion at the joint. By turning the screw, Fig. 2, the point may be moved a very fine distance, thus making it very convenient for taking measure-

'ments from scales, or dividing distances into equal parts. The spring should be pretty stiff.

5. *Bow compasses.* These are for drawing small circles both in pencil and ink. There are some forms made, where the pen and pencil points can be exchanged as in the larger

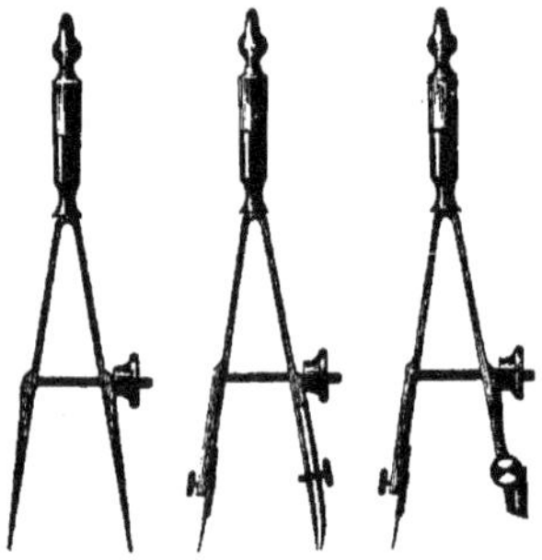

FIG. 3.

compasses. It is more convenient, however, to have .. separate instruments, one for the pen, and the other for the pencil, as shown in Fig. 3. See that the springs are strong.

There are other forms of compasses, which are convenient at times, but not necessary to buy at first. Among these are the proportional and beam compasses.

6. *Proportional compasses.* These are useful for enlarging or reducing drawings. The simplest form, shown in Fig. 4, is called halves and wholes; where the shorter legs are half the length of the others, so that the distance between the points of the shorter legs will be one half of that between the points at the other end.

Fig. 5 shows another form of these compasses, similar in principle to the last, but constructed so that the position of the joint can be changed, thus giving different proportions between the extremities at either end. To adjust the instrument, close it, and after unscrewing the nut, move the slide along until the mark across it coincides with the required number, then clamp the nut.

Four scales are sometimes engraved upon these compasses, called lines, circles, planes, and solids. The last two are omitted upon many of the instruments, as they are of little use.

FIG. 4.

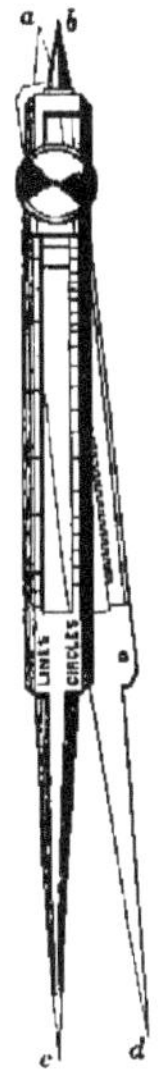

FIG. 5.

If the mark is brought to $\frac{1}{3}$ in the scale of lines, the distance *ab* will be one-third of *cd*. If the mark is brought to 8 in the scale of circles, *ab* will be the chord of the eighth part of the circumference of a circle whose radius is *cd*. Place the mark at 4 in the scale of planes, and *ab* will be the side of a square, or radius of a circle whose area is one-fourth that of the square or circle formed with *cd*. In the scale of solids, with the mark at 4, *ab* will be the diameter of a sphere or edge of a cube whose solidity is one-fourth that of a sphere or cube whose diameter or edge is *cd*.

The graduation of these instruments cannot always be relied upon, and the accuracy of the proportions is also affected by any change in the length of the legs, occasioned by use or breaking. It would be well to test their accuracy before purchasing.

7. *Beam compasses.* These are for describing larger arcs than would be possible with the other compasses. There are different forms of these. In all of them there is a beam of wood, or metal, with two collars, one carrying a pen or pencil point, and the other a needle point. Fig. 6 shows a convenient form of this instrument. In this the tops of the collars are left open so that they can be used on any straight edge.

being clamped to it by means of screws. The needle point is clamped at one end, while the other collar can be clamped at any distance from it. By turning the screw *a* the point *b* can be moved slightly, thus enabling one to adjust nicely the

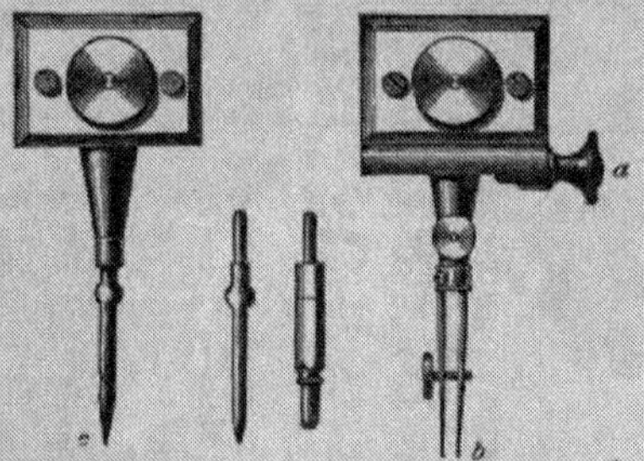

FIG. 6.

distance between *b* and *c*. In some forms there is a scale upon the beam, but this is not necessary and makes it more expensive.

8. *Drawing pen.* Fig. 7. This is made of two flat pointed steel blades, one of which has a hinge-joint at its base, thus allowing the blades to be sufficiently separated for cleaning

FIG. 7.

or sharpening. The distance between the points is regulated by means of a screw connecting the two blades. This distance determines the width of the lines. Do not select one in which the blades are much curved.

9. *Drawing board.* This is an indispensable part of the draughtsman's outfit. It should be made of a thoroughly seasoned light wood; pine is generally used. A board twenty-eight inches long, twenty inches wide, and about one inch thick is a convenient size. Each end should be finished

with a cleat, as shown in Fig. 8, to prevent warping. Each side should be rubbed to a smooth plane surface, with fine

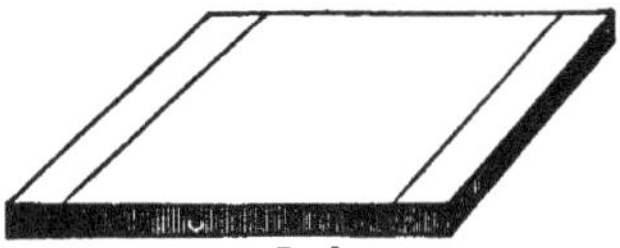

FIG. 8.

sand-paper. The edges should be straight and at right angles to each other.

10. T *square.* This consists of a long thin blade, with a head at right angles to it; fig. 9 is a good pattern, where the

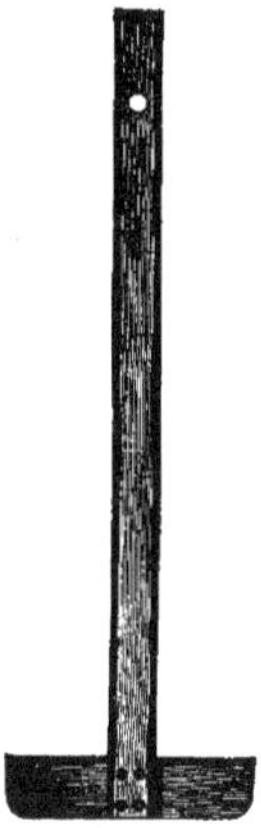

FIG 9.

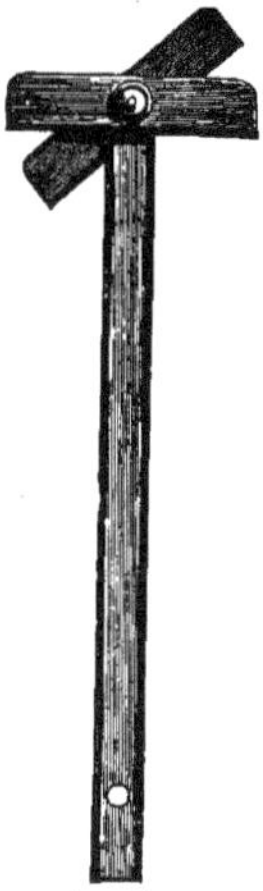

FIG. 10.

blade is simply laid upon the head and screwed to it. Any fine-grained hard wood will do for material, pear-wood is very good. Sometimes metal is used, and for accuracy it would be the best; but as it rusts and tarnishes easily, the paper is liable to be soiled. The blade should be about the same length as the board. For a blade thirty inches in length, in order to be sufficiently stiff, the width should be at least two and a half inches, and the thickness one-eighth of an inch. The head is generally made of one piece, although sometimes of two, one on either side of the blade, as shown in fig. 10. One of these pieces is fixed while the other can be clamped at any angle with the blade; so that, if the square is turned over and used with this side of the head against the edge of the board, parallel lines may be drawn making a corresponding angle with the sides of the board. This is not used very much, as it cannot be clamped sufficiently tight to prevent displacement by a slight rap, or any great pressure upon the blade.

11. *Triangles.* These are made of different materials, as wood, metal, rubber, etc., the last being the best; metal triangles are open to the same objection that metal squares are. Triangles are made solid or open, as shown in fig. 11, the

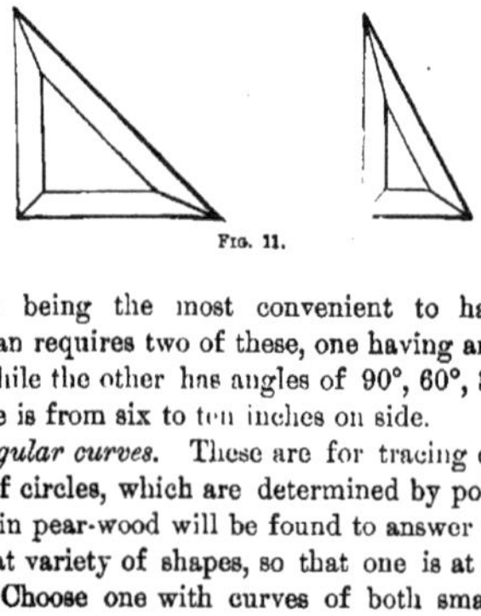

FIG. 11.

open ones being the most convenient to handle. The draughtsman requires two of these, one having angles of 90°, 45°, 45°, while the other has angles of 90°, 60°, 30°. A convenient size is from six to ten inches on side.

12. *Irregular curves.* These are for tracing curves, other than arcs of circles, which are determined by points. Those made of thin pear-wood will be found to answer well. They have a great variety of shapes, so that one is at a loss which to select. Choose one with curves of both small and large radius.

13. *India ink.* It is important to have this material of the best quality, as it is used exclusively for all black lines. Good India ink, when broken across, should have a shining and somewhat golden lustre. If an end of it is wetted and rubbed on the thumb-nail, it should have a pasty feel, free from grains, and exhale an odor of musk; when dried the end should present a shiny and golden-hued surface. Ink of inferior quality is of a dull bluish color, and when wetted and rubbed on the nail feels granular; also when rubbed up in water it settles; whereas good ink remains thoroughly diffused through the water.

14. *Colors.* Windsor and Newton's water colors are considered the best. There are two sizes of cakes, called the whole and half cakes. The moist colors which come in porcelain dishes are equally good, and are preferred by some, as the cakes are liable to crack and crumble.

15. *Ink saucers.* These come in nests of four or six, and are very convenient for preserving the colors after they are prepared. One forms a cover for another and thus keeps out the dust, besides keeping the colors moist for some time.

16. *Pencils.* These should be of the hardest and best quality. A. W. Faber's hexagonal pencils are the best. *HH* and *HHH* are good numbers for mechanical drawing.

17. *Brushes.* The best brushes are made of sable hair, of which there are two varieties, the red and black. The red is somewhat the cheapest, but is about as good as the black. Camel's-hair brushes will answer very well, if one does not want to afford the sable. In selecting brushes see that they come to a point when moistened with water; they should keep this point when used.

18. *India rubber.* Fine vulcanized rubber is the best for removing pencil marks. Sponge rubber is good for cleaning drawings.

19. *Thumb tacks.* These are for fastening the paper to the drawing board, when it is not necessary to stretch it. The best have the steel point riveted into the head. The top of the head should be slightly rounded, the edges being thin, so as to allow the T square to pass over readily.

20. *Horn centre.* This is used in case many circles are to

be drawn from the same centre. The needle point rests upon this instead of the paper, to prevent the wearing of a large hole. It is made of a piece of transparent horn, with three little steel points to prevent slipping.

21. *Drawing paper.*—Watman's drawing paper is considered the best. It comes in sheets of standard sizes, as follows:

Cap	13 in.	by	17	Elephant	23 in.	by	28
Demy	15 "	"	20	Columbier	23 "	"	34
Medium	17 "	"	22	Atlas	26 "	"	34
Royal	19 "	"	24	Double Elephant	27 "	"	40
Super Royal	19 "	"	27	Antiquarian	31 "	"	53
Imperial	22 "	"	30	Emperor	48 "	"	68

There are two kinds of this paper, the rough- or cold-pressed, and the smooth- or hot-pressed; the smooth paper is better for finished line drawings, while the rough surface takes color better; does not show erasures, and is better for general work. On holding the paper up to the light the maker's name is seen in water lines, and when it can be read, the nearest surface is considered the right side. If there is any difference between the two, it is supposed to be in favor of this side. The double elephant sheet is of a good weight and size for general work. For smaller sizes cut it in halves or quarters.

22. *Tracing paper.* This is a thin paper prepared so as to be sufficiently transparent to allow the lines of a drawing to show through, for the purpose of copying. It comes in sheets or by the roll. The best paper is tough, transparent, and without any greasiness.

23. *Tracing cloth.* This is for the same purpose as tracing paper. It is better than paper for preserving copies, or for those that are to be subjected to any wear, as in the case of working drawings. It comes in rolls of twenty-four yards, and of different widths. That which has a dull surface on one side is better for pencil marks or for tinting.

SCALES.

24. As it would be impossible in most cases to make a drawing the same size as the object, it is necessary to resort to the use of scales in order to preserve the relative positions

of the lines, and also to be able to determine what proportion the drawing bears to the object. These scales consist of distances of different lengths, divided with great accuracy. Various materials are used in their construction, such as ivory, wood, metal, paper, etc. Ivory is the best, but quite expensive, while those made of boxwood are good, and are generally used. Metal is expensive and tarnishes easily, while paper soon wears out.

It is well in making a drawing to use as large a scale as convenient, so that the small parts of the object may be brought out distinctly and accurately.

The scale of a drawing should always be given upon it, and in the case of a working drawing, the measurements also. By giving the measurements the time of the workman is saved, since he follows the dimensions rather than the drawing, in case they differ.

The dimensions are given in figures, using one accent to indicate feet and two accents for inches, as 2', read two feet, and 3'', three inches. Where feet and inches are to be written, the figures are separated by a comma simply, as 6', 4''. Where only inches are to be written, use a cipher in place of feet, as 0', 6''. This is not always necessary, but upon drawings where many of the dimensions are given in feet and fractions of a foot, it is well to use the cipher, as it may save mistakes in reading.

To indicate the points between which the measurement reads, small arrow heads are used at the points; as seen upon Pl. XVI. Fig. 144. When the arrow heads are some distance apart, they are connected by a fine dotted line. This line may be broken at the centre to allow the measurements to be inserted, or the line may be continuous, and the figures be placed just above it or on it. To make the measurements more noticeable, red ink is generally used for the figures and arrow heads, and blue ink for the dotted lines. All the horizontal measurements should be written from left to right, the vertical being written from the bottom to the top.

25. *A scale of equal parts.* (Pl. I. Fig. 7.) This is a small flat instrument of ivory. On both sides of this instrument we shall find a number of lines drawn lengthwise, and divided crosswise by short lines, against which numbers are

written. It is not our object, in this place, to give a full description of this scale, but simply of that portion which is termed the scale of equal parts. A scale of equal parts consists of a number of inches, or of any fractional part of an inch, set off along a line; the first inch, or fractional part to the left, being subdivided into ten or twelve equal portions. When the divisions of the line are inches, the scale is sometimes termed an *inch scale;* if the divisions are each three quarters of an inch, it is termed a *three quarter inch scale;* and so on, for any other fractional part of an inch. These different scales are usually placed on the same side of the ivory scale; the inch scale being at the bottom, the three quarter inch scale next above; next the half inch scale, and so on. The inch scale is usually marked IN. on the left; the three quarter inch scale with the fraction $\frac{3}{4}$; the others, in like manner, with the fractions $\frac{1}{2}$, $\frac{1}{4}$, and so on. The first division of each of these scales is usually subdivided, along the bottom line of the scale, into ten equal parts, by short lines; and just above these short lines will be found others, somewhat shorter, which divide the same division into twelve equal parts. It is not usual to place any number against the first division; against the short line which marks the second division, the number 1 is written; at the third division the number 2; and so on to the right.

26. *Manner of using the scale.* Geometrical drawings of objects are usually made on a smaller scale than the real size of the object. In making the geometrical drawing of a house, for example, the drawing would have to be very much smaller than the house, in order that a sheet of paper of moderate dimensions may contain it. We must then, in this case, as in all others, select a suitable scale for the object to be represented. Let us suppose that the scale chosen for the example in question is the inch scale; and that each inch on the drawing shall correspond to ten feet on the house. As a foot contains twelve inches, it is plain, that an inch on the drawing will correspond to 120 inches on the house; thus any line on the drawing will be the one hundred and twentieth part of the corresponding line on the house; and were we to make a model of the house, on the same scale as

the drawing, the height or the breadth of the model would be exactly the one hundred and twentieth part of the height or the breadth of the house. By bearing these remarks in mind, the manner of using this, or any other scale, will appear clearer. Suppose, for example, we wish to take off from the scale, by a pair of dividers, the distance of twenty-three feet; we observe, in the first place, that as each inch corresponds to ten feet, two inches will correspond to twenty feet; and as each tenth of an inch corresponds to one foot three tenths will correspond to three feet. We then place one point of the dividers at the division marked 2, and extend the other point to the left through the two divisions of an inch each, and thence along the third division so as to take in three tenths. From the scale, here described, we cannot take off any fractional part of a foot, with accuracy. If we had wished to have taken off twenty-three feet and a half, for example, we might have extended the point of the dividers to the middle between the division of three tenths and four tenths; but, as this middle point is not marked on the scale, the accuracy of the operation will depend upon the skill with which we can judge of distances by the eye. To avoid any error, from want of skill, we must resort to one of the scales of the fractional parts of an inch. Taking the half inch scale, for example, its principal divisions being halves of an inch, will, therefore, correspond to five feet; the first of its principal divisions being subdivided, like the one on the inch scale, one tenth of it will correspond to half a foot, or six inches. So that from this scale we can take off any number of feet and half feet. The quarter inch scale being the half of the half inch scale, its small subdivisions will correspond to a quarter of a foot, or to three inches. The small subdivisions on the eighth of an inch scale, in like manner, correspond to one inch and a half. We thus observe that, by suitably using one of the above scales, we can take off any of the fractional parts of a foot on the inch scale, corresponding to a half, a quarter, or an eighth.

Let us now suppose, as a second example in the use of the inch scale, that we had to make a drawing of a house on a scale of one inch to twelve feet. We observe, in the first place, as twelve feet contain 144 inches, and as one inch, on the drawing, corresponds to 144 inches on the house in its true size, every line on the drawing will be the one hundred and forty-fourth part of the corresponding lines on the house. In this case, instead of using the division of the inch subdivided into tenths, we use the divisions of twelfths, which are just above the tenths; each twelfth corresponding to one foot. We next observe, in using the twelfths, what we found in using the tenths; that is, we cannot obtain, from the inch scale, any part corresponding to a fractional part of a foot; but, taking the half inch scale, we find the first half inch subdivided in the same way as the inch scale into twelfths; and, therefore, each twelfth on the half inch scale will correspond to half a foot, or six inches. In like manner the twelfths on the quarter inch scale will correspond to three inches; and the twelfths on the eighth of an inch scale to one inch and a half.

27. *Diagonal scale of equal parts.* (Pl. I. Fig. 8.) In the two examples of the use of an ordinary scale of equal parts, we found, that the smallest fractional part of a foot, that any of the scales examined would give, was one inch and a half. But, as all measurements of objects not larger than a house are commonly taken either in feet and inches, or in feet and the decimal divisions of a foot, it is very desirable to have a scale from which we can obtain either the tenths of a foot, if the decimal numeration is used; or the inches, or twelfths, when the duodecimal numeration is used. To effect these purposes, a scale, called a diagonal scale of equal parts, has been imagined; and this scale is frequently found on the small ivory scale, on which the other scales of equal parts are marked. A diagonal scale of equal parts may be either an inch scale, or a scale of any fractional part of an inch. The first inch, or division, is divided into ten, or twelve equal parts; the other inches to the right are numbered like the ordinary scales. Below the top line, on which the inches are marked off, we find either ten, or twelve lines, drawn parallel to the top line, and at equal distances from each other. We next observe perpendicular lines, drawn from the top line, across the parallel lines, to the bottom line, at the points on

the top line which mark the divisions of inches. But, from the subdivisions on the top line, we find oblique lines drawn to the bottom line; these oblique lines being also parallel to each other, and at equal distances apart. The direction of these oblique lines, termed diagonal lines, and from which the scale takes its name, is now to be carefully noticed, in order to obtain a right understanding of the use of the scale. By examining, in the first place, the bottom line of the scale, we observe that it is divided, in all respects, precisely like the top line. In the next place, we observe, that the first diagonal line to the left, 10, is drawn from the end of the top line, to the point *m*, which marks the first subdivision to the left on the bottom line. The other diagonal lines, we observe, are drawn parallel to the first one, on the left, and from the points of the subdivisions on the top line; the last diagonal line, on the right, being drawn from the last subdivision on the top line, to the end of the first division of the bottom line. On examining the perpendicular lines, we find, that they divide all the parallel lines, from top to bottom, into equal parts of an inch each. We find, also, that all the subdivisions, on the same parallel lines, made by the diagonal lines, are equal between the diagonal lines, each being equal to the top subdivisions. But when we examine the small divisions, on the parallel lines, contained between the first perpendicular line, 10—*n*, on the left, and the diagonal line next to it, we find these small divisions increase in length from the top to the bottom. In like manner we find that the small divisions, on the parallel lines, between the diagonal line, 1—*r*, on the right, and the perpendicular, 0—*r*, next to it, decrease in length from the top to bottom. Now, it is by means of these decreasing subdivisions that we get the tenths, or twelfths of one of the top subdivisions, according as we find ten or twelve parallel lines below the top line.

Let us suppose, for example, that we have ten parallel lines below the top line; then the small subdivision, on the first parallel line, below the top line, contained between the diagonal line, 1—*r*, on the right, and the perpendicular, 0—*r*, would be nine tenths of the top subdivision; that is nine tenths of a foot, if the top subdivision corresponds to one foot. The next small division below this would be eight tenths; the next below seven tenths; and so on down Now, if we take the small subdivisions, between the perpendicular line, on the left, and the first diagonal line, 10—m, the one below the top line will be one tenth of the top subdivision; the next below this two tenths; and so on, increasing by one tenth, as we proceed towards the bottom.

Let us suppose, for an example in the use of this scale, that the drawing is made to a scale of one inch to ten feet; and that we wish to take off from the scale sixteen feet and seven tenths. With the dividers slightly open in one hand, we run the point of the dividers down along the perpendicular, marked 0—*r*, next to the diagonal line on the right, until we come to the parallel line on which the small division seven tenths is found; this will be the third line below the top line. We place the point of the dividers on this parallel line, at *a*, where the perpendicular line, numbered 0—*r*, crosses it, and we extend the other point to the right, to *b*, to the perpendicular marked 1, along the parallel line, to take in one inch, or ten feet. We then keep the right point of the dividers fixed, at *b*; and extend the other point to the left, to *c*, taking in the small division seven tenths, and six of the subdivisions along the parallel line. The length, thus taken in between the two points of the dividers, will be the required distance on the scale.

From the description of the diagonal scale, and the example of its use just explained, the arrangement of, and the manner of using any other diagonal scale will be easily learned. We have first to count the number of parallel lines below the top line, and this will show us the smallest fractional part of the equal subdivisions of the top line that we can obtain, by means of the scale. If, for example, we should find one hundred of these lines below the top line, then we could obtain from the scale, as small a fraction of the top subdivisions as one hundredth; and counting downwards on the left, or upwards on the right, the short lines, between the extreme diagonal lines and the perpendicular lines next to them, we could obtain from the one hundredth to ninety nine hundredths of the top subdivisions.

Remarks. In the preceding examples we have taken the scales as corresponding to feet, because dimensions of objects of ordinary magnitude are usually expressed in feet. When the drawing represents objects of considerable extent, we then should use a scale of an inch to so many yards, or miles; as in the case of a map representing a field, or an entire country. When the drawing represents objects whose principal dimensions are less than a foot we then use a scale of an inch to so many inches. In some cases where we wish to represent very minute objects, which cannot be drawn accurately of their natural size, we use a *magnified* scale, that is a scale which gives the dimensions on the drawing a certain number of times greater than those of the object represented. For example, in a drawing made to a scale of three inches to one inch, the dimensions on the drawing would be three times those of the corresponding lines on the object.

28. A convenient form of diagonal scale for obtaining twelfths of a foot, is shown in Fig. 12, where ab, bc, represent

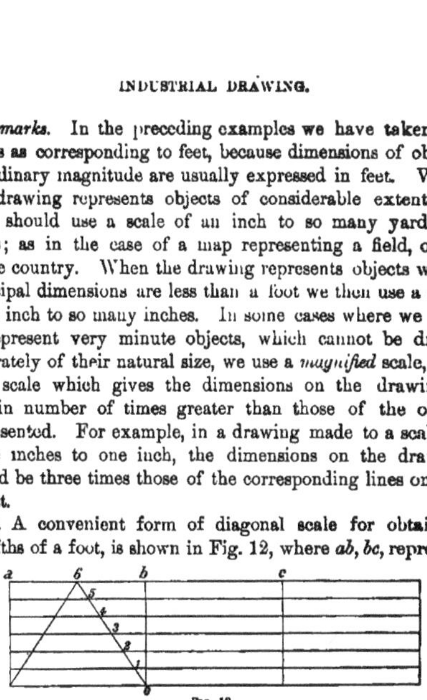

FIG. 12.

feet, while the horizontal distances of the points 1, 2, 3, etc., from the vertical line through b are each equal to a corresponding number of inches.

29. The scales represented in Figs. 7 and 8, Pl. I, although used to some extent, are rather short and not as convenient to use as those where the graduation runs to the edge, so that by laying the scale on the paper the required distance can be marked off directly without using the dividers. The frequent use of the dividers in taking distances from the scales, defaces the lines of the scale and should be avoided. In Fig. 13 are shown sections of scales in general use. These are all made

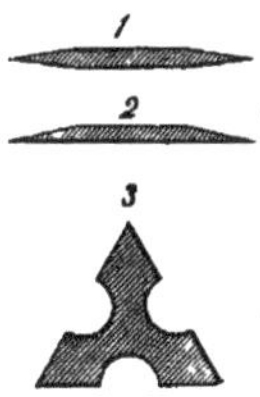

FIG. 13.

with thin edges, and with the graduation running to the very edge. On Nos. 1 and 2 there would be one, or possibly two scales for each edge, while on No. 3 there can be at least six scales in all, two to each edge, one on either side.

30. Fig. 14 gives a side view of Nos. 1 or 2. There are four scales upon this, two upon each edge, one being double

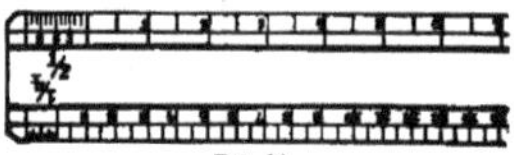

FIG. 14.

the other. The scales are duodecimally divided, the divisions representing feet and inches. The following scales are the most useful: $\frac{1}{8}$, $\frac{1}{4}$, $\frac{1}{2}$, 1, $\frac{3}{8}$, $\frac{3}{4}$, $1\frac{1}{2}$, 3. Two flat ones, or one triangular, will contain all of these.

31. Fig. 15 represents what is called a chain scale. Such scales are numbered 10, 20, 30, 40, 50, 60, according to the

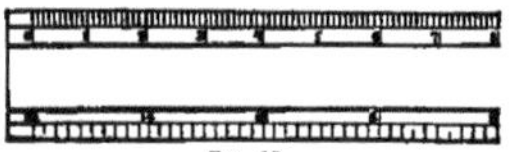

FIG. 15.

number of divisions contained in an inch, and are the scales in common use. The upper scale in Fig. 15 is numbered 20, that is, an inch is divided into 20 equal parts and might be used in practice for a scale of two or twenty chains to the inch; two or twenty feet to the inch, or two or twenty miles to the inch. One triangular, or three flat scales, will contain all of those mentioned above. The duodecimally divided scales are most useful for mechanical and geometrical drawing, while the chain scales, as their name indicates, are used mostly for plotting surveys.

32. After the drawing of an object has been completed, it is necessary to state upon it the ratio between the lines of the drawing and those of the object. This is often done by the use of a fraction, as a scale of $\frac{1}{2}$, $\frac{1}{4}$, $\frac{1}{8}$, etc. It is understood in such cases that the numerator refers to the drawing and the denominator to the object, and that the numerator is equal

to the denominator; for example in the scale $\frac{1}{4}$ we should understand that one inch on the drawing equals four inches on the object. In the scale $\frac{1}{8}$ 1 in. = 8 in. or $1\frac{1}{2}''$ = 1 foot. Instead of always expressing scales by the use of fractions, it is often stated what the scale is to a foot, as for example, "Scale $\frac{1}{2}$ in. = 1 foot," this expressed fractionally would be $\frac{1}{24}$. Scale $\frac{3}{4}$ in. = 1 foot would be the same as $\frac{1}{16}$.

33. *Protractor.* This is the instrument in most common use for laying off angles. It consists of a semicircle of thin metal or horn (Fig. 16), the circumference of which is divided

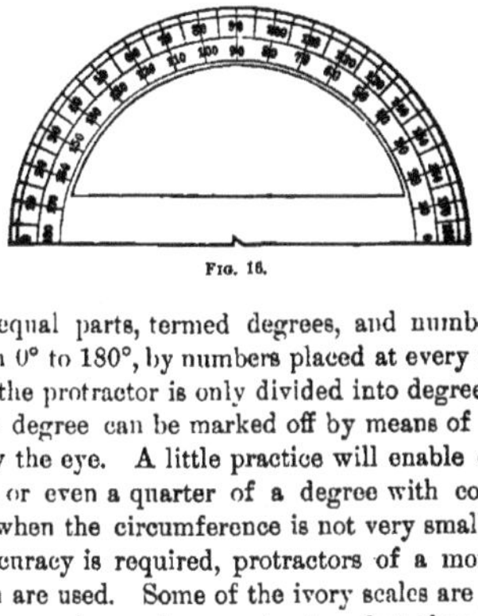

FIG. 16.

into 180 equal parts, termed degrees, and numbered, both ways, from 0° to 180°, by numbers placed at every tenth division. As the protractor is only divided into degrees, subdivisions of a degree can be marked off by means of it only by judging by the eye. A little practice will enable one to set off a half, or even a quarter of a degree with considerable accuracy, when the circumference is not very small. Where greater accuracy is required, protractors of a more complicated form are used. Some of the ivory scales are graduated so that they can be used as protractors, but they cannot be depended upon for accurate work. Horn protractors are convenient to use as they are transparent, but they are liable to warp. Tracing paper has recently been used to print protractors upon. Although not very durable, they have this advantage that they may be made of larger sizes, some being fourteen inches in diameter; being upon tracing paper, they are transparent, and also cheap.

There are other forms of scales more or less complex, and seldom used, which it is not necessary to describe here.

CHAPTER II.

USE AND CARE OF INSTRUMENTS.

1. Good tools are not only necessary for good work, but they should be kept in perfect order. This is particularly true in drawing. The draughtsman should keep at hand a clean old linen rag, and a piece of soft washleather, to be used for cleaning and wiping the instruments before and after using. The pen should be wiped dry before laying it aside, and the soil from perspiration cleaned with the washleather in like manner. With proper care a set of good instruments will last a lifetime.

2. *Compasses.* In describing circles keep both legs nearly vertical. This can be accomplished by means of the joint in each leg. By keeping the needle in a vertical position, it will not make a larger hole than necessary in the paper. Usually one hand is sufficient when describing circles; but when the lengthening bar is used, it is better to steady the needle point with one hand, while the circle is described with the other. When inking a circle, complete it before taking the pen from the paper, because without great care the place where the lines join will show.

3. *Dividers.* These are used for transferring distances from one part of a drawing to another, or from scales to the drawing. One hand is sufficient for their use; but care must be taken when transferring distances not to change the position of the points by clumsy handling. A little care and practice will enable one to manage them easily. When taking any distance with the dividers, open the points wider than necessary, and then bring to the required distance by pressing them together. In case it is required to lay off the same distance a number of times on a straight line, it is better to step the distance off, keeping one of the points on the line all the

time. In doing this, do not turn the instrument continuously in one direction, but reverse at each step, so that the moving point will pass alternately to the right and left of the line. A single trial will convince one, by the ease with which the instrument can be handled, of the advantage of the last method. Care should be taken when using the dividers not to injure the surface of the paper. When laying off distances, do not make holes in the paper; a very slight prick is sufficient, and this can afterwards be marked with the pencil.

4. *Drawing pen.* This is one of the most important instruments, and should never be of inferior quality. It is used for inking the lines of a drawing after it has been pencilled. The ink can be placed between the blades by means of a small brush or a strip of paper; but a more convenient way is to dip the edges of the pen into the ink, and they will generally take up enough; in case they do not, breathe upon them, and then they will readily take the ink. After taking the ink in this way, always wipe the outside of the blades. When inking, incline the pen slightly to the right in the direction of the line, taking care that both points touch the paper. Do not press too hard against the ruler, nor try to keep the point of the pen too near the ruler. If the line is to be heavy, or broad, the pen should be moved along rather slowly, otherwise the edges of the line will appear rough. Always draw the lines from left to right. In case the ink does not flow readily from the pen, try it upon a piece of waste paper, or outside the border line; a piece of blotting paper is also good for this purpose. If these means fail, pass between the blades the corner of a piece of firm paper. When the ink gets too thick, it dries rapidly in the pen and occasions considerable annoyance; in such a case, add a little water to the ink, and mix well before using.

5. *Sharpening pen.* As the pen is used a great deal, the points are worn away, changing their form as well as thickness, making it impossible to do nice work. Every draughtsman should be able to sharpen his pen and keep it in good order; with a little practice and attention to the following directions, one will soon be able to sharpen a pen. Having obtained a fine grained oilstone, first screw the points together,

then draw the pen over the stone, keeping it in a perpendicular plane, and turning it at the same time, so that the curve at the point shall take the shape shown in No. 1, Fig. 17.

FIG. 17.

This is a better shape than either Nos. 2 or 3, although 3 might do for heavy lines; but for all lines, 1 is the best shape. It is well, however, to have two pens; one being kept sharp for fine lines, while the other is used for heavy lines, and need not be sharpened as often. Having obtained the right shape, separate the points a little by means of the screw, and then lay each blade in turn upon the stone—keeping the pen at an angle of about 30° with the face of the stone—and grind off the thickness so as to bring to an edge along the point of this curve. For fine lines this edge should be pretty thin; not a knife edge, which would cut the paper. See that the edges of both blades are of the same thickness, and the points of the same length; then take the screw out and opening the blades, apply the inside of each to the stone just enough to take off any edge that may have been turned over. Next, screw up the blades, and try the points on the thumb nail to see if the edges are too sharp; if they cut the nail, the sharp edge should be taken off by drawing the pen very lightly over the stone as in the first step. Next, try the pen with ink on paper, and the character of the line made will show whether anything more is needed.

6. *Drawing board.* The sides should be plane surfaces, and their accuracy may be tested by placing the edge of a ruler across the board in several positions, and observing whether it coincides throughout, in every position, with the surface. The edges of the board should be perfectly straight, and if one cannot detect any inaccuracy by the eye alone, they can be tested by applying a straight edge. It is not essential, however, that the edges should be exactly at right angles to each other, provided the head of the square is used only on one edge for any given drawing.

7. *T square.* By placing the head against any edge of the board, and moving it along, at the same time drawing lines along the edge of the blade in its successive positions, we have a series of parallel lines. If now the head is placed against either adjoining edge, and lines are drawn as before, we shall have two sets of parallel lines at right angles to each other; that is, if the two edges of the board are exactly at right angles, and also the blade of the square exactly at right angles to the head. Now, as it is impossible to be sure that these angles are correct at all times, and as the lines drawn while the head is moved along any edge would be parallel, whether the blade be at right angles to the head or not, it is better to use the head upon only one edge, and depend upon the triangles for perpendicular lines. It is customary and more convenient to use the head upon the left-hand edge of the board, controlling its movements with the left hand, while the right is free to draw the lines. In moving from one position to another, take hold of the head instead of the blade. Always see that the head is against the edge before drawing a line, and use the upper edge in ruling.

8. *Triangles.* As there are two triangles, having the angles 90°, 45°, 45°, and 90°, 60°, 30°, respectively, it is evident that, by placing either of these triangles against the blade of the square, lines may be drawn making corresponding angles. As before suggested, this is the best way to draw perpendiculars. In case parallel lines are to be drawn, making angles different from those of the triangles, it may be possible to

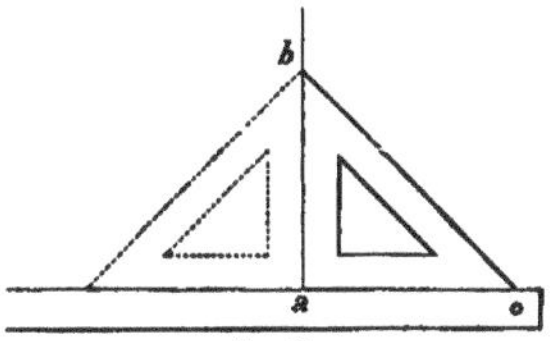

FIG. 18.

accomplish it by a combination of both triangles with the square; but it is difficult to hold so many pieces in place, so that it is better to use either one with the square, moving the blade so that the edge of the triangle shall coincide with a line already drawn at the desired angle; then, by holding the blade in place, and moving the triangle, lines may be drawn parallel to the first. To test the right angle of the triangle, place it against the square as in Fig. 18, and draw the line *a b*, then turn the triangle over, as in the dotted position, and draw another line along the vertical edge, taking care that the two lines start from the same point *a*. Now, if these lines correspond throughout, the angle at the base is a right angle; if there is any deviation, it will indicate what change should be made to correct it.

Manner of using the triangles for drawing lines which are to be either parallel or perpendicular to another line.

Let *A B* (Pl. I. Fig. 4) be a line to which it is required to draw parallel lines which shall respectively pass through the points, *C*, *D*, *E*, etc., on either side of *A B*.

1st. Place the longest side, *a b*, of the triangle so as to coincide accurately with the given line; and, if its other sides are unequal, taking care to have the next longest of the two, *a c*, towards the left hand. 2d. Keeping the triangle accurately in this position, with the left hand, place the edge of the ruler against the side, *a c*, and secure it also in its position with the left hand. 3d. Having the instruments in this position, slide the triangle along the edge of the ruler towards one of the given points, as *C* for example, until the side, *a b*, is brought so near the point that a line drawn with the pencil along *a b* will pass accurately through the point. 4th. Keep the triangle firmly in this position, with one of the fingers of the left hand, and with the right draw the pencil line through the point. Proceed in the same way with respect to the other points.

Remarks. When practicable, the first position of the triangle should be so chosen that the side, *a b*, can be brought in succession to pass through the different points without having to change the position of the ruler.

After drawing each line the triangle should be brought back to its first position, in order to detect any error from an accidental cnange in the position of the ruler during the operation; and it will generally be found not only most convenient but an aid to accuracy to draw the line through the highest point first, and so on downwards; as the eye will the more readily detect any inaccuracy, in comparing the positions of the lines as they are successively drawn. It will also be found most convenient to place the triangle first against the ruler and adjust them together, in the first position along *A B*.

It will readily appear that either side of the triangle may be placed against the ruler, or the given line. The draftsman will be guided on this point by the positions and lengths of the required parallels.

Let *A B* (Pl. I. Fig. 5) be a line to which it is required to draw a perpendicular at a point, *C*, upon the line, or through a point, *D*, exterior to it.

1st. Place the longest side, *a b*, of the triangle against the given line, and directly beneath the given point *C*, or *D*, with the ruler against *a c*, as in the last case.

2d. Confining the ruler firmly with the left hand, shift the position of the triangle so as to bring the other shorter side, *b c*, against the ruler.

3d. Slide the triangle along the ruler, until the longest side, *a b*, is brought upon the given point *C*, or *D*; and, confining it in this position, draw with the pencil a line through *C*, or *D*. The line so drawn is the required perpendicular.

Another method of drawing a perpendicular in like cases is to place the ruler against the given line, and, holding it firmly in this position, to place one of the shorter sides of the triangle against the edge of the ruler, and then slide the triangle along this edge until the other shorter side is brought upon the given point, when, the triangle being confined in this position, the required perpendicular can be drawn. But this is usually neither so accurate nor so convenient a method as the preceding one.

Remark. The accuracy of the two methods just described will depend upon the accuracy of the triangle. If its right angle is not perfectly accurate, the required perpendicular will not be true. This method also should only be resorted to for perpendiculars of short lengths. In other cases one of the methods to be described farther on should be used as being less liable to error.

9. *Irregular curves.* Having determined the points through which the curve is to pass, the edge of the instrument is shifted about until it is brought in a position to coincide with three or more consecutive points *a*, *d*, *c* (Pl. I. Fig. 11) of the curve *x–y* to be traced. When the position chosen satisfies the eye, that portion of the curve is traced in pencil which will pass through the points coinciding with the edge of the instrument. The instrument is again shifted so as to bring several points, contiguous to the one or other end of the portion of the curve just traced, to coincide, as before, with the edge of the instrument; taking care that the new portion of the curve shall form a continuation of the portion already traced. The operation is continued in this way until the entire curve is traced in pencil; it is then put in ink by going over the pencil line with the pen, using the instrument as a guide, as at first.

The successful use of this instrument demands some attention and skill on the part of the draughtsman, in judging by the eye the direction of the curve from the position of its points. When thus employed, curves of the most complicated forms can be traced with the greatest accuracy.

When similar curves are to be drawn on both sides of a line—as in an ellipse—mark on the edge of the instrument the limits of the part used in drawing the curve on one side, and then turn it over and draw the opposite side between the same limits.

10. *Preparation of ink.* Place a few drops of water in the saucer and rub the ink in it until the liquid is pretty thick and black. After a little experience one can tell by the appearance when it has arrived at the proper consistency for use; it is not well, however, to trust to sight alone, but also to test it by making a wide line with the drawing pen upon a piece of paper, to see if it is perfectly black when dry. In testing in this way, go over the line only once. The cake should always be wiped dry after using to prevent cracking. Keep the saucer covered when not filling the pen. Ink may be kept moist for some time in a covered saucer; but if it

should happen to dry, it is better to wash it all out and start anew.

11. *Pencils.* For drawing straight lines the pencil should not be cut to a round point, but to a flat thin edge like a wedge; the flat side being laid against the edge of the ruler when drawing lines. It is well to have another pencil sharpened to a round point for making dots and marking points. For the compasses the pencil point should be round.

When the pencil becomes dull, or makes a heavy line, it may be sharpened by rubbing on any hard surface, as a piece of rough paper, a piece of fine sand paper, or a fine file. Long pencils are more convenient to handle; when they get short, trim them down for the compasses.

12. *Stretching paper.* When it is desired to make a small line drawing, requiring no tinting, nor much time for its completion, it is sufficient to fasten the paper to the board with thumb-tacks; but for large drawings, and especially those requiring any tinting or shading, it is necessary to stretch the paper by wetting, and then fasten to the board with mucilage.

To do this, place the sheet of paper upon the board, right side up, and turn up each edge of the paper against a ruler placed upon it about half an inch from the edge. Then take a perfectly clean sponge, and with clean water moisten the upper surface, omitting the edges that are turned up; in doing this, do not rub the paper, but merely press the sponge upon all parts. Let it stand with a little water upon the surface for about fifteen minutes—less time might do, but that will always ensure a good stretch—after that sop up the standing water, and then fasten each edge of the paper to the board with thick mucilage. After fastening one edge, it is better to fasten the opposite edge next, instead of either adjoining edge. Rub the edges down with the thumb to secure a firm joint. Leave the board in a horizontal position while the paper is drying, taking care not to place near the fire.

Some prefer not to wet that side of the paper upon which the drawing is to be made. There is no objection to it, if one is only careful not to injure the surface by rubbing, and to use clean water; besides, it is a little more convenient, for the edges are not likely to get wet, as they are turned up; it also saves the trouble of turning the paper over, during which operation the board is likely to get wet, and the mucilage will not be so likely to hold.

When stretching a large sheet where the centre is apt to dry before the edges, so that there is danger of their being pulled up, lay a damp cloth upon the centre, away from the edges, and let it remain until they become dry.

13. *Pencilling a drawing.* This consists in locating the lines of the drawing properly and accurately upon the paper. In doing this, do not make any unnecessary lines, or any lines unnecessarily long; a little attention given to this will make a much neater drawing, and there will be less liability to make mistakes when inking. The lines should be fine and merely dark enough to be seen. As a rule it is better to complete the drawing in pencil before inking; to this rule, however, there are exceptions; as in complicated drawings of machinery where it is well to ink some parts before finishing the pencilling of the whole.

14. *Inking a drawing.* It is customary in inking a drawing to ink all the circles and arcs before the right lines, as it is easier to make the lines meet the arcs than the arcs the lines. When there are a number of small concentric circles to be inked, commence with the smallest.

After inking all the circles, ink the horizontal lines next, commencing at the top and working down; then ink the vertical lines, commencing at the left and going to the right. Where there are to be lines of different widths, ink those of the same width before changing the pen. By having a little system one will work more rapidly.

When inking a complicated drawing before or after it is entirely pencilled, ink first those parts that are in front, and work back, thus avoiding the danger of making lines full that should be dotted.

To obtain the best effect in a line drawing, the ink should be perfectly black, and the lines smooth and even; the thickness of the fine and heavy lines should be proportioned to each other and to the scale of the drawing. The shade lines should also be correctly located. There is another thing that adds much to the looks of a drawing, and that is perfect intersections of lines, as in the case of two lines meeting at a point neither line should stop before reaching the point, nor run beyond, as is more likely to occur.

If the drawing is to be shaded, do not use black ink for the outlines, as light ink will blend into the shading better; it is well, too, to make the lines fine.

It is sometimes found necessary to ink a straight line so that it shall taper. This is easily accomplished by moving one end of the ruler slightly back, the other end remaining fixed, and going over the line again. Where a number of lines meet at a point, care must be taken in inking, not to make a large blot at the intersection; it is better to draw the lines from rather than towards the point; wait for each line to dry before drawing the next. Where there are a great many lines, the angle between them being small, they will unavoidably meet, before reaching the point; so that in inking it is not well to start each line from the point, but only from where it would meet the last line. Let about every third line start from the point.

15. *Accuracy.* In both the construction of a drawing in pencil and the inking, accuracy should be the aim of the draughtsman. No matter how simple the drawing, let the construction be exact. The importance of this is apt to be lost sight of in the class room and upon elementary work, but will be manifest when one comes to the construction of drawings for use. Begin right, then, and cultivate accuracy as a habit.

16. *Cleaning a drawing.* To remove pencil lines a piece of vulcanized India rubber is necessary; but to remove dirt there is nothing better than a piece of stale bread, using the inside of a crust. This seems to remove the dirt without affecting the ink lines, and leaves the paper with a fine gloss. Do not rely, however, upon the possibility of cleaning a drawing when finished; never allow it to get very much soiled. Always dust with a brush, the drawing board, paper, and instruments, before commencing work. When a drawing is to occupy much time, paste a piece of waste paper on the edge of the drawing board, to fold over the drawing when

not at work. By cutting the paper, one can arrange so as to cover part of the drawing while working on another part.

17. *Cutting off a drawing.* To remove the paper from the board after the drawing is finished; place the ruler so as to coincide with a pencil line, drawn just inside the line of the mucilage, and then run the knife along the ruler.

Before cutting off a drawing see that it is perfectly dry, as it will wrinkle if part of the sheet is damp. When cutting take the edges in order round the board; not crossing from one edge to the opposite, and let each cut commence from the last one.

18. *Tracing.* It is often necessary to have one or more copies of a drawing. By the use of tracing paper or cloth, these can be taken from the drawing already made, thus saving much time. The paper or cloth should be large enough to allow the tacks, which hold it down, to clear the drawing; weights may be used in case it is not, but they are apt to be in the way. Some of the tracing cloth has one side dull, for the use of a pencil, if desired; let the tracing be made upon the glazed side. Tracing cloth will take color, but the tint should be somewhat thicker for this purpose than for ordinary tinting. Apply the tint to the dull side of the cloth; do not try to tint large surfaces.

19. *Accuracy of scales.* To test the accuracy of the graduation, take any distance with the dividers, from the scale, and compare it with a similar distance, at different parts of the scale. It is well to test the graduation near the ends, as it is more likely to be inaccurate there. Another way of testing is by placing two scales together to see if they correspond.

CHAPTER III.

CONSTRUCTION OF PROBLEMS OF POINTS AND STRAIGHT LINES.

Prob. 1. (Pl. I. Fig. 18.) *To draw a straight line through two given points.* Let *A* and *B* be two given points, pricked into the surface either by the sharp point of a needle, or of a lead pencil.

1st. Make with the lead pencil a small o, or round thus ⊙, enclosing each point, for the purpose of guiding the eye in finding the point.

2d. Place the edge of the ruler in such a position near the points that the point of the lead pencil, or other instrument used, pressed against and drawn along the edge of the ruler, will pass accurately through the points.

3d. Place the pencil upon, or a little beyond the point *A*, on the left, and draw it steadily along the edge of the ruler until its point is brought to the point *B*, on the right, or a short distance beyond it.

Remark. To draw a straight line accurately, so as to avoid any breaks, or undulations in its length, and have its breadth uniform, demands considerable practice and skill. The pressure of fingers and thumb on the pencil should be firm but gentle, as well as the pressure of the pencil against the edge of the ruler and upon the surface of the drawing. We should endeavor to get into the habit of beginning the line exactly at the one point and finishing it with the same precision at the other; this is indispensable in the case of ink lines, but although not so important in pencil lines, as they are easily effaced, still it aids in giving firmness to the hand and accuracy to the eye to practise it in all cases. The small round ⊙ placed about the dot will be found a very useful adjunct both to the hand and eye in all cases. Drawing ink lines of various degrees of breadth with the ordinary steel or quill pen will be also found excellent practice under this head.

Lines in drawing are divided into several classes (Pl. I. Fig. 13 bis) as *full*, *broken*, *dotted*, and *broken and dotted*, &c.: these again are divided into *fine*, *medium*, and *heavy*, according to the breadth of the line. A fine line is the one of least breadth that can be distinctly traced with the drawing pen; the medium line is twice the breadth of the fine; and the heavy is at least twice the breadth of the medium.

The coarse broken line consists of short lines of about $\frac{1}{8}$ of an inch in length, with blank spaces of the same length between them. The fine broken lines and spaces are $\frac{1}{32}$ of an inch.

The dotted line consists of small elongated dots with spaces of the same between.

The broken and dotted consists of short lines from $\frac{1}{16}$ to $\frac{1}{4}$ of an inch with spaces equal in length to the lines divided by one, two, or three dots at equal distances from each other and the ends of the lines.

These lines may also be fine, medium, or heavy.

When a line is traced with quite pale ink it is termed a *faint* line.

The lines of a problem which are either given or are to be found should be traced in full lines either fine or medium.

The lines of construction should be broken or dotted.

The outlines of an object that can be seen by a spectator from the point of view in which it is represented should be full, and either fine, medium, or heavy, according to the particular effect that the draftsman wishes to give. The portions of the outline that cannot be seen from the assumed point of view, but which are requisite to give a complete idea of the object, should be dotted or broken.

The other lines are used for conventional purposes by the draftsman to show the connexion between the parts of a problem, &c., &c.

Prob. 2. (Pl. II. Fig. 14.) *To set off a given distance along a straight line, from a given point on it.*

Let *C—D* be the line, and *A* the given point.

1st. Mark the given point *A*, as in the preceding problem.

2d. Take off the given distance, from the scale of equal parts, with the dividers.

3d. Set one foot of the dividers on *A*, and bring the other foot upon the line, and mark the point *B*, either by pricking the surface with the foot of the dividers, or by a small dot made on the line with the sharp point of a lead pencil.

When the distance to be set off is too small to be taken off from the scale with accuracy, proceed as follows:—

1st. Take off in the dividers any convenient distance greater than the given distance, and set it off from *A* to *b*.

2d. Take off the length by which *A b* is greater than the given distance and set it off from *b* to *c*, towards *A*; the part *A c* will be the required distance.

Remark. A given distance, as the length of a line, or the distance between two given points, is sometimes required to be set off along some given line of a drawing. This is done by a series of operations precisely the same as just described. In using the dividers, they must be held without stiffness, care being taken not to alter the opening given to them, in taking off the distances, until the correctness of the result has been carefully verified, by going over the operation a second time. Particular care should be paid to the manner of holding the dividers in pricking points with them, to avoid changing their opening, as well as making too large a hole in the drawing surface.

Prob. 3. (Pl. II. Fig. 15.) *To set off, along a straight line, any number of given equal distances.*

Let *C D* be the straight line, and the given number of equal distances be eight.

1st. Commence by marking a point *A*, on the line, in the usual manner, as a starting point.

2d. The number of equal divisions being even, take off in the dividers from the scale their sum, and set it off from *A* to 8, and mark the point 8.

3d. Take from the scale half the sum total, and set it off from *A* to 4; taking care to ascertain that the dividers will accurately extend from 4 to 8, before marking the point 4.

4th. Take off from the scale the fourth of the sum total, and set it off respectively from *A* to 2, and 4 to 6; taking care to verify, as in the preceding operation, the distances 2—4, and 6—8.

5th. Take off from the scale the given equal part, and set it off from *A* to 1; from 2 to 3, &c.; taking care to verify the distances as before.

Remark. When the number of equal distances is odd, commence by setting off from the starting point, as just described, an even number of equal distances, either greater or smaller than the given odd number by one, taking in preference the even number which with its parts is divisible by two; if, for example, the odd number is 7, then take 8 as the even number to be first set off; if it is 5 then take 4 as the even number. Having as in the first example, set off 8 parts we take only the seven required parts; and in the second having set off 4 parts only we add on the remaining fifth part to complete the required whole.

The reason for using the operations just given instead of setting off each equal part in succession, commencing at the starting point, is, if there should be the least error in taking off the first equal part from the scale, this error will increase in proportion to the total number of equal parts set off, so that the whole distance will be so much the longer or shorter than it ought to be, by the length of the error in the first equal distance multiplied by the number of times it has been repeated.

Prob. 4. (Pl. II. Fig. 16.) *From a point on a right line to set off any number of successive unequal distances.*

Let *C D* be the given line, and *A* the point from which the first distance is to be reckoned; and, for example, let the distances be respectively *A b* equal 20 feet; *b c* equal 8; *c d* equal 15 feet; and *d B* equal 25 feet.

1st. Commence by adding into one sum the total number of distances, which in this case is 68 feet.

2d. Take off from the scale of equal parts this total, and set it off from *A* to *B*.

3d. Add up the three first distances of which the total is 43 feet; take this off from the scale, and set it off from *A* to *d*.

4th. Take off the distance *d B* in the dividers, and apply it to the scale to verify the accuracy of the construction.

5th. Set off successively the distances *A b* equal 20 feet; and *A c* equal 28 feet; and verify by the scale the distances *b c*, and *c d*.

Remark The object of performing the operations in the manner here laid down is to avoid carrying forward any inaccuracy that might be made were the respective distances set off separately. The verifications will serve to check, as well as to discover any error that may have been made in any part of the construction.

Prob. 5. (Pl. II. Fig. 17.) *To divide a given line, or the distances between two given points, into a given number of equal parts.*

Let *A B* be the distance to be divided; and let, for example, the number of its equal parts be four.

Take off the distance *A B* in the dividers, and apply it to the scale of equal parts, then see whether the number of equal parts that it measures on the scale is exactly divisible by 4, or the number of parts into which *A B* is to be divided. If this division can be performed, the quotient will be one of the required equal parts of *A B* Having found the length of one of the equal parts proceed to divide *A B* precisely in the same way as in *Prob.* 3.

If *A B* cannot be divided in this way, we shall be obliged to use the ruler and triangle, in addition to the dividers and scale of equal parts, to perform the requisite operations, and proceed as follows:—

1st. Through the point *B*, draw with the ruler and pencil a straight line, which extend above and below the line *A B*, so that the whole length shall be longer than the longest side of the triangle used. The line *C D* should make nearly a right angle with *A B*.

2d. Take off from the scale of equal parts any distance

greater than *A B*, which is exactly divisible by 4, or the number of parts into which *A B* is to be divided.

3d. Place one foot of the dividers at *A*, and bring the other foot upon the line *C D*, and mark this second point 4, in the usual way.

4th. Draw a straight line through *A* and 4.

5th. Divide, in the usual way, the distance *A* 4 into its four equal parts *A* 1, &c., and mark the points 1, 2, 3, &c.

6th. With the ruler, triangle, and pencil draw lines parallel to *C D*, through the points 3, 2, and 1; and mark the points *d*, *c*, and *b*, where these parallel lines cross *A B*. The distances *A b*, *b c*, *c d*, and *d B* will be equal to each other, and each the one fourth of *A B*.

Remarks. The distance *A* 4 may be taken any length greater than *A B* the line to be divided. It will generally be found most convenient to take a length over twice that of *A B*.

The line *B C* is drawn so as to make nearly a right angle with *A B*, in order that the points where the lines parallel to it cross *A B* may be distinctly marked. Attention to the selection of lines of construction is of importance, as the accuracy of the solution will greatly depend on this choice. In this *Prob.*, for example, the line *C D* might have been taken making any angle, however acute, with *A B*, without affecting the principle of the solution; but the practical result might have been very far from accurate, had the angle been very acute, from the difficulty of ascertaining with accuracy, by the eye alone, the exact point at which two lines intersect which make a very acute angle between them, such as the lines drawn from the points 1, 2, 3, &c., parallel to *C D*, would have made with *A B* had the angle between it and *C D* been very acute. The same remarks apply to the selection of arcs of circles by which points are to be found as in figs. 18, 19, &c. The radii in such cases should be so chosen that the arcs will not intersect in a very acute angle.

Prob. 6. (Pl. II. Fig. 18.) *From a point on a given line to construct a perpendicular to the line.*

Let *C D* be the given line, and *A* the point at which it is required to construct the perpendicular.

1st. Having fitted the pencil point to the dividers, open the legs to any convenient distance, and having placed the steel point at *A*, mark, by describing a small arc across the given line with the pencil point, two points *b* and *c*, on either side of *A*, and at equal distances from it.

2d. Place the steel point at *b*, and open the legs until the pencil point is brought accurately on the point *c*; then from *b*, with the distance *b c*, describe with the pencil point a small arc above and below the line, and as nearly as the eye can judge just over and under the point *A*.

3d. Preserving carefully the same opening of the dividers, shift the steel point to the point *c*, and describe from it small arcs above and below the line, and mark with care the points where they cross the two described from *b*.

4th. With the ruler and pencil, draw a line through the points *A* and *B*, extend it above *B* as far as necessary; this is the required perpendicular.

Remarks. The accuracy of the preceding construction will depend in a great degree upon a judicious selection of the equal distances set off on each side of *A* in the first place; in the opening of the dividers *b c* with which the arcs are described; and upon the care taken in handling the instruments and marking the requisite points.

With respect to the two equal distances *A b* and *A c*, they may be taken as has been already said of any length we please, but it will be seen that the longer they are taken, provided the whole distance *b c* can be conveniently taken off with the dividers, the smaller will be the chances of error in the construction. Because the greater the distance *b c* the farther will the point *B*, where the two arcs cross, be placed from *A*, and any error therefore that may happen to be made, in marking the point of crossing of the arcs at *B*, will throw the required perpendicular less out of its true position than if the same error had been made nearer to the point *A*; moreover, it is easier to draw a straight line accurately through two points at some distance apart than when they are near each other; particularly if the line is required to be extended beyond either or both of the points; for if any error is made in the part of the line joining the two points it will increase the more the farther the line is extended either way beyond the points.

With respect to the distance *b c*, with which the arcs are described, this might have been taken of any length provided it were greater than *A b*. But it will be found on trial, if a distance much less than the three fourths of, or much greater than *b c*, is taken, to describe the arcs with, that their point of crossing cannot be marked as accurately as they can be when the distance *b c* is used.

Attention to a judicious selection of distances, &c., used in making a construction, where they can be taken at pleasure, is of great importance in attaining accuracy. Where points, like *B*, are to be found, by the crossing of arcs, or of straight lines, we should endeavor to give the lines such a position that the point of crossing can be distinctly made out, and accurately marked; and this will, in all cases, be effected by avoiding to place the lines in a very oblique position to each other.

A further point to secure accuracy of construction is to obtain means of proof, or verification. In the construction just made, the point *d* will serve as a means of verification; for the perpendicular, if prolonged below *A*, should pass accurately through the point *d* if the construction is correct.

Prob. 7. (Pl. II. Fig. 19.) *From a point, at or near the extremity of a given line, to construct a perpendicular to the line.*

Let *C D* be the line, and *A* the point.

In this case the distance *A C* being too short to use it as in the last *Prob.*, and there not being room to extend the line beyond *C*, a different process must be used.

1st. Mark any point as *a* above *C D*, and between *A* and *D*.

2d. Place the foot of the dividers at *a*, and open the legs until the pencil point is brought accurately on *A*; then describe an arc to cross *C D* at *b*, and produce it from *A* so far above it that a straight line drawn through *b* and *a* will cross the arc above *A*.

3d. Mark the point *b*, and with the ruler and pencil draw a straight line through *a* and *b*, and prolong it to cross the arc at *B*.

4th. Mark the point *B*; and with the ruler and pencil draw a line through *A* and *B*. This will be the required perpendicular.

Prob. 8 (Pl. II. Fig. 18.) *From a given point, above or below a given line, to draw a perpendicular to the line.*

Let *C D* be the given line, and *B* the given point.

1st. Take any opening of the dividers with the pencil point, and placing the steel point at *B* describe two small arcs, crossing *C D* at *b* and *c*; and mark carefully these points.

2d. Without changing the opening of the dividers, place the steel points successively at *b* and *c*, from which describe two arcs below *C D*, and mark the point *d* where they cross.

3d. With the pencil and ruler draw a line through *B d*. This is the required perpendicular.

Remark. The distance *B c*, taken to describe the first arcs, should as nearly as the eye can judge be equal to that *b c* between them, unless the given point is very near the given line.

Verification. If the construction is accurate, the distance *A b* will be found equal to *A c*; and *A B* equal to *A d*.

Prob. 9. (Pl. II. Fig. 19.) *To construct the perpendicular when the point is nearly over the end of the given line.*

Let *B* be the given point, and *C D* the given line.

1st. Take off any equal number of equal distances from the scale with the dividers and pencil point.

2d. Place the steel point at *B*, and, with the distance taken off, describe an arc to cross *C D* at *b*; and mark the point *b*.

3d. Draw a line through *B b*.

4th. Take off half the distance *B b*, and set it off from either *B*, or *b* to *a*, and mark the point *a*.

5th. Place the steel point of the dividers at *a*, and stretching the pencil point to *b*, or *B*, describe an arc to cross *C D* at *A*, and mark the point *A*.

6th. Draw a line through *A* and *B*. This is the required perpendicular.

Verification. Produce *B A* below *C D*, and set off *A d* equal to *A B*; if the construction is accurate *b d* will be found equal to *B b*.

Prob. 10 (Pl. II. Figs. 18, 19.) ***From a given point of a line to set off a point at a given distance above or below the line.***

Let A be the given point on the line CD.

1st. By *Prob.* 6, or 7, according to the position of A, construct a perpendicular at A to CD.

2d. Take off the given distance and set it off from A along the perpendicular, according as the point is required above or below the line.

Remark. If the point may be set off, at pleasure, above or below CD, we may either construct a perpendicular at pleasure, and set off the point as just described, or we may take the following method, which is more convenient and expeditious, and, with a little practice, will be found as accurate as either of the preceding.

Take off the given distance in the dividers. Then place one foot of the dividers upon the paper, and describing an arc lightly with the other, notice whether it just touches, crosses, or does not reach the given line. If it crosses, the position taken for the point is too near the line, and the foot of the dividers must be shifted farther off; if the arc does not meet the line the foot of the dividers must be brought nearer to the line. If the arc just touches the line the point where the stationary foot of the dividers is placed being marked will be a point at the required distance from the given line.

Verification. The correctness of this method may be verified by describing from a point set off by either of the other methods an arc with the given distance, which will be found just to touch the given line.

Prob. 11. (Pl. II. Fig. 20.) *Through a given point to draw a line parallel to a given line.*

Let A be the given point; CD the given line.

1st. Place one foot of the dividers at A, and bring the other foot in a position such that it will describe an arc that shall just touch CD at b.

2d. Without changing the opening of the dividers place one foot at a point B, near the other end of CD, so that the arc described with this opening will just touch the line at a.

3d. Having marked the point B, draw through $A\,B$ a line. This will be the required parallel.

Verification. Having constructed the two perpendiculars $A\,b$, and $B\,c$, to $C\,D$, the distance $b\,c$ will be found equal to $A\,B$ if the construction is accurate.

Prob. 12. (Pl. II. Fig. 20.) *To draw at a given distance from a given line a parallel to the line.*

Let $C\,D$ be the given line.

1st. Take off in the dividers the given distance at which the parallel line is to be drawn.

2d. Find, by either of the preceding methods, a point A, near one end of $C\,D$, and a point B near the other, at the given distance from $C\,D$.

3d. Having marked these points draw a line through them. This is the required parallel.

Verification. The same proof may be used for this as in *Prob.* 11.

Prob. 13. (Pl. II. Fig. 21.) *To transfer an angle; or, from a point, on a given line, to draw a line which shall make with the given line an angle equal to one between two other lines on the drawing.*

Let the given angle to be transferred be the one $b\,a\,c$ between the lines $a\,b$ and $a\,c$. Let $D\,E$ be the given line, and A the point, at which a line is to be so drawn as to make with $D\,E$ an angle at A equal to the given angle.

1st. With the dividers and pencil point describe, from a, with any opening, an arc, and mark the points b and c, where it crosses the lines containing the angle.

2d. Without changing this opening, shift the foot of the dividers to A, and describe from thence an arc as nearly as the eye can judge somewhat greater than the one $b\,c$, and mark the point B where it crosses $D\,E$.

3d. Place the foot of the dividers at b, and extend the pencil point to c.

4th. Shift the foot of the dividers to B, and, with the same opening, describe a small arc to cross the first at C.

5th. Having marked the point C, draw a line through $A\,C$. This line will make with $D\,E$ the required angle.

Prob. 14. (Pl. II. Fig. 22.) *From a point of a given line, to draw a line making an angle of 60° with the given line.*

Let $D E$ be the given line, and A the given point.

1st. Take any distance in the dividers and pencil point, and set it off from A to B.

2d. From A and B, with the same opening, describe an arc, and mark the point C where the arcs cross.

3d. Draw a line through A C. This line will make with the given one the required angle of 60°.

Prob. 15. (Pl. II. Fig. 22.) *From a point on a given line to draw a line making an angle of 45° with it.*

Let B be the given point on the line $D E$.

1st. Set off any distance $B a$, along $D E$, from B.

2d. Construct by *Prob.* 6 a perpendicular to $D E$ at a.

3d. Set off on this perpendicular $a c$ equal to $a B$.

4th. Having marked the point c, draw through $B c$ a line. This will make with $D E$ the required angle of 45°.

Prob. 16. (Pl. II. Fig. 23.) *To divide a given angle into two equal parts.*

Let $B A C$ be the given angle.

1st. With any opening of the dividers and pencil point, describe an arc from the point A, and mark the points b and c, where it crosses the sides $A B$ and $A C$ of the angle.

2d. Without changing the opening of the dividers, describe from b and c an arc, and mark the point D where the arcs cross.

3d. Draw a line through $A D$. This line will divide the given angle into equal parts.

Verification. If we draw a line through $b c$, and mark the point d where it crosses $A D$; the distance $b d$ will be found equal to $d c$, and the line $b c$ perpendicular to $A D$, if the construction is accurate.

Remarks. Should it be found that the point of crossing at D of the arcs described from b and c is not well defined, owing to the obliquity of the arcs, a shorter or longer distance than $A b$ may be taken with which to describe them, without making any change in the points b and c first set off.

Prob. 17. (Pl. II. Fig. 24.) *To find the line which will divide into two equal parts the angle contained between two given lines, when the angular point, or point of meeting of the two lines, is not on the drawing.*

Let *A B* and *C D* be the two given lines.

1st. By *Prob.* 10 set off a point at *b* at any distance taken at pleasure from *A B*, and by *Prob.* 11 draw through this point a line parallel to *A B*.

2d. Set off a point *d* at the same distance from *D C* as *b* is from *A B*, and draw through it a parallel to *D C*; and mark the point *c* where these parallel lines cross.

3d. Divide the angle *b c d* between the two parallels into two equal parts, by *Prob.* 16. The dividing line *c a* will also divide into two equal parts the angle between the given lines.

Verification. If from any point, as *o*, on the line *c a*, a perpendicular *o m* be drawn to *A B*, and another *o n* to *C D*, these two perpendiculars will be found equal if the construction is accurate.

CONSTRUCTION OF PROBLEMS OF ARCS OF CIRCLES, STRAIGHT LINES, AND POINTS.

Prob. 18. (Pl. II. Fig. 25.) *Through two given points to describe an arc of a circle with a given radius.*

Let *B* and *C* be the two points.

1st. Take off the given distance in the dividers and pencil point, and with it describe an arc from *B* and *C* respectively, and mark the point *A* where the arcs cross.

2d. Without changing the opening of the dividers, describe an arc from the point *A* through *B* and *C*, which will be the one required.

Prob. 19. (Pl. II. Fig. 26.) *To find the centre of a circle, or arc, the circumference of which can be described through three given points, and to describe it.*

Let *A*, *B*, and *C* be the three given points

1st. Take off the distance *B A* between the intermediate point and one of the exterior points, as *A*, with the dividers and pencil point, and with this opening describe two arcs from *B*, on either side of *B A*.

2d. With the same opening describe from *A* two like arcs, and mark the points *a* and *b* where these cross the two described from *B*.

3d. Draw a line through *a b*.

4th. With the distance *B C* in the dividers describe, from *B* and *C*, arcs as in the preceding case, and mark the points *c* and *d* where these cross; and then draw a line through *c d*.

5th. Having marked the point *O* where the two lines thus drawn cross, place the steel point of the dividers at *O*, and extending the pencil point to *A*, or either of the three given points, describe an arc, or a complete circle, with this opening. This will be the required arc or circle.

Verification. The fact that the arc or circle is found to pass accurately through the three points is the best proof of the correctness of the operations.

Prob. 20. (Pl. II. Fig. 26.) *At a point on an arc or the circumference of a circle to construct a tangent to the arc or the circle.*

Let *D* be the given point and *O* the centre of the circle.

1st. Draw through *D* a radius *O D*, and prolong it outwards from the arc.

2d. At *D* construct by *Prob.* 6 a perpendicular *E D F* to *O D*. This is the required tangent.

If the centre of the arc or the circle is not given, proceed as follows:—

1st. With any convenient opening in the dividers and pencil point (Fig. 26) set off from *D* the same arc on each side of it, and mark the points *A* and *B*.

2d. Take off the distance *A B* and describe with it arcs from *A* and *B* on each side of the given arc, and mark the points *a* and *b* where they cross.

3d. Draw a line through *a b*.

4th. Construct a perpendicular to *a b* at *D*. This is the required tangent.

Verification. Having set off from *D* the same distance on each side of it along *a b*, and having set off also any distance from *D* along *E F*, the distance from this last point to the other two set off on *a b* will be found equal, if the construction is accurate.

Remarks. It sometimes happens that the point to which a tangent is required is so near the extremity of the arc, as at *A*, or *C*, that the method last explained cannot be applied. In such a case we must first find the centre of the arc, or circle, which will be done by marking two other points, as *B* and *A*, on the arc, and by *Prob.* 19 finding the centre *O* of the circle of which this arc is a portion of the circumference. Having thus found the centre, the tangent at *C* will be constructed by the first method in this *Prob.*

Prob. 21. (Pl. II. Fig. 27.) *At a given point on the circumference of a given circle, to construct a circle, or arc, of a given radius tangent to the given circle.*

Let *B* be the given point, and *D* the centre, which is either given, or has been found by *Prob.* 19.

1st. Through *DB* draw the radius, which extend outwards if the centres of the required circle and of the given one are to lie on opposite sides of a tangent line to the first circle at *B*; or, in the contrary case, extend it, if requisite, from *D* in the opposite direction.

2d. From *B* set off along this line the length of the given radius of the required circle to *C*, or to *A*.

3d. From *C*, or *A*, with the distance *CB*, or *AB*, describe a circle. This is the one required.

Prob. 22. (Pl. II. Fig. 28.) *From a given point without a given circle, to draw two tangents to the circle.*

Let *A* be the centre of the given circle, and *B* the given point.

1st. Through *AB* draw a line.

2d. Divide the distance *AB* into two equal parts by *Prob.* 5.

3d. From *C*, with the radius *CA*, describe an arc, and mark the points *D*, and *E*, where it crosses the circumference of the given circle.

4th. From *B* draw lines through *D* and *E*. These lines are the required tangents.

Verification. If lines are drawn from *A*, to *D* and *E*, they will be found perpendicular respectively to the tangents, if the construction is accurate.

Remark. In this *Prob.*, as in most geometrical constructions, many of the lines of construction need not be actually drawn, either in whole, or in part. In this case, for example, a small portion of the line A—B, at its middle point, is alone necessary to determine this point. In like manner, the points L and E could have been marked, without describing the arc actually, but by simply dotting the points required. In this manner, a draftsman, by a skilful selection of his lines of construction, and using only such of them, in whole, or in part, as are indispensably requisite for the solution, may, in complicated constructions, avoid confusion from the intersection of a multiplicity of lines of construction, and abridge his labor.

Prob. 23. (Pl. II. Fig. 29.) *To draw a tangent to two given circles.*

Let A be the centre of one of the circles, and AC its radius; B the centre, and BE the radius of the other.

1st. Through AB draw a line.

2d. From C set off CD equal to BE.

3d. From A, with the radius AD, equal to the difference between the radii of the given circles, describe a circle.

4th. From B by *Prob.* 22 draw a tangent BD to this last circle, and through the tangential point D, a radius AC to the given circle.

5th. Through C draw a line parallel to BD. This line will touch the other given circle, and is the required tangent.

Verification. CE will be found equal to BD, if the construction is accurate.

Prob. 24. (Pl. II. Fig. 30.) *Having two lines that make an angle, to construct within the angle, a circle with a given radius tangent to the two given lines.*

Let AB and AC be the two given lines containing the angle.

1st. By *Prob.* 16 construct the line AD which divides the given angle into two equal parts.

2d. By *Prob.* 10 set off a point b at a distance from AB equal to the given radius, and through this point draw the line ab parallel to AB, and mark the point a where it crosses AD.

3d. From *a*, with the given radius, describe a circle. This is the one required.

Verification. The distances *Ac*, and *Ad*, will be found equal, if the construction is accurate.

Prob. 25. (Pl. II. Fig. 31.) *Having two lines containing an angle, and a given radius of a circle, to construct, as in the last case, this circle tangent to the two lines; and then to construct another circle which shall be tangent to the last and also to the two lines.*

Let *AB* and *CD* be the two lines, the point of meeting of which is not on the drawing.

1st. By *Prob.* 17 find the line *EF* that equally divides the angle between the lines.

2d. By *Prob.* 24 construct the circle, with the given radius *ac*, tangent to these two lines.

3d. At *b*, where *EF* crosses the circumference, draw by *Prob.* 20 a tangent to the circle, and mark the point *d* where it crosses *AB*.

4th. From *d*, set off *de* equal to *db*, and mark the point *e*.

5th. At *e* construct by *Prob.* 6 a perpendicular *ef*, to *AB*, and mark the point *f*, where it crosses *EF*.

6th. From *f*, with the radius *fe*, describe a circle. This is tangent to the first circle, and to the two given lines.

Remark. In like manner a third circle might be constructed tangent to the second and to the two given lines; and so on as many in succession as may be wanted.

Prob. 26. (Pl. III. Fig. 32.) *Having a circle and right line given, to construct a circle of a given radius which shall be tangent to the given circle and right line.*

Let *C* be the centre of the given circle, and *AB* the given line.

1st. By *Prob.* 12 draw a line parallel to *AB*, and at a distance *BG* from it, equal to the given radius.

2d. Draw a radius *CD* through any point *D* of the given circle, and prolong it outwards.

3d. From *D* set off, along the radius, a distance *DE* equal to *BG*, or the given radius.

4th. From *C*, with the distance *CE*, describe an arc

[illegible]

[illegible]

[illegible]

[illegible]

[illegible]

[illegible] the given point [illegible]

[illegible] the given [illegible]

[illegible]

[illegible]

[illegible]

[illegible]

[illegible] the given line, [illegible]

[illegible] perpendicular [illegible] the given [illegible]

[illegible] the given [illegible]

[illegible] I mean the [illegible] perpendicular [illegible] the line [illegible]

[illegible] where this perpendicular crosses the

one at a; and with ac describe a circle. This is the one required.

Prob. 29. (Pl. III. Fig. 35.) *Having two circles, to construct a third which shall be tangent to one of them at a given point, and also touch the other.*

Let C and B be the centres of the two given circles; and D the given point on one of them, at which the required circle is to be tangent to it.

1st. Through CD draw a line, which prolong each way from C and D.

2d. From D set off towards C the distance DA equal to the radius BF of the other given circle.

3d. Through AB draw a line, and by *Probs.* 5 and 6, bisect AB by the perpendicular GE.

4th. Mark the point E, where the perpendicular crosses the line CD prolonged; and with the distance ED describe a circle from E. This is the one required.

Prob. 30. (Pl. III. Fig. 36.) *Having a given distance, or line, and the perpendicular which bisects it, to construct three arcs of circles, the radii of two of which shall be equal, and of a given length, and their centres on the given line; and the third shall pass through a given point on the perpendicular and be tangent to the other two circles.*

Let AB be the given line, and D the given point on the perpendicular to AB through its middle point C; and let the distance CD be less than AC, the half of AB.

1st. Take any distance, *less than* CD, and set it off from A and B, to b and c, and mark these two points for the centres of the two arcs of the equal given radii less than CD.

2d. Set off from D the distance Dc equal to Ab, and through bc draw a line.

3d. Bisect bc by a perpendicular, by *Probs.* 5 and 6, and mark the point d where it crosses the perpendicular to AB prolonged below it, the point d is the centre of the third arc.

4th. Draw a line through db, and prolong it; and also one through dc which prolong.

5th. From b, with the distance bA, describe an arc from A to m on the line db prolonged; and one, from the other centre c, from B to n on the line dc prolonged.

[illegible] distance *dD*, describe an arc around [illegible] prolonged. This is the third arc [illegible] the other two where they cross the [illegible] and *n*.

[illegible] termed a *half oval*, or a *three centre* [illegible] curve, on the other side of *AB*, [illegible] distance *Cg* equal to *Cd*, and [illegible] from *b* and *e* around to lines [illegible] by connecting these arcs [illegible] radius equal to *Dd*.

[illegible] *a given line and the* [illegible] *lines drawn through a* [illegible] *and each making the same* [illegible] *of four arcs of circles* [illegible] *and their centres to lie* [illegible] *from its extremities; each* [illegible] *to be tangent respec-* [illegible] *the perpendicular* [illegible]

[illegible] given point on the bisect- [illegible] the two lines, drawn [illegible] the perpendicular. [illegible] distance to *b* and *a*, for [illegible] which distance must, [illegible] *distance from* [illegible] *B*. [illegible] *Bn*. [illegible] a distance *Bd* [illegible]

4th. [illegible] set this distance by a [illegible]

5th. [illegible] where this last perpen- [illegible] through *ab* a line, and [illegible]

6th. [illegible] describe an arc, which [illegible] is one of the first required arcs.

7th. From *c*, with [illegible] distance *cB*, describe an arc. This is one of the second required arcs.

8th. Through *a*, and the point *f*, where *bc* crosses the perpendicular *BA* prolonged, draw a line.

9th. From *a*, set off *ae* equal to *bc*.

10th. From *a* and *e*, with radii respectively equal to *bC*, and *cB*, describe arcs. These are the others required; and *CBD* the required curve.

Remark. If the construction is accurate, the perpendicular through *BA* will bisect the distance *ec*.

This curve is termed a *four centre obtuse* or *pointed* curve, according as the distance *AB* is less or greater than *AC*.

Prob. 32. (Pl. III. Fig. 38.) *Having a line, and the perpendicular which bisects it, and a given point on the perpendicular; to construct a curve formed of five arcs of circles, the consecutive arcs to be tangent; the centres of two of the arcs to be on the given line, and at equal distances from its extremities; the radii of the two arcs, respectively tangent to these two, to be equal, and of a given length; and the centre of the fifth arc, which is to be tangent to these two last, to lie on the given perpendicular.*

Let *AB* be the given line, and *C* the point on its bisecting perpendicular *LC*.

1st. Take any distance, *less than LC*, and set it off from *B* to *D*, and from *A* to *f*.

2d. From *C* set off *CG* equal to *BD*, and draw a line from *G* to *D*.

3d. Bisect the distance *DG* by a perpendicular; and mark the point *E*, where this perpendicular crosses the perpendicular *LC* prolonged.

4th. Draw a line from *E* to *D*.

5th. Take any distance, *less than CE*, equal to the given radius of the second arc, and set it off from *C* to *F*.

6th. Through *F* draw a line *FH* parallel to *AB*.

7th. Take off *GF*, the difference between *CF* and *CG*, and with it describe an arc from *D*; and mark the points *a* and *b* where it crosses the lines *DE* and *FH*.

8th. Take any point *c* on this arc, between the points *a* and *b*, and draw from it a line to *F*.

9th. Bisect the line *cF* by a perpendicular, and mark the point *I* where it crosses the perpendicular *CL* prolonged.

10th. From c draw a line through D and prolong it; and another from I prolonged through c.

11th. From c draw a perpendicular to CI; and from d, where it crosses CI, set off dq equal to cd, and mark the point q.

12th. From I draw a line through q and prolong it; and one from q prolonged through f.

13. From D and f, with the distance BD, describe the arcs Bm, and Ap; from c and q, with the distance cm, or qp, describe the arcs mn, and po; and from I with the distance IC, describe the arc no. The curve BCA is the one required.

Remarks. This curve is also termed a semi oval; and from the number of arcs of which it is composed, a *curve of five centres.*

Prob. 33. (Pl. III. Fig. 39.) *Having two parallel lines, to construct a curve of three centres which shall be tangent to the two parallels at their extremities.*

Let AB and CD be the given parallels; and B and D the points at which the required curve is to be drawn tangent.

1st. From B construct a perpendicular to AB, and mark the point b where it crosses CD; and also a perpendicular at D to CD.

2d. From B, set off any distance Bc less than the half of Bb; and through c draw a line parallel to AB, and mark the point d where it crosses the perpendicular to CD.

3d. From d, set off along dc prolonged, the distance de equal to dB.

4th. Taking de, as the radius of the first arc, construct a quarter oval by *Prob.* 30 through the points e and D.

5th. Prolong the arc described from e to the point B. The curve BeD is the one required.

Remark. This curve is termed a scotia of two centres.

Prob. 34. (Pl. III. Fig. 40.) *Having two parallels, to construct a quarter of a curve of five centres tangent to them at their extremities.*

Let AB and CD be the given parallels, and B and D their extremities.

1st. Proceed, as in the last case, to draw the perpendiculars

at *B*, and *D*, and a parallel to *AB* through a point *c*, taken on the first perpendicular, at a distance from *B* less than the half of *Bl*.

2d. Set off from *c* a distance *ca* equal to *cB*; and on *ac* and *Dd* describe the quarter oval by *Prob.* 32.

3d. Prolong the first arc from *a* to *B*, which will complete the required curve.

Remark. This curve is termed a *scotia* of three centres.

Prob. 35. (Pl. III. Fig. 41.) *Having two parallels and a given point on each, to construct two equal arcs which shall be tangent to each other and respectively tangent to the parallels at the given points.*

Let *AB* and *CD* be the two parallels; *B* and *D* the given points.

1st. Draw a line through *BD*, and bisect the distance *BD*.

2d. Bisect each half *BE*, and *ED* by perpendiculars.

3d. From *B*, and *D* draw perpendiculars to *AB* and *CD*, and mark the points *a*, and *b*, where they cross the bisecting perpendiculars.

4th. From *a*, with the distance *aE*, describe an arc to *B*; and from *b*, with the same distance, an arc *ED*. These are the required arcs.

Prob. 36. (Pl. III. Fig. 42.) *Having two parallels, and a point on each, to construct two equal arcs which shall be tangent to each other, have their centres respectively on the parallels, and pass through the given points.*

Let *AB* and *CD* be the parallels, *B* and *D* the given points.

1st. Join *BD* by a line and bisect it.

2d. Bisect each half *BE*, and *ED* by a perpendicular; and mark the points *a* and *b*, where the perpendiculars cross the parallels.

3d. From *a*, with *aB*, describe the arc *BE*; and from *b*, with the same distance, the arc *DE*. These are the required arcs.

CONSTRUCTION OF PROBLEMS OF LINES AND RECTILINEAR FIGURES.

Prob. [illegible] *the sides of a triangle to construct* [illegible]

Let [illegible] be the lengths of the given sides.

1st. Draw a line, and set off upon it the longest side *AB*.

2d. From the point [illegible] radius equal to *AC*, one of the remaining sides, describe an arc.

3d. From the point [illegible] the third side *BC*, describe a second arc, and mark the point [illegible] where the arcs cross.

4th. Draw lines from [illegible] and *B*. The figure *ACB* is the one required.

Remark. The side [illegible] might have been set off from *B*, and [illegible] would have given an equal triangle [illegible] constructed [illegible] vertex would have been placed differently.

Remark. This construction is also used to find the position of a point when its distances from two other given points are given. We proceed to make the construction in this case like the preceding. It will be seen that the required point can take four different positions with respect to the two others. Two of them [illegible] triangle, will be on one side of the line joining the given points, and the other two on the [illegible] side of the line.

Prob. [illegible] *the side of a square to construct* [illegible]

Let *AB* be the given side.

1st. Draw a line and set off *AB* upon it.

2d. Construct perpendiculars at *A* and *B* to *AB*.

3d. From *A* and *B* set off the given side on these perpendiculars to *C* and [illegible] draw a line from *C* to *D*. The figure *ABCD* is the one required.

Prob. [illegible] *the two sides of a parallelogram, and the angle* [illegible] *them, to construct the figure.*

Let *AB* and *AC* be the given sides; and *E* the given angle.

1st. Draw a line, and set off AB upon it.

2d Construct at A an angle equal to the given one by *Prob.* 13.

3d. Set off, along the side of this angle, from A, the other given line AC.

4th. From C, with the distance AB describe an arc, and from B with the distance AC describe another arc.

5th. From the point D, where the arcs cross, draw lines to C, and B. The figure $ABDC$ is the one required.

Prob. 40. (Pl. III. Fig. 46.) *To circumscribe a given triangle by a circle.*

Let ABC be the given triangle.

As the circumference of the required circle must be described through the three given points A, B and C, its centre and radius will be found precisely as in *Prob.* 19.

Prob. 41. (Pl. III. Fig. 47.) *In a given triangle to inscribe a circle.*

Let ABC be the given triangle.

1st. By *Prob.* 16 construct the lines bisecting the angles A, and C; and mark the point D where these lines cross.

2d. From D by *Prob.* 8 construct a perpendicular DE, to AC.

3d. From D, with the distance DE, describe a circle. This is the one required.

Prob. 42. (Pl. IV. Fig. 48.) *In a given circle to inscribe a square.*

Let O be the centre of the given circle.

1st. Through O draw a diameter AB, and a second diameter CD perpendicular to it.

2d. Draw the lines AC, CB, BD, and DA. The figure $ADBC$ is the one required.

Prob. 43. (Pl. IV. Fig. 48.) *In a given circle to inscribe a regular octagon.*

1st. Having inscribed a square in the circle bisect each of its sides; and through the bisecting points and the centre O draw radii.

2d. Draw lines from the points d, b, a, c, where these radii meet the circumference, to the adjacent points D, A, &c. The figure $dAbC$ &c. is the one required.

tions, many of the lines of construction need not be actually drawn, either in whole, or in part. In this case, for example, a small portion of the line A—B, at its middle point, is alone necessary to determine this point. In like manner, the points L and E could have been marked, without describing the arc actually, but by simply dotting the points required. In this manner, a draftsman, by a skilful selection of his lines of construction, and using only such of them, in whole, or in part, as are indispensably requisite for the solution, may, in complicated constructions, avoid confusion from the intersection of a multiplicity of lines of construction, and abridge his labor.

Prob. 23. (Pl. II. Fig. 29.) *To draw a tangent to two given circles.*

Let A be the centre of one of the circles, and AC its radius; B the centre, and BE the radius of the other.

1st. Through AB draw a line.

2d. From C set off CD equal to BE.

3d. From A, with the radius AD, equal to the difference between the radii of the given circles, describe a circle.

4th. From B by *Prob.* 22 draw a tangent BD to this last circle, and through the tangential point D, a radius AC to the given circle.

5th. Through C draw a line parallel to BD. This line will touch the other given circle, and is the required tangent.

Verification. CE will be found equal to BD, if the construction is accurate.

Prob. 24. (Pl. II. Fig. 30.) *Having two lines that make an angle, to construct within the angle, a circle with a given radius tangent to the two given lines.*

Let AB and AC be the two given lines containing the angle.

1st. By *Prob.* 16 construct the line AD which divides the given angle into two equal parts.

2d. By *Prob.* 10 set off a point b at a distance from AB equal to the given radius, and through this point draw the line ab parallel to AB, and mark the point a where it crosses

3d. From *a*, with the given radius, describe a circle. This is the one required.

Verification. The distances *Ac*, and *Ad*, will be found equal, if the construction is accurate.

Prob. 25. (Pl. II. Fig. 31.) *Having two lines containing an angle, and a given radius of a circle, to construct, as in the last case, this circle tangent to the two lines; and then to construct another circle which shall be tangent to the last and also to the two lines.*

Let *AB* and *CD* be the two lines, the point of meeting of which is not on the drawing.

1st. By *Prob.* 17 find the line *EF* that equally divides the angle between the lines.

2d. By *Prob.* 24 construct the circle, with the given radius *ab*, tangent to these two lines.

3d. At *b*, where *EF* crosses the circumference, draw by *Prob.* 20 a tangent to the circle, and mark the point *d* where it crosses *AB*.

4th. From *d*, set off *de* equal to *db*, and mark the point *e*.

5th. At *e* construct by *Prob.* 6 a perpendicular *ef*, to *AB*, and mark the point *f*, where it crosses *EF*.

6th. From *f*, with the radius *fe*, describe a circle. This is tangent to the first circle, and to the two given lines.

Remark. In like manner a third circle might be constructed tangent to the second and to the two given lines; and so on as many in succession as may be wanted.

Prob. 26. (Pl. III. Fig. 32.) *Having a circle and right line given, to construct a circle of a given radius which shall be tangent to the given circle and right line.*

Let *C* be the centre of the given circle, and *AB* the given line.

1st. By *Prob.* 12 draw a line parallel to *AB*, and at a distance *BG* from it, equal to the given radius.

2d. Draw a radius *CD* through any point *D* of the given circle, and prolong it outwards.

3d. From *D* set off, along the radius, a distance *DE* equal to *BG*, or the given radius.

4th. From *C*, with the distance *CE*, describe an arc

and mark the point *F* where it crosses the line parallel to *AB*.

5th. From the point *F*, with the given radius describe a circle. This is the one required.

Remarks. If the construction is accurate a line drawn from *F* to *C* will pass through the point where the circles touch, and one drawn from *F* perpendicular to *AB* will pass through the point where the circle touches the line.

If from the centre *C*, a perpendicular is drawn to *AB*, and the points *a*, *b* and *d* where the perpendicular crosses the line and the given circle are marked, it will be found that the given radius cannot be less than one half of *ab* nor greater than one half of *ad*.

Prob. 27. (Pl. III. Fig. 33.) *Having a circle and right line given, to construct a circle which shall be tangent to the given circle at a given point, and also to the line.*

Let *C* be the centre of the given circle, *D* the given point on its circumference, and *AB* the given line.

1st. By *Prob.* 20 construct a tangent to the given circle at the point *D*; prolong it to cross the given line, and mark the point *A* where it crosses.

2d. By *Prob.* 16 construct the line *AE* which bisects the angle between the tangent and the given line.

3d. Through *CD* draw a radius, and prolong it to cross the bisecting line at *E*.

4th. Mark the point *E*, and with the distance *ED* describe a circle. This is the required circle.

Prob. 28. (Pl. III. Fig. 34.) *Having a circle and right line, to construct a circle which shall be tangent to the given circle, and also to the line at a given point on it.*

Let *C* be the centre of the given circle; *AB* the given line, and *a* the given point on it.

1st. By *Prob.* 6 construct a perpendicular at *a* to the given line.

2d. From *a* set off *ab* equal to the radius *Cd* of the given circle.

3d. Draw a line through *bC*, and by *Prob.* 5 bisect the distance *bC* by a perpendicular to the line *bC*.

4th. Mark the point *c*, where this perpendicular crosses the

one at a; and with ac describe a circle. This is the one required.

Prob. 29. (Pl. III. Fig. 85.) *Having two circles, to construct a third which shall be tangent to one of them at a given point, and also touch the other.*

Let C and B be the centres of the two given circles; and D the given point on one of them, at which the required circle is to be tangent to it.

1st. Through CD draw a line, which prolong each way from C and D.

2d. From D set off towards C the distance DA equal to the radius BF of the other given circle.

3d. Through AB draw a line, and by *Probs.* 5 and 6, bisect AB by the perpendicular GE.

4th. Mark the point E, where the perpendicular crosses the line CD prolonged; and with the distance ED describe a circle from E. This is the one required.

Prob. 30. (Pl. III. Fig. 86.) *Having a given distance, or line, and the perpendicular which bisects it, to construct three arcs of circles, the radii of two of which shall be equal, and of a given length, and their centres on the given line; and the third shall pass through a given point on the perpendicular and be tangent to the other two circles.*

Let AB be the given line, and D the given point on the perpendicular to AB through its middle point C; and let the distance CD be less than AC, the half of AB.

1st. Take any distance, *less than* CD, and set it off from A and B, to b and c, and mark these two points for the centres of the two arcs of the equal given radii less than CD.

2d. Set off from D the distance Dc equal to Ab, and through bc draw a line.

3d. Bisect bc by a perpendicular, by *Probs.* 5 and 6, and mark the point d where it crosses the perpendicular to AB prolonged below it, the point d is the centre of the third arc.

4th. Draw a line through db, and prolong it; and also one through dc which prolong.

5th. From b, with the distance bA, describe an arc from A to m on the line db prolonged; and one, from the other centre c, from B to n on the line dc prolonged.

6th. From *d*, with the distance *dD*, describe an arc around to the two lines *db*, and *de* prolonged. This is the third arc required, and touches the other two where they cross the lines *db* and *de* prolonged at *m* and *n*.

Remark. This curve is termed a *half oval*, or a *three centre curve*. The other half of the curve, on the other side of *AB*, can be drawn by setting off a distance *Cg* equal to *Cd*, and by continuing the arcs described from *b* and *e* around to lines drawn from *g*, through *b* and *e*; and by connecting these arcs by another described from *g*, with a radius equal to *Dd*.

Prob. 31. (Pl. III. Fig. 37.) *Having a given line and the perpendicular that bisects it; also two lines drawn through a given point, on the perpendicular, and each making the same angle with it; to construct a curve formed of four arcs of circles, two of these arcs to have equal given radii, and their centres to lie on the given line, and at equal distances from its extremities; each of the other arcs to have equal radii, and to be tangent respectively to one of the given lines where it crosses the perpendicular and also to one of the first arcs.*

Let *CD* be the given line; *B* the given point on the bisecting perpendicular; and *Bm*, *Bn*, the two lines, drawn through *B*, making the same angle with the perpendicular.

1st. From *C* and *D*, set off the same distance to *b* and *a*, for the given radii of the two first arcs; which distance must, in all cases, be taken *less than the perpendicular distance from the point b* or *a*, *to one of the given lines through B*.

2d. At *B* draw a perpendicular to the line *Bm*.

3d. Set off from *B*, along this perpendicular, a distance *Bd* equal *Cb*.

4th. Draw a line through *bd*, and bisect this distance by a perpendicular.

5th. Having marked the point *c*, where this last perpendicular crosses the one at *B*, draw through *cb* a line, and prolong it beyond *b*.

6th. From *b*, with the distance *bC*, describe an arc, which prolong to the line through *bc*; this is one of the first required arcs.

7th. From *c*, with a distance *cB*, describe an arc. This is one of the second required arcs.

8th. Through *a*, and the point *f*, where *bc* crosses the perpendicular *BA* prolonged, draw a line.

9th. From *a*, set off *ae* equal to *bc*.

10th. From *a* and *e*, with radii respectively equal to *bC*, and *eB*, describe arcs. These are the others required; and *CBD* the required curve.

Remark. If the construction is accurate, the perpendicular through *BA* will bisect the distance *ec*.

This curve is termed a *four centre obtuse* or *pointed* curve, according as the distance *AB* is less or greater than *AC*.

Prob. 32. (Pl. III. Fig. 38.) *Having a line, and the perpendicular which bisects it, and a given point on the perpendicular; to construct a curve formed of five arcs of circles, the consecutive arcs to be tangent; the centres of two of the arcs to be on the given line, and at equal distances from its extremities; the radii of the two arcs, respectively tangent to these two, to be equal, and of a given length; and the centre of the fifth arc, which is to be tangent to these two last, to lie on the given perpendicular.*

Let *AB* be the given line, and *C* the point on its bisecting perpendicular *LC*.

1st. Take any distance, *less than LC*, and set it off from *B* to *D*, and from *A* to *f*.

2d. From *C* set off *CG* equal to *BD*, and draw a line from *G* to *D*.

3d. Bisect the distance *DG* by a perpendicular; and mark the point *E*, where this perpendicular crosses the perpendicular *LC* prolonged.

4th. Draw a line from *E* to *D*.

5th. Take any distance, *less than CE*, equal to the given radius of the second arc, and set it off from *C* to *F*.

6th. Through *F* draw a line *FH* parallel to *AB*.

7th. Take off *GF*, the difference between *CF* and *CG*, and with it describe an arc from *D*; and mark the points *a* and *b* where it crosses the lines *DE* and *FH*.

8th. Take any point *c* on this arc, between the points *a* and *b*, and draw from it a line to *F*.

9th. Bisect the line *cF* by a perpendicular, and mark the point *I* where it crosses the perpendicular *CL* prolonged.

10th. From c draw a line through D and prolong it; and another from I prolonged through e.

11th. From e draw a perpendicular to CI; and from d, where it crosses CI, set off dg equal to ed, and mark the point g.

12th. From I draw a line through g and prolong it; and one from g prolonged through f.

13. From D and f, with the distance BD, describe the arcs Bm, and Ap; from c and g, with the distance cm, or gp, describe the arcs mn, and po; and from I with the distance IC, describe the arc no. The curve BCA is the one required.

Remarks. This curve is also termed a semi oval; and, from the number of arcs of which it is composed, a *curve of five centres.*

Prob. 33. (Pl. III. Fig. 39.) *Having two parallel lines, to construct a curve of three centres which shall be tangent to the two parallels at their extremities.*

Let AB and CD be the given parallels; and B and D the points at which the required curve is to be drawn tangent.

1st. From B construct a perpendicular to AB, and mark the point b where it crosses CD; and also a perpendicular at D to CD.

2d. From B, set off any distance Bc *less than the half of* Bb; and through c draw a line parallel to AB, and mark the point d where it crosses the perpendicular to CD.

3d. From c, set off, along cd prolonged, the distance ca equal to cB.

4th. Taking ca, as the radius of the first arc, construct a quarter oval by *Prob.* 30 through the points a and D.

5th. Prolong the arc described from c to the point B. The curve BaD is the one required.

Remark. This curve is termed a *scotia* of two centres.

Prob. 34. (Pl. III. Fig. 40.) *Having two parallels, to construct a quarter of a curve of five centres tangent to them at their extremities.*

Let AB and CD be the given parallels, and B and D their extremities.

1st. Proceed, as in the last case, to draw the perpendiculars

at B, and D, and a parallel to AB through a point c, taken on the first perpendicular, at a distance from B less than the half of Bl.

2d. Set off from c a distance ca equal to cB; and on ad and Dd describe the quarter oval by *Prob.* 32.

3d. Prolong the first arc from a to B, which will complete the required curve.

Remark. This curve is termed a *scotia* of three centres.

Prob. 35. (Pl. III. Fig. 41.) *Having two parallels and a given point on each, to construct two equal arcs which shall be tangent to each other and respectively tangent to the parallels at the given points.*

Let AB and CD be the two parallels; B and D the given points.

1st. Draw a line through BD, and bisect the distance BD.

2d. Bisect each half BE, and ED by perpendiculars.

3d. From B, and D draw perpendiculars to AB and CD, and mark the points a, and b, where they cross the bisecting perpendiculars.

4th. From a, with the distance aE, describe an arc to B; and from b, with the same distance, an arc ED. These are the required arcs.

Prob. 36. (Pl. III. Fig. 42.) *Having two parallels, and a point on each, to construct two equal arcs which shall be tangent to each other, have their centres respectively on the parallels, and pass through the given points.*

Let AB and CD be the parallels, B and D the given points.

1st. Join BD by a line and bisect it.

2d. Bisect each half BE, and ED by a perpendicular; and mark the points a and b, where the perpendiculars cross the parallels.

3d. From a, with aB, describe the arc BE; and from b, with the same distance, the arc DE. These are the required arcs.

Construction of Problems of Circles and Rectilineal Figures.

Prob. 37. (Pl. III. Fig. 43.) *Having the sides of a triangle to construct the figure.*

Let *AC*, *BC*, and *AB* be the lengths of the given sides.

1st. Draw a line, and set off upon it the longest side *AB*.

2d. From the point *A*, with a radius equal to *AC*, one of the remaining sides, describe an arc.

3d. From the point *B*, with the third side *BC*, describe a second arc, and mark the point *C* where the arcs cross.

4th. Draw lines from *C*, to *A* and *B*. The figure *ACB* is the one required.

Remark. The side *AC* might have been set off from *B*, and *BC* from *A*; this would have given an equal triangle to the one constructed, but its vertex would have been placed differently.

Remark. This construction is also used to find the position of a point when its distances from two other given points are given. We proceed to make the construction in this case like the preceding. It will be seen, that the required point can take four different positions with respect to the two others. Two of them, like the vertex of the triangle, will lie on one side of the line joining the given points, and the other two on the other side of the line.

Prob. 38. (Pl. III. Fig. 44.) *Having the side of a square to construct the figure.*

Let *AB* be the given side.

1st. Draw a line, and set off *AB* upon it.

2d. Construct perpendiculars at *A*, and *B*, to *AB*.

3d. From *A* and *B*, set off the given side on these perpendiculars to *C* and *D*; and draw a line from *C* to *D*. The figure *ABCD* is the one required.

Prob. 39. (Pl. III. Fig. 45.) *Having the two sides of a parallelogram, and the angle contained by them, to construct the figure.*

Let *AB*, and *AC* be the given sides; and *E* the given angle.

1st. Draw a line, and set off AB upon it.

2d Construct at A an angle equal to the given one by *Prob.* 13.

3d. Set off, along the side of this angle, from A, the other given line AC.

4th. From C, with the distance AB describe an arc, and from B with the distance AC describe another arc.

5th. From the point D, where the arcs cross, draw lines to C, and B. The figure $ABDC$ is the one required.

Prob. 40. (Pl. III. Fig. 46.) *To circumscribe a given triangle by a circle.*

Let ABC be the given triangle.

As the circumference of the required circle must be described through the three given points A, B and C, its centre and radius will be found precisely as in *Prob.* 19.

Prob. 41. (Pl. III. Fig. 47.) *In a given triangle to inscribe a circle.*

Let ABC be the given triangle.

1st. By *Prob.* 16 construct the lines bisecting the angles A, and C; and mark the point D where these lines cross.

2d. From D by *Prob.* 8 construct a perpendicular DE, to AC.

3d. From D, with the distance DE, describe a circle. This is the one required.

Prob. 42. (Pl. IV. Fig. 48.) *In a given circle to inscribe a square.*

Let O be the centre of the given circle.

1st. Through O draw a diameter AB, and a second diameter CD perpendicular to it.

2d. Draw the lines AC, CB, BD, and DA. The figure $ADBC$ is the one required.

Prob. 43. (Pl. IV. Fig. 48.) *In a given circle to inscribe a regular octagon.*

1st. Having inscribed a square in the circle bisect each of its sides; and through the bisecting points and the centre O draw radii.

2d. Draw lines from the points d, b, a, c, where these radii meet the circumference, to the adjacent points D, A, &c. The figure $dAbC$ &c. is the one required.

tions, many of the lines of construction need not be actually drawn, either in whole, or in part. In this case, for example, a small portion of the line $A—B$, at its middle point, is alone necessary to determine this point. In like manner, the points L and E could have been marked, without describing the arc actually, but by simply dotting the points required. In this manner, a draftsman, by a skilful selection of his lines of construction, and using only such of them, in whole, or in part, as are indispensably requisite for the solution, may, in complicated constructions, avoid confusion from the intersection of a multiplicity of lines of construction, and abridge his labor.

Prob. 23. (Pl. II. Fig. 29.) *To draw a tangent to two given circles.*

Let A be the centre of one of the circles, and AC its radius; B the centre, and BE the radius of the other.

1st. Through AB draw a line.

2d. From C set off CD equal to BE.

3d. From A, with the radius AD, equal to the difference between the radii of the given circles, describe a circle.

4th. From B by *Prob.* 22 draw a tangent BD to this last circle, and through the tangential point D, a radius AC to the given circle.

5th. Through C draw a line parallel to BD. This line will touch the other given circle, and is the required tangent.

Verification. CE will be found equal to BD, if the construction is accurate.

Prob. 24. (Pl. II. Fig. 30.) *Having two lines that make an angle, to construct within the angle, a circle with a given radius tangent to the two given lines.*

Let AB and AC be the two given lines containing the angle.

1st. By *Prob.* 16 construct the line AD which divides the given angle into two equal parts.

2d. By *Prob.* 10 set off a point b at a distance from AB equal to the given radius, and through this point draw the line ab parallel to AB, and mark the point a where it crosses AD.

3d. From a, with the given radius, describe a circle. This is the one required.

Verification. The distances *Ac*, and *Ad*, will be found equal, if the construction is accurate.

Prob. 25. (Pl. II. Fig. 31.) *Having two lines containing an angle, and a given radius of a circle, to construct, as in the last case, this circle tangent to the two lines; and then to construct another circle which shall be tangent to the last and also to the two lines.*

Let *AB* and *CD* be the two lines, the point of meeting of which is not on the drawing.

1st. By *Prob.* 17 find the line *EF* that equally divides the angle between the lines.

2d. By *Prob.* 24 construct the circle, with the given radius *ac*, tangent to these two lines.

3d. At *b*, where *EF* crosses the circumference, draw by *Prob.* 20 a tangent to the circle, and mark the point *d* where it crosses *AB*.

4th. From *d*, set off *de* equal to *db*, and mark the point *e*.

5th. At *e* construct by *Prob.* 6 a perpendicular *ef*, to *AB*, and mark the point *f*, where it crosses *EF*.

6th. From *f*, with the radius *fe*, describe a circle. This is tangent to the first circle, and to the two given lines.

Remark. In like manner a third circle might be constructed tangent to the second and to the two given lines; and so on as many in succession as may be wanted.

Prob. 26. (Pl. III. Fig. 32.) *Having a circle and right line given, to construct a circle of a given radius which shall be tangent to the given circle and right line.*

Let *C* be the centre of the given circle, and *AB* the given line.

1st. By *Prob.* 12 draw a line parallel to *AB*, and at a distance *BG* from it, equal to the given radius.

2d. Draw a radius *CD* through any point *D* of the given circle, and prolong it outwards.

3d. From *D* set off, along the radius, a distance *DE* equal to *BG*, or the given radius.

4th. From *C*, with the distance *CE*, describe an arc

and mark the point *F* where it crosses the line parallel to *AB*.

5th. From the point *F*, with the given radius describe a circle. This is the one required.

Remarks. If the construction is accurate a line drawn from *F* to *C* will pass through the point where the circles touch, and one drawn from *F* perpendicular to *AB* will pass through the point where the circle touches the line.

If from the centre *C*, a perpendicular is drawn to *AB*, and the points *a*, *b* and *d* where the perpendicular crosses the line and the given circle are marked, it will be found that the given radius cannot be less than one half of *ab* nor greater than one half of *ad*.

Prob. 27. (Pl. III. Fig. 33.) *Having a circle and right line given, to construct a circle which shall be tangent to the given circle at a given point, and also to the line.*

Let *C* be the centre of the given circle, *D* the given point on its circumference, and *AB* the given line.

1st. By *Prob.* 20 construct a tangent to the given circle at the point *D*; prolong it to cross the given line, and mark the point *A* where it crosses.

2d. By *Prob.* 16 construct the line *AE* which bisects the angle between the tangent and the given line.

3d. Through *CD* draw a radius, and prolong it to cross the bisecting line at *E*.

4th. Mark the point *E*, and with the distance *ED* describe a circle. This is the required circle.

Prob. 28. (Pl. III. Fig. 34.) *Having a circle and right line, to construct a circle which shall be tangent to the given circle, and also to the line at a given point on it.*

Let *C* be the centre of the given circle; *AB* the given line, and *a* the given point on it.

1st. By *Prob.* 6 construct a perpendicular at *a* to the given line.

2d. From *a* set off *ab* equal to the radius *Cd* of the given circle.

3d. Draw a line through *bC*, and by *Prob.* 5 bisect the distance *bC* by a perpendicular to the line *bC*.

4th. Mark the point *c*, where this perpendicular crosses the

one at a; and with ac describe a circle. This is the one required.

Prob. 29. (Pl. III. Fig. 85.) *Having two circles, to construct a third which shall be tangent to one of them at a given point, and also touch the other.*

Let C and B be the centres of the two given circles; and D the given point on one of them, at which the required circle is to be tangent to it.

1st. Through CD draw a line, which prolong each way from C and D.

2d. From D set off towards C the distance DA equal to the radius BF of the other given circle.

3d. Through AB draw a line, and by *Probs.* 5 and 6, bisect AB by the perpendicular GE.

4th. Mark the point E, where the perpendicular crosses the line CD prolonged; and with the distance ED describe a circle from E. This is the one required.

Prob. 30. (Pl. III. Fig. 86.) *Having a given distance, or line, and the perpendicular which bisects it, to construct three arcs of circles, the radii of two of which shall be equal, and of a given length, and their centres on the given line; and the third shall pass through a given point on the perpendicular and be tangent to the other two circles.*

Let AB be the given line, and D the given point on the perpendicular to AB through its middle point C; and let the distance CD be less than AC, the half of AB.

1st. Take any distance, *less than* CD, and set it off from A and B, to b and c, and mark these two points for the centres of the two arcs of the equal given radii less than CD.

2d. Set off from D the distance Dc equal to Ab, and through bc draw a line.

3d. Bisect bc by a perpendicular, by *Probs.* 5 and 6, and mark the point d where it crosses the perpendicular to AB prolonged below it, the point d is the centre of the third arc.

4th. Draw a line through db, and prolong it; and also one through dc which prolong.

5th. From b, with the distance bA, describe an arc from A to m on the line db prolonged; and one, from the other centre c, from B to n on the line dc prolonged.

6th. From *d*, with the distance *dD*, describe an arc around to the two lines *dh* and *dr* prolonged. This is the third arc required, and touches the other two where they cross the lines *df* and *de* prolonged at *m* and *n*.

Remark. This curve is termed a *half oval*, or a *three centre curve.* The other half of the curve, on the other side of *AB*, can be drawn by setting off a distance *Cg* equal to *Cd*, and by continuing the arcs described from *b* and *e* around to lines drawn from *g*, through *b* and *e*; and by connecting these arcs by another described from *g*, with a radius equal to *Dd*.

Prob. 31. (Pl. III. Fig. 37.) *Having a given line and the perpendicular that bisects it; also two lines drawn through a given point, on the perpendicular, and each making the same angle with it; to construct a curve formed of four arcs of circles, two of these arcs to have equal given radii, and their centres to lie on the given line, and at equal distances from its extremities; each of the other arcs to have equal radii, and to be tangent respectively to one of the given lines where it crosses the perpendicular and also to one of the first arcs.*

Let *CD* be the given line; *B* the given point on the bisecting perpendicular; and *Bm*, *Bn*, the two lines, drawn through *B*, making the same angle with the perpendicular.

1st. From *C* and *D*, set off the same distance to *b* and *a*, for the given radii of the two first arcs; which distance must, in all cases, be taken *less than the perpendicular distance from the point b* or *a*, *to one of the given lines through B.*

2d. At *B* draw a perpendicular to the line *Bm*.

3d. Set off from *B* along this perpendicular, a distance *Bd* equal *Cb*.

4th. Draw a line through *bd*, and bisect this distance by a perpendicular.

5th. Having marked the point *c*, where this last perpendicular crosses the one at *B*, draw through *cb* a line, and prolong it beyond *b*.

6th. From *b*, with the distance *bC*, describe an arc, which prolong to the line through *bc*; this is one of the first required arcs.

7th. From *c*, with a distance *cB*, describe an arc. This is one of the second required arcs.

8th. Through *a*, and the point *f*, where *bc* crosses the perpendicular *BA* prolonged, draw a line.

9th. From *a*, set off *ae* equal to *bc*.

10th. From *a* and *e*, with radii respectively equal to *bC*, and *eB*, describe arcs. These are the others required; and *CBD* the required curve.

Remark. If the construction is accurate, the perpendicular through *BA* will bisect the distance *ec*.

This curve is termed a *four centre obtuse* or *pointed* curve, according as the distance *AB* is less or greater than *AC*.

Prob. 32. (Pl. III. Fig. 38.) *Having a line, and the perpendicular which bisects it, and a given point on the perpendicular; to construct a curve formed of five arcs of circles, the consecutive arcs to be tangent; the centres of two of the arcs to be on the given line, and at equal distances from its extremities; the radii of the two arcs, respectively tangent to these two, to be equal, and of a given length; and the centre of the fifth arc, which is to be tangent to these two last, to lie on the given perpendicular.*

Let *AB* be the given line, and *C* the point on its bisecting perpendicular *LC*.

1st. Take any distance, *less than LC*, and set it off from *B* to *D*, and from *A* to *f*.

2d. From *C* set off *CG* equal to *BD*, and draw a line from *G* to *D*.

3d. Bisect the distance *DG* by a perpendicular; and mark the point *E*, where this perpendicular crosses the perpendicular *LC* prolonged.

4th. Draw a line from *E* to *D*.

5th. Take any distance, *less than CE*, equal to the given radius of the second arc, and set it off from *C* to *F*.

6th. Through *F* draw a line *FH* parallel to *AB*.

7th. Take off *GF*, the difference between *CF* and *CG*, and with it describe an arc from *D*; and mark the points *a* and *b* where it crosses the lines *DE* and *FH*.

8th. Take any point *c* on this arc, between the points *a* and *b*, and draw from it a line to *F*.

9th. Bisect the line *cF* by a perpendicular, and mark the point *I* where it crosses the perpendicular *CL* prolonged.

10th. From c draw a line through D and prolong it; and another from I prolonged through c.

11th. From c draw a perpendicular to CI; and from d, where it crosses CI, set off dg equal to cd, and mark the point g.

12th. From I draw a line through g and prolong it; and one from g prolonged through f.

13. From D and f, with the distance BD, describe the arcs Bm, and Ap; from c and g, with the distance cm, or gp, describe the arcs mn, and po; and from I with the distance IC, describe the arc no. The curve BCA is the one required.

Remarks. This curve is also termed a semi oval; and, from the number of arcs of which it is composed, a *curve of five centres.*

Prob. 33. (Pl. III. Fig. 39.) *Having two parallel lines, to construct a curve of three centres which shall be tangent to the two parallels at their extremities.*

Let AB and CD be the given parallels; and B and D the points at which the required curve is to be drawn tangent.

1st. From B construct a perpendicular to AB, and mark the point b where it crosses CD; and also a perpendicular at D to CD.

2d. From B, set off any distance Bc *less than the half of* Bb; and through c draw a line parallel to AB, and mark the point d where it crosses the perpendicular to CD.

3d. From c, set off, along cd prolonged, the distance ca equal to cB.

4th. Taking ca, as the radius of the first arc, construct a quarter oval by *Prob.* 30 through the points a and D.

5th. Prolong the arc described from c to the point B. The curve BaD is the one required.

Remark. This curve is termed a *scotia* of two centres.

Prob. 34. (Pl. III. Fig. 40.) *Having two parallels, to construct a quarter of a curve of five centres tangent to them at their extremities.*

Let AB and CD be the given parallels, and B and D their extremities.

1st. Proceed, as in the last case, to draw the perpendiculars

at *B*, and *D*, and a parallel to *AB* through a point *c*, taken on the first perpendicular, at a distance from *B* less than the half of *Bi*.

2d. Set off from *c* a distance *ca* equal to *cB*; and on *ai* and *Dd* describe the quarter oval by *Prob.* 32.

3d. Prolong the first arc from *a* to *B*, which will complete the required curve.

Remark. This curve is termed a *scotia* of three centres.

Prob. 35. (Pl. III. Fig. 41.) *Having two parallels and a given point on each, to construct two equal arcs which shall be tangent to each other and respectively tangent to the parallels at the given points.*

Let *AB* and *CD* be the two parallels; *B* and *D* the given points.

1st. Draw a line through *BD*, and bisect the distance *BD*.

2d. Bisect each half *BE*, and *ED* by perpendiculars.

3d. From *B*, and *D* draw perpendiculars to *AB* and *CD*, and mark the points *a*, and *b*, where they cross the bisecting perpendiculars.

4th. From *a*, with the distance *aE*, describe an arc to *B*; and from *b*, with the same distance, an arc *ED*. These are the required arcs.

Prob. 36. (Pl. III. Fig. 42.) *Having two parallels, and a point on each, to construct two equal arcs which shall be tangent to each other, have their centres respectively on the parallels, and pass through the given points.*

Let *AB* and *CD* be the parallels, *B* and *D* the given points.

1st. Join *BD* by a line and bisect it.

2d. Bisect each half *BE*, and *ED* by a perpendicular; and mark the points *a* and *b*, where the perpendiculars cross the parallels.

3d. From *a*, with *aB*, describe the arc *BE*; and from *b*, with the same distance, the arc *DE*. These are the required arcs.

Construction of Problems of Circles and Rectilineal Figures.

Prob. 37. (Pl. III. Fig. 43.) *Having the sides of a triangle to construct the figure.*

Let AC, BC, and AB be the lengths of the given sides.

1st. Draw a line, and set off upon it the longest side AB.

2d. From the point A, with a radius equal to AC, one of the remaining sides, describe an arc.

3d. From the point B, with the third side BC, describe a second arc, and mark the point C where the arcs cross.

4th. Draw lines from C, to A and B. The figure ACB is the one required.

Remark. The side AC might have been set off from B, and BC from A; this would have given an equal triangle to the one constructed, but its vertex would have been placed differently.

Remark. This construction is also used to find the position of a point when its distances from two other given points are given. We proceed to make the construction in this case like the preceding. It will be seen, that the required point can take four different positions with respect to the two others. Two of them, like the vertex of the triangle, will lie on one side of the line joining the given points, and the other two on the other side of the line.

Prob. 38. (Pl. III. Fig. 44.) *Having the side of a square to construct the figure.*

Let AB be the given side.

1st. Draw a line, and set off AB upon it.

2d. Construct perpendiculars at A, and B, to AB.

3d. From A and B, set off the given side on these perpendiculars to C and D; and draw a line from C to D. The figure $ABCD$ is the one required.

Prob. 39. (Pl. III. Fig. 45.) *Having the two sides of a parallelogram, and the angle contained by them, to construct the figure.*

Let AB, and AC be the given sides; and E the given angle.

1st. Draw a line, and set off *AB* upon it.

2d Construct at *A* an angle equal to the given one by *Prob.* 13.

3d. Set off, along the side of this angle, from *A*, the other given line *AC*.

4th. From *C*, with the distance *AB* describe an arc, and from *B* with the distance *AC* describe another arc.

5th. From the point *D*, where the arcs cross, draw lines to *C*, and *B*. The figure *ABDC* is the one required.

Prob. 40. (Pl. III. Fig. 46.) *To circumscribe a given triangle by a circle.*

Let *ABC* be the given triangle.

As the circumference of the required circle must be described through the three given points *A*, *B* and *C*, its centre and radius will be found precisely as in *Prob.* 19.

Prob. 41. (Pl. III. Fig. 47.) *In a given triangle to inscribe a circle.*

Let *ABC* be the given triangle.

1st. By *Prob.* 16 construct the lines bisecting the angles *A*, and *C*; and mark the point *D* where these lines cross.

2d. From *D* by *Prob.* 8 construct a perpendicular *DE*, to *AC*.

3d. From *D*, with the distance *DE*, describe a circle. This is the one required.

Prob. 42. (Pl. IV. Fig. 48.) *In a given circle to inscribe a square.*

Let *O* be the centre of the given circle.

1st. Through *O* draw a diameter *AB*, and a second diameter *CD* perpendicular to it.

2d. Draw the lines *AC*, *CB*, *BD*, and *DA*. The figure *ADBC* is the one required.

Prob. 43. (Pl. IV. Fig. 48.) *In a given circle to inscribe a regular octagon.*

1st. Having inscribed a square in the circle bisect each of its sides; and through the bisecting points and the centre *O* draw radii.

2d. Draw lines from the points *d*, *b*, *a*, *c*, where these radii meet the circumference, to the adjacent points *D*, *A*, &c. The figure *dAbC* &c. is the one required.

Remark. By bisecting the sides of the octagon, and drawing radii through the points of bisection, and then drawing lines from the points where these radii meet the circumference to the adjacent points of the octagon, a figure of sixteen equal sides can be inscribed, and in like manner one of 32 sides, &c.

Prob. 44. (Pl. IV. Fig. 49.) *To inscribe in a given circle a regular hexagon.*

Let *O* be the centre of the given circle.

1st. Having taken off the radius *OA*, commence at *A*, and set it off from *A* to *B*, and from *A* to *F*, on the circumference.

2d. From *B* set off the same distance to *C*; and from *C* to *D*, and so on to *F*.

3d. Draw lines between the adjacent points. The figure *ABC* &c. is the one required.

Remark. By a process similar to the one employed for constructing an octagon from a square, we can, from the hexagon, construct a figure of 12 sides; then one of 24; and so on doubling the number of sides.

Prob. 45. (Pl. IV. Fig. 49.) *To inscribe in a given circle an equilateral triangle.*

Having, as in the last problem, constructed a regular hexagon, draw lines between the alternate angles, as *AC*, *CE*, and *EA*; the figure thus formed is the one required.

Prob. 46. (Pl. IV. Fig. 50.) *To inscribe in a given circle a regular pentagon.*

Let *O* be the centre of the given circle.

1st. Draw a diameter of the circle *AB*, and a second one *CD* perpendicular to it.

2d. Bisect the radius *OB*, and from the point of bisection *a* set off the distance *aC*, to *b*, along *AB*.

3d. From *C*, with the radius *Cb*, describe an arc, and mark the points *H*, and *I*, where it crosses the circumference of the given circle.

4th. From *H*, and *I*, set off the same distance to *G* and *K* on the circumference.

5th. Draw the lines *CH*, *HG*, *GK*, *KI*, and *IC*. The figure *CHGKI* is the one required.

Prob. 47. *To construct a regular figure, the sides of which shall be respectively equal to a given line.*

Let AB be the given line.

First Method. (Pl. IV. Fig. 50.)

1st. Construct any circle, and inscribe within it a regular figure, by one of the preceding *Probs.* of the same number of sides as the one required.

Let us suppose for example that the one required is a pentagon.

2d. Having constructed this inscribed figure, draw from the centre of the circle, through the angular points of the figure, lines; and prolong them outwards, if the side of the inscribed figure is less than the given line.

3d. Prolong any one of the sides, as CI, of the inscribed figure, and set off along it, from the angular point C, a distance Cm equal to the given line.

4th. Through m, draw a line parallel to the line drawn from O through C, and mark the point n, where it crosses the line drawn from O through I.

5th. Through n, draw a line parallel to CI, and mark the point o, where it crosses the line OC prolonged.

6th. From O, set off, along the other lines drawn from C through the other angular points, the distances Op, Oq, and Or, each equal to Om, or On.

7th. The points o, p, r, and n being joined by lines; the figure $opqrn$ is the one required.

Second Method. (Pl. IV. Fig. 51.)

1st. Draw a line and set off the given line AB upon it.

2d. At B construct a perpendicular to AB.

3d. From B, with BA, describe an arc Aa.

4th. Divide this arc into as many equal parts as number of sides in the required figure; and mark the points of division from a, 1, 2, 3, &c.

5th. From A, with AB, describe an arc, and mark the point c where it crosses the arc Aa.

6th. From B draw a line through the division point 2.

7th. From c, set off the distance $c2$, to b, on the arc Bc.

and mark the point *F* where it crosses the line parallel to *AB*.

5th. From the point *F*, with the given radius describe a circle. This is the one required.

Remarks. If the construction is accurate a line drawn from *F* to *C* will pass through the point where the circles touch, and one drawn from *F* perpendicular to *AB* will pass through the point where the circle touches the line.

If from the centre *C*, a perpendicular is drawn to *AB*, and the points *a*, *b* and *d* where the perpendicular crosses the line and the given circle are marked, it will be found that the given radius cannot be less than one half of *ab* nor greater than one half of *ad*.

Prob. 27. (Pl. III. Fig. 33.) *Having a circle and right line given, to construct a circle which shall be tangent to the given circle at a given point, and also to the line.*

Let *C* be the centre of the given circle, *D* the given point on its circumference, and *AB* the given line.

1st. By *Prob.* 20 construct a tangent to the given circle at the point *D*; prolong it to cross the given line, and mark the point *A* where it crosses.

2d. By *Prob.* 16 construct the line *AE* which bisects the angle between the tangent and the given line.

3d. Through *CD* draw a radius, and prolong it to cross the bisecting line at *E*.

4th. Mark the point *E*, and with the distance *ED* describe a circle. This is the required circle.

Prob. 28. (Pl. III. Fig. 34.) *Having a circle and right line, to construct a circle which shall be tangent to the given circle, and also to the line at a given point on it.*

Let *C* be the centre of the given circle; *AB* the given line, and *a* the given point on it.

1st. By *Prob.* 6 construct a perpendicular at *a* to the given line.

2d. From *a* set off *ab* equal to the radius *Cd* of the given circle.

3d. Draw a line through *bC*, and by *Prob.* 5 bisect the distance *bC* by a perpendicular to the line *bC*.

4th. Mark the point *c*, where this perpendicular crosses the

one at *a*; and with *ac* describe a circle. This is the one required.

Prob. 29. (Pl. III. Fig. 35.) *Having two circles, to construct a third which shall be tangent to one of them at a given point, and also touch the other.*

Let *C* and *B* be the centres of the two given circles; and *D* the given point on one of them, at which the required circle is to be tangent to it.

1st. Through *CD* draw a line, which prolong each way from *C* and *D*.

2d. From *D* set off towards *C* the distance *DA* equal to the radius *BF* of the other given circle.

3d. Through *AB* draw a line, and by *Probs.* 5 and 6, bisect *AB* by the perpendicular *GE*.

4th. Mark the point *E*, where the perpendicular crosses the line *CD* prolonged; and with the distance *ED* describe a circle from *E*. This is the one required.

Prob. 30. (Pl. III. Fig. 36.) *Having a given distance, or line, and the perpendicular which bisects it, to construct three arcs of circles, the radii of two of which shall be equal, and of a given length, and their centres on the given line; and the third shall pass through a given point on the perpendicular and be tangent to the other two circles.*

Let *AB* be the given line, and *D* the given point on the perpendicular to *AB* through its middle point *C*; and let the distance *CD* be less than *AC*, the half of *AB*.

1st. Take any distance, *less than CD*, and set it off from *A* and *B*, to *b* and *e*, and mark these two points for the centres of the two arcs of the equal given radii less than *CD*.

2d. Set off from *D* the distance *Dc* equal to *Ab*, and through *bc* draw a line.

3d. Bisect *bc* by a perpendicular, by *Probs.* 5 and 6, and mark the point *d* where it crosses the perpendicular to *AB* prolonged below it, the point *d* is the centre of the third arc.

4th. Draw a line through *db*, and prolong it; and also one through *de* which prolong.

5th. From *b*, with the distance *bA*, describe an arc from *A* to *m* on the line *db* prolonged; and one, from the other centre *e*, from *B* to *n* on the line *de* prolonged.

6th. From *d*, with the distance *dD*, describe an arc around to the two lines *db*, and *de* prolonged. This is the third arc required, and touches the other two where they cross the lines *db* and *de* prolonged at *m* and *n*.

Remark. This curve is termed a *half oval*, or a *three centre curve.* The other half of the curve, on the other side of *AB*, can be drawn by setting off a distance *Cg* equal to *Cd*, and by continuing the arcs described from *b* and *e* around to lines drawn from *g*, through *b* and *e*; and by connecting these arcs by another described from *g*, with a radius equal to *Dd*.

Prob. 31. (Pl. III. Fig. 37.) *Having a given line and the perpendicular that bisects it; also two lines drawn through a given point, on the perpendicular, and each making the same angle with it; to construct a curve formed of four arcs of circles, two of these arcs to have equal given radii, and their centres to lie on the given line, and at equal distances from its extremities; each of the other arcs to have equal radii, and to be tangent respectively to one of the given lines where it crosses the perpendicular and also to one of the first arcs.*

Let *CD* be the given line; *B* the given point on the bisecting perpendicular; and *Bm*, *Bn*, the two lines, drawn through *B*, making the same angle with the perpendicular.

1st. From *C* and *D*, set off the same distance to *b* and *a*, for the given radii of the two first arcs; which distance must, in all cases, be taken *less than the perpendicular distance from the point b or a, to one of the given lines through B.*

2d. At *B* draw a perpendicular to the line *Bm*.

3d. Set off from *B*, along this perpendicular, a distance *Bd* equal *Cb*.

4th. Draw a line through *bd*, and bisect this distance by a perpendicular.

5th. Having marked the point *c*, where this last perpendicular crosses the one at *B*, draw through *cb* a line, and prolong it beyond *b*.

6th. From *b*, with the distance *bC*, describe an arc, which prolong to the line through *bc*; this is one of the first required arcs.

7th. From *c*, with a distance *cB*, describe an arc. This is one of the second required arcs.

8th. Through a, and the point f, where bc crosses the perpendicular BA prolonged, draw a line.

9th. From a, set off ae equal to bc.

10th. From a and e, with radii respectively equal to bC, and eB, describe arcs. These are the others required; and CBD the required curve.

Remark. If the construction is accurate, the perpendicular through BA will bisect the distance ec.

This curve is termed a *four centre obtuse* or *pointed* curve, according as the distance AB is less or greater than AC.

Prob. 32. (Pl. III. Fig. 38.) *Having a line, and the perpendicular which bisects it, and a given point on the perpendicular; to construct a curve formed of five arcs of circles, the consecutive arcs to be tangent; the centres of two of the arcs to be on the given line, and at equal distances from its extremities; the radii of the two arcs, respectively tangent to these two, to be equal, and of a given length; and the centre of the fifth arc, which is to be tangent to these two last, to lie on the given perpendicular.*

Let AB be the given line, and C the point on its bisecting perpendicular LC.

1st. Take any distance, *less than* LC, and set it off from B to D, and from A to f.

2d. From C set off CG equal to BD, and draw a line from G to D.

3d. Bisect the distance DG by a perpendicular; and mark the point E, where this perpendicular crosses the perpendicular LC prolonged.

4th. Draw a line from E to D.

5th. Take any distance, *less than* CE, equal to the given radius of the second arc, and set it off from C to F.

6th. Through F draw a line FH parallel to AB.

7th. Take off GF, the difference between CF and CG, and with it describe an arc from D; and mark the points a and b where it crosses the lines DE and FH.

8th. Take any point c on this arc, between the points a and b, and draw from it a line to F.

9th. Bisect the line cF by a perpendicular, and mark the point I where it crosses the perpendicular CL prolonged.

10th. From *c* draw a line through *D* and prolong it; and another from *I* prolonged through *e*.

11th. From *e* draw a perpendicular to *CI*; and from *d*, where it crosses *CI*, set off *dg* equal to *ed*, and mark the point *g*.

12th. From *I* draw a line through *g* and prolong it; and one from *g* prolonged through *f*.

13. From *D* and *f*, with the distance *BD*, describe the arcs *Bm*, and *Ap*; from *e* and *g*, with the distance *em*, or *gp*, describe the arcs *mn*, and *po*; and from *I* with the distance *IC*, describe the arc *no*. The curve *BCA* is the one required.

Remarks. This curve is also termed a semi oval; and, from the number of arcs of which it is composed, a *curve of five centres.*

Prob. 33. (Pl. III. Fig. 39.) *Having two parallel lines, to construct a curve of three centres which shall be tangent to the two parallels at their extremities.*

Let *AB* and *CD* be the given parallels; and *B* and *D* the points at which the required curve is to be drawn tangent.

1st. From *B* construct a perpendicular to *AB*, and mark the point *b* where it crosses *CD*; and also a perpendicular at *D* to *CD*.

2d. From *B*, set off any distance *Bc less than the half of Bb*; and through *c* draw a line parallel to *AB*, and mark the point *d* where it crosses the perpendicular to *CD*.

3d. From *c*, set off, along *cd* prolonged, the distance *ca* equal to *cB*.

4th. Taking *ca*, as the radius of the first arc, construct a quarter oval by *Prob.* 30 through the points *a* and *D*.

5th. Prolong the arc described from *c* to the point *B*. The curve *BaD* is the one required.

Remark. This curve is termed a *scotia* of two centres.

Prob. 34. (Pl. III. Fig. 40.) *Having two parallels, to construct a quarter of a curve of five centres tangent to them at their extremities.*

Let *AB* and *CD* be the given parallels, and *B* and *D* their extremities.

1st. Proceed, as in the last case, to draw the perpendiculars

at *B*, and *D*, and a parallel to *AB* through a point *c*, taken on the first perpendicular, at a distance from *B* less than the half of *Bl*.

2d. Set off from *c* a distance *ca* equal to *cB*; and on *ad* and *Dd* describe the quarter oval by *Prob.* 32.

3d. Prolong the first arc from *a* to *B*, which will complete the required curve.

Remark. This curve is termed a *scotia* of three centres.

Prob. 35. (Pl. III. Fig. 41.) *Having two parallels and a given point on each, to construct two equal arcs which shall be tangent to each other and respectively tangent to the parallels at the given points.*

Let *AB* and *CD* be the two parallels; *B* and *D* the given points.

1st. Draw a line through *BD*, and bisect the distance *BD*.

2d. Bisect each half *BE*, and *ED* by perpendiculars.

3d. From *B*, and *D* draw perpendiculars to *AB* and *CD*, and mark the points *a*, and *b*, where they cross the bisecting perpendiculars.

4th. From *a*, with the distance *aE*, describe an arc to *B*; and from *b*, with the same distance, an arc *ED*. These are the required arcs.

Prob. 36. (Pl. III. Fig. 42.) *Having two parallels, and a point on each, to construct two equal arcs which shall be tangent to each other, have their centres respectively on the parallels, and pass through the given points.*

Let *AB* and *CD* be the parallels, *B* and *D* the given points.

1st. Join *BD* by a line and bisect it.

2d. Bisect each half *BE*, and *ED* by a perpendicular; and mark the points *a* and *b*, where the perpendiculars cross the parallels.

3d. From *a*, with *aB*, describe the arc *BE*; and from *b*, with the same distance, the arc *DE*. These are the required arcs.

CONSTRUCTION OF PROBLEMS OF CIRCLES AND RECTILINEAL FIGURES.

Prob. 37. (Pl. III. Fig. 43.) *Having the sides of a triangle to construct the figure.*

Let AC, BC, and AB be the lengths of the given sides.

1st. Draw a line, and set off upon it the longest side AB.

2d. From the point A, with a radius equal to AC, one of the remaining sides, describe an arc.

3d. From the point B, with the third side BC, describe a second arc, and mark the point C where the arcs cross.

4th. Draw lines from C, to A and B. The figure ACB is the one required.

Remark. The side AC might have been set off from B, and BC from A; this would have given an equal triangle to the one constructed, but its vertex would have been placed differently.

Remark. This construction is also used to find the position of a point when its distances from two other given points are given. We proceed to make the construction in this case like the preceding. It will be seen, that the required point can take four different positions with respect to the two others. Two of them, like the vertex of the triangle, will lie on one side of the line joining the given points, and the other two on the other side of the line.

Prob. 38. (Pl. III. Fig. 44.) *Having the side of a square to construct the figure.*

Let AB be the given side.

1st. Draw a line, and set off AB upon it.

2d. Construct perpendiculars at A, and B, to AB.

3d. From A and B, set off the given side on these perpendiculars to C and D; and draw a line from C to D. The figure $ABCD$ is the one required.

Prob. 39. (Pl. III. Fig. 45.) *Having the two sides of a parallelogram, and the angle contained by them, to construct the figure.*

Let AB, and AC be the given sides; and E the given angle.

1st. Draw a line, and set off AB upon it.

2d Construct at A an angle equal to the given one by *Prob.* 13.

3d. Set off, along the side of this angle, from A, the other given line AC.

4th. From C, with the distance AB describe an arc, and from B with the distance AC describe another arc.

5th. From the point D, where the arcs cross, draw lines to C, and B. The figure $ABDC$ is the one required.

Prob. 40. (Pl. III. Fig. 46.) *To circumscribe a given triangle by a circle.*

Let ABC be the given triangle.

As the circumference of the required circle must be described through the three given points A, B and C, its centre and radius will be found precisely as in *Prob.* 19.

Prob. 41. (Pl. III. Fig. 47.) *In a given triangle to inscribe a circle.*

Let ABC be the given triangle.

1st. By *Prob.* 16 construct the lines bisecting the angles A, and C; and mark the point D where these lines cross.

2d. From D by *Prob.* 8 construct a perpendicular DE, to AC.

3d. From D, with the distance DE, describe a circle. This is the one required.

Prob. 42. (Pl. IV. Fig. 48.) *In a given circle to inscribe a square.*

Let O be the centre of the given circle.

1st. Through O draw a diameter AB, and a second diameter CD perpendicular to it.

2d. Draw the lines AC, CB, BD, and DA. The figure $ADBC$ is the one required.

Prob. 43. (Pl. IV. Fig. 48.) *In a given circle to inscribe a regular octagon.*

1st. Having inscribed a square in the circle bisect each of its sides; and through the bisecting points and the centre O draw radii.

2d. Draw lines from the points d, b, a, c, where these radii meet the circumference, to the adjacent points D, A, &c. The figure $dAbC$ &c. is the one required.

Remark. By bisecting the sides of the octagon, and drawing radii through the points of bisection, and then drawing lines from the points where these radii meet the circumference to the adjacent points of the octagon, a figure of sixteen equal sides can be inscribed, and in like manner one of 32 sides, &c.

Prob. 44. (Pl. IV. Fig. 49.) *To inscribe in a given circle a regular hexagon.*

Let *O* be the centre of the given circle.

1st. Having taken off the radius *OA*, commence at *A*, and set it off from *A* to *B*, and from *A* to *F*, on the circumference.

2d. From *B* set off the same distance to *C*; and from *C* to *D*, and so on to *F*.

3d. Draw lines between the adjacent points. The figure *ABC* &c. is the one required.

Remark. By a process similar to the one employed for constructing an octagon from a square, we can, from the hexagon, construct a figure of 12 sides; then one of 24; and so on doubling the number of sides.

Prob. 45. (Pl. IV. Fig. 49.) *To inscribe in a given circle an equilateral triangle.*

Having, as in the last problem, constructed a regular hexagon, draw lines between the alternate angles, as *AC*, *CE*, and *EA*; the figure thus formed is the one required.

Prob. 46. (Pl. IV. Fig. 50.) *To inscribe in a given circle a regular pentagon.*

Let *O* be the centre of the given circle.

1st. Draw a diameter of the circle *AB*, and a second one *OD* perpendicular to it.

2d. Bisect the radius *OB*, and from the point of bisection *a* set off the distance *aC*, to *b*, along *AB*.

3d. From *C*, with the radius *Cb*, describe an arc, and mark the points *H*, and *I*, where it crosses the circumference of the given circle.

4th. From *H*, and *I*, set off the same distance to *G* and *K* on the circumference.

5th. Draw the lines *CH*, *HG*, *GK*, *KI*, and *IC*. The figure *CHGKI* is the one required.

Prob. 47. *To construct a regular figure, the sides of which shall be respectively equal to a given line.*

Let AB be the given line.

First Method. (Pl. IV. Fig. 50.)

1st. Construct any circle, and inscribe within it a regular figure, by one of the preceding *Probs.* of the same number of sides as the one required.

Let us suppose for example that the one required is a pentagon.

2d. Having constructed this inscribed figure, draw from the centre of the circle, through the angular points of the figure, lines; and prolong them outwards, if the side of the inscribed figure is less than the given line.

3d. Prolong any one of the sides, as CI, of the inscribed figure, and set off along it, from the angular point C, a distance Cm equal to the given line.

4th. Through m, draw a line parallel to the line drawn from O through C, and mark the point n, where it crosses the line drawn from O through I.

5th. Through n, draw a line parallel to CI, and mark the point o, where it crosses the line OC prolonged.

6th. From O, set off, along the other lines drawn from C through the other angular points, the distances Op, Oq, and Or, each equal to Om, or On.

7th. The points o, p, r, and n being joined by lines; the figure $opqrn$ is the one required.

Second Method. (Pl. IV. Fig. 51.)

1st. Draw a line and set off the given line AB upon it.

2d. At B construct a perpendicular to AB.

3d. From B, with BA, describe an arc Aa.

4th. Divide this arc into as many equal parts as number of sides in the required figure; and mark the points of division from a, 1, 2, 3, &c.

5th. From A, with AB, describe an arc, and mark the point c where it crosses the arc Aa.

6th From B draw a line through the division point 2.

7th. From c, set off the distance $c2$, to b, on the arc Bc.

3d. [illegible] draw a line through [illegible] and mark the point [illegible] crosses [illegible].

4th. [illegible] with the distance [illegible] or [illegible], describe a [illegible]

5th. Set off the distance [illegible] on the circumference.

6th. Draw [illegible] &c. This is the [illegible]

[illegible]

2d. Bisect the angle, as *DOB*, between any two of these lines of division, and prolong out the bisecting line.

3d. Construct a tangent to the given circle at either *B*, or *D*, and mark the point *a* where this tangent crosses the bisecting line.

4th. From *a*, set off *aB* to *b*, along the bisecting line.

5th. At *b* construct a perpendicular to *Oa*, and mark the point *c* where it crosses *OB*.

6th. From *c*, with the distance *cB*, describe a circle. This is one of the required circles.

7th. From the other points of division, *D*, &c., set off the same distance *Bc*, and from the points thus set off with this distance describe circles. These are the other required circles.

Prob. 51. (Pl. IV. Fig. 52.) *To circumscribe a given circle by a given number of circles tangent to it, and to each other.*

1st. Having divided the given circle into a number of equal parts, the same as the given number of required circles: bisect, in the same way, the angle between any two adjacent lines of division.

Let us take for illustration six as the number of required circles.

2d. Prolong outwards one of the lines of division, as *OD'*, and also the line, as *Od*, that bisects the angle between it and the adjacent line of division *Oa*. Construct a tangent at *D'* to the given circle; and mark the point *f* where it crosses the bisecting line.

3d. From *f*, set off *fD'* to *d*, along the bisecting line; and at *d*, construct a perpendicular to this line, and mark the point *g* where it crosses the line *OD'*.

4th. From *g*, with the distance *gD'*, or *gd*, describe a circle. This is one of the required circles.

5th. Prolong outwards the other lines of division; and set off along them, from the points where they cross the circumference, the distance *D'g*; and from these points with this distance describe circles. These are the remaining required circles.

6th. From d, with the distance dD, describe an arc around to the two lines db, and de prolonged. This is the third arc required, and touches the other two where they cross the lines db and de prolonged at m and n.

Remark. This curve is termed a *half oval*, or a *three cent.e curve.* The other half of the curve, on the other side of AB, can be drawn by setting off a distance Cg equal to Cd, and by continuing the arcs described from b and e around to lines drawn from g, through b and e; and by connecting these arcs by another described from g, with a radius equal to Dd.

Prob. 31. (Pl. III. Fig. 37.) *Having a given line and the perpendicular that bisects it; also two lines drawn through a given point, on the perpendicular, and each making the same angle with it; to construct a curve formed of four arcs of circles, two of these arcs to have equal given radii, and their centres to lie on the given line, and at equal distances from its extremities; each of the other arcs to have equal radii, and to be tangent respectively to one of the given lines where it crosses the perpendicular and also to one of the first arcs.*

Let CD be the given line; B the given point on the bisecting perpendicular; and Bm, Bn, the two lines, drawn through B, making the same angle with the perpendicular.

1st. From C and D, set off the same distance to b and a, for the given radii of the two first arcs; which distance must, in all cases, be taken *less than the perpendicular distance from the point* b or a, *to one of the given lines through* B.

2d. At B draw a perpendicular to the line Bm.

3d. Set off from B, along this perpendicular, a distance Bd equal Cb.

4th. Draw a line through bd, and bisect this distance by a perpendicular.

5th. Having marked the point c, where this last perpendicular crosses the one at B, draw through cb a line, and prolong it beyond b.

6th. From b, with the distance bC, describe an arc, which prolong to the line through bc; this is one of the first required arcs.

7th. From c, with a distance cB, describe an arc. This is one of the second required arcs.

8th. Through a, and the point f, where bc crosses the perpendicular BA prolonged, draw a line.

9th. From a, set off ae equal to bc.

10th. From a and e, with radii respectively equal to bC, and cB, describe arcs. These are the others required; and CBD the required curve.

Remark. If the construction is accurate, the perpendicular through BA will bisect the distance ec.

This curve is termed a *four centre obtuse* or *pointed* curve, according as the distance AB is less or greater than AC.

Prob. 32. (Pl. III. Fig. 38.) *Having a line, and the perpendicular which bisects it, and a given point on the perpendicular; to construct a curve formed of five arcs of circles, the consecutive arcs to be tangent; the centres of two of the arcs to be on the given line, and at equal distances from its extremities; the radii of the two arcs, respectively tangent to these two, to be equal, and of a given length; and the centre of the fifth arc, which is to be tangent to these two last, to lie on the given perpendicular.*

Let AB be the given line, and C the point on its bisecting perpendicular LC.

1st. Take any distance, *less than* LC, and set it off from B to D, and from A to f.

2d. From C set off CG equal to BD, and draw a line from G to D.

3d. Bisect the distance DG by a perpendicular; and mark the point E, where this perpendicular crosses the perpendicular LC prolonged.

4th. Draw a line from E to D.

5th. Take any distance, *less than* CE, equal to the given radius of the second arc, and set it off from C to F.

6th. Through F draw a line FH parallel to AB.

7th. Take off GF, the difference between CF and CG, and with it describe an arc from D; and mark the points a and b where it crosses the lines DE and FH.

8th. Take any point c on this arc, between the points a and b, and draw from it a line to F.

9th. Bisect the line cF by a perpendicular, and mark the point I where it crosses the perpendicular CL prolonged.

10th. From *c* draw a line through *D* and prolong it; and another from *I* prolonged through *e:*

11th. From *e* draw a perpendicular to *CI;* and from *d*, where it crosses *CI*, set off *dg* equal to *cd*, and mark the point *g*.

12th. From *I* draw a line through *g* and prolong it; and one from *g* prolonged through *f*.

13. From *D* and *f*, with the distance *BD*, describe the arcs *Bm*, and *Ap;* from *e* and *g*, with the distance *em*, or *gp*, describe the arcs *mn*, and *po;* and from *I* with the distance *IC*, describe the arc *no*. The curve *BCA* is the one required.

Remarks. This curve is also termed a semi oval; and, from the number of arcs of which it is composed, a *curve of five centres.*

Prob. 33. (Pl. III. Fig. 39.) *Having two parallel lines, to construct a curve of three centres which shall be tangent to the two parallels at their extremities.*

Let *AB* and *CD* be the given parallels; and *B* and *D* the points at which the required curve is to be drawn tangent.

1st. From *B* construct a perpendicular to *AB*, and mark the point *b* where it crosses *CD;* and also a perpendicular at *D* to *CD*.

2d. From *B*, set off any distance *Bc less than the half of Bb;* and through *c* draw a line parallel to *AB*, and mark the point *d* where it crosses the perpendicular to *CD*.

3d. From c, set off, along *cd* prolonged, the distance *ca* equal to *cB*.

4th. Taking *ca*, as the radius of the first arc, construct a quarter oval by *Prob.* 30 through the points *a* and *D*.

5th. Prolong the arc described from *c* to the point *B*. The curve *BaD* is the one required.

Remark. This curve is termed a *scotia* of two centres.

Prob. 34. (Pl. III. Fig. 40.) *Having two parallels, to construct a quarter of a curve of five centres tangent to them at their extremities.*

Let *AB* and *CD* be the given parallels, and *B* and *D* their extremities.

1st. Proceed, as in the last case, to draw the perpendiculars

at *B*, and *D*, and a parallel to *AB* through a point *c*, taken on the first perpendicular, at a distance from *B* less than the half of *Bl*.

2d. Set off from *c* a distance *ca* equal to *cB*; and on *al* and *Dd* describe the quarter oval by *Prob.* 32.

3d. Prolong the first arc from *a* to *B*, which will complete the required curve.

Remark. This curve is termed a *scotia* of three centres.

Prob. 35. (Pl. III. Fig. 41.) *Having two parallels and a given point on each, to construct two equal arcs which shall be tangent to each other and respectively tangent to the parallels at the given points.*

Let *AB* and *CD* be the two parallels; *B* and *D* the given points.

1st. Draw a line through *BD*, and bisect the distance *BD*.

2d. Bisect each half *BE*, and *ED* by perpendiculars.

3d. From *B*, and *D* draw perpendiculars to *AB* and *CD*, and mark the points *a*, and *b*, where they cross the bisecting perpendiculars.

4th. From *a*, with the distance *aE*, describe an arc to *B*; and from *b*, with the same distance, an arc *ED*. These are the required arcs.

Prob. 36. (Pl. III. Fig. 42.) *Having two parallels, and a point on each, to construct two equal arcs which shall be tangent to each other, have their centres respectively on the parallels, and pass through the given points.*

Let *AB* and *CD* be the parallels, *B* and *D* the given points.

1st. Join *BD* by a line and bisect it.

2d. Bisect each half *BE*, and *ED* by a perpendicular; and mark the points *a* and *b*, where the perpendiculars cross the parallels.

3d. From *a*, with *aB*, describe the arc *BE*; and from *b*, with the same distance, the arc *DE*. These are the required arcs.

Construction of Problems on Triangles and Rectilineal Figures.

Prob. 37. (Pl. III. Fig. 43.) *Having the sides of a triangle to construct the figure.*

Let *AC*, *BC* and *AB* be the lengths of the given sides.

1st. Draw a line, and set off upon it the longest side *AB*.

2d. From the point *A*, with a radius equal to *AC* one of the remaining sides, describe an arc.

3d. From the point *B*, with the third side *BC*, describe a second arc, and mark the point *C* where the arcs cross.

4th. Draw lines from *C* to *A* and *B*. The figure *ACB* is the one required.

Remark. The side *AC* might have been set off from *B*, and *BC* from *A*; this would have given an equal triangle to the one constructed, but its vertex would have been placed differently.

Remark. This construction is also used to find the position of a point when its distances from two other given points are given. We proceed to make the construction in this case like the preceding. It will be seen that the required point can take four different positions with respect to the two others. Two of them, like the vertex of the triangle, will lie on one side of the line joining the given points, and the other two on the other side of the line.

Prob. 38. (Pl. III. Fig. 44.) *Having the side of a square to construct the figure.*

Let *AB* be the given side.

1st. Draw a line, and set off *AB* upon it.

2d. Construct perpendiculars at *A*, and *B*, to *AB*.

3d. From *A* and *B*, set off the given side on these perpendiculars to *C* and *D*; and draw a line from *C* to *D*. The figure *ABCD* is the one required.

Prob. 39. (Pl. III. Fig. 45.) *Having the two sides of a parallelogram, and the angle contained by them, to construct the figure.*

Let *AB*, and *AC* be the given sides; and *E* the given angle.

1st. Draw a line, and set off AB upon it.

2d Construct at A an angle equal to the given one by *Prob.* 13.

3d. Set off, along the side of this angle, from A, the other given line AC.

4th. From C, with the distance AB describe an arc, and from B with the distance AC describe another arc.

5th. From the point D, where the arcs cross, draw lines to C, and B. The figure $ABDC$ is the one required.

Prob. 40. (Pl. III. Fig. 46.) *To circumscribe a given triangle by a circle.*

Let ABC be the given triangle.

As the circumference of the required circle must be described through the three given points A, B and C, its centre and radius will be found precisely as in *Prob.* 19.

Prob. 41. (Pl. III. Fig. 47.) *In a given triangle to inscribe a circle.*

Let ABC be the given triangle.

1st. By *Prob.* 16 construct the lines bisecting the angles A, and C; and mark the point D where these lines cross.

2d. From D by *Prob.* 8 construct a perpendicular DE, to AC.

3d. From D, with the distance DE, describe a circle. This is the one required.

Prob. 42. (Pl. IV. Fig. 48.) *In a given circle to inscribe a square.*

Let O be the centre of the given circle.

1st. Through O draw a diameter AB, and a second diameter CD perpendicular to it.

2d. Draw the lines AC, CB, BD, and DA. The figure $ADBC$ is the one required.

Prob. 43. (Pl. IV. Fig. 48.) *In a given circle to inscribe a regular octagon.*

1st. Having inscribed a square in the circle bisect each of its sides; and through the bisecting points and the centre O draw radii.

2d. Draw lines from the points d, b, a, c, where these radii meet the circumference, to the adjacent points D, A, &c. The figure $dAbC$ &c. is the one required.

Remark. [illegible] sides [illegible] of 12 sides, &c.

Prob. [illegible] *To inscribe in a given circle a regular* [illegible].

Let [illegible] be the centre of the given circle.

1st. [illegible] and [illegible] on the circumference.

2d. From [illegible] set off the same distance [illegible] and from *C* to [illegible].

3d. Draw lines between the adjacent points. The figure *ABC* &c. is the one required.

Remark. By a process similar to the one employed for constructing [illegible] from a square, we can, from the hexagon, construct a figure of 12 sides; then one of 24; and so on, doubling the number of sides.

Prob. [illegible] *To inscribe in a given circle an equilateral triangle.*

Having, as in the last problem, constructed a regular hexagon, draw lines between the alternate angles, as *AC*, *CE*, and *EA*. The figure thus formed is the one required.

Prob. [illegible] *To inscribe in a given circle a regular pentagon.*

Let *O* be the centre of the given circle.

1st. Draw a diameter of the circle *AB* and a second one *CD* perpendicular to it.

2d. Bisect the radius [illegible] and from the point of bisection [illegible] set off the distance [illegible] along *AB*.

3d. From *C*, with the radius [illegible], describe an arc, and mark the points *H*, and *I*, where it crosses the circumference of the given circle.

4th. From *H*, and *I*, set off the same distance to *G* and *K* on the circumference.

5th. Draw the lines *CH*, *HG*, *GK*, *KI*, and *IC*. The figure *CHGKI* is the one required.

Prob. 47. *To construct a regular figure, the sides of which shall be respectively equal to a given line.*

Let AB be the given line.

First Method. (Pl. IV. Fig. 50.)

1st. Construct any circle, and inscribe within it a regular figure, by one of the preceding *Probs.* of the same number of sides as the one required.

Let us suppose for example that the one required is a pentagon.

2d. Having constructed this inscribed figure, draw from the centre of the circle, through the angular points of the figure, lines; and prolong them outwards, if the side of the inscribed figure is less than the given line.

3d. Prolong any one of the sides, as CI, of the inscribed figure, and set off along it, from the angular point C, a distance Cm equal to the given line.

4th. Through m, draw a line parallel to the line drawn from O through C, and mark the point n, where it crosses the line drawn from O through I.

5th. Through n, draw a line parallel to CI, and mark the point o, where it crosses the line OC prolonged.

6th. From O, set off, along the other lines drawn from C through the other angular points, the distances Op, Oq, and Or, each equal to Om, or On.

7th. The points o, p, r, and n being joined by lines; the figure $opqrn$ is the one required.

Second Method. (Pl. IV. Fig. 51.)

1st. Draw a line and set off the given line AB upon it.

2d. At B construct a perpendicular to AB.

3d. From B, with BA, describe an arc Aa.

4th. Divide this arc into as many equal parts as number of sides in the required figure; and mark the points of division from a, 1, 2, 3, &c.

5th. From A, with AB, describe an arc, and mark the point c where it crosses the arc Aa.

6th. From B draw a line through the division point 2.

7th. From c, set off the distance $c2$, to b, on the arc Bc, and mark the point F where it crosses the line parallel to AB.

5th. From the point F, with the given radius describe a circle. This is the one required.

Remarks. If the construction is accurate a line drawn from F to C will pass through the point where the circles touch, and one drawn from F perpendicular to AB will pass through the point where the circle touches the line.

If from the centre C, a perpendicular is drawn to AB, and the points a, b and d where the perpendicular crosses the line and the given circle are marked, it will be found that the given radius cannot be less than one half of ab nor greater than one half of ad.

Prob. 27. (Pl. III. Fig. 33.) *Having a circle and right line given, to construct a circle which shall be tangent to the given circle at a given point, and also to the line.*

Let C be the centre of the given circle, D the given point on its circumference, and AB the given line.

1st. By *Prob.* 20 construct a tangent to the given circle at the point D; prolong it to cross the given line, and mark the point A where it crosses.

2d. By *Prob.* 16 construct the line AE which bisects the angle between the tangent and the given line.

3d. Through CD draw a radius, and prolong it to cross the bisecting line at E.

4th. Mark the point E, and with the distance ED describe a circle. This is the required circle.

Prob. 28. (Pl. III. Fig. 34.) *Having a circle and right line, to construct a circle which shall be tangent to the given circle, and also to the line at a given point on it.*

Let C be the centre of the given circle; AB the given line, and a the given point on it.

1st. By *Prob.* 6 construct a perpendicular at a to the given line.

2d. From a set off ab equal to the radius Cd of the given circle.

3d. Draw a line through bC, and by *Prob.* 5 bisect the distance bC by a perpendicular to the line bC.

4th. Mark the point c, where this perpendicular crosses the one at *a*; and with *ac* describe a circle. This is the one required.

Prob. 29. (Pl. III. Fig. 35.) *Having two circles, to construct a third which shall be tangent to one of them at a given point, and also touch the other.*

Let *C* and *B* be the centres of the two given circles; and *D* the given point on one of them, at which the required circle is to be tangent to it.

1st. Through *CD* draw a line, which prolong each way from *C* and *D*.

2d. From *D* set off towards *C* the distance *DA* equal to the radius *BF* of the other given circle.

3d. Through *AB* draw a line, and by *Probs.* 5 and 6, bisect *AB* by the perpendicular *GE*.

4th. Mark the point *E*, where the perpendicular crosses the line *CD* prolonged; and with the distance *ED* describe a circle from *E*. This is the one required.

Prob. 30. (Pl. III. Fig. 36.) *Having a given distance, or line, and the perpendicular which bisects it, to construct three arcs of circles, the radii of two of which shall be equal, and of a given length, and their centres on the given line; and the third shall pass through a given point on the perpendicular and be tangent to the other two circles.*

Let *AB* be the given line, and *D* the given point on the perpendicular to *AB* through its middle point *C*; and let the distance *CD* be less than *AC*, the half of *AB*.

1st. Take any distance, *less than CD*, and set it off from *A* and *B*, to *b* and *e*, and mark these two points for the centres of the two arcs of the equal given radii less than *CD*.

2d. Set off from *D* the distance *Dc* equal to *Ab*, and through *bc* draw a line.

3d. Bisect *bc* by a perpendicular, by *Probs.* 5 and 6, and mark the point *d* where it crosses the perpendicular to *AB* prolonged below it, the point *d* is the centre of the third arc.

4th. Draw a line through *db*, and prolong it; and also one through *de* which prolong.

5th. From *b*, with the distance *bA*, describe an arc from *A* to *m* on the line *db* prolonged; and one, from the other centre *e*, from *B* to *n* on the line *de* prolonged.

6th. From *d*, with the distance *dD*, describe an arc around to the two lines *db*, and *de* prolonged. This is the third arc required, and touches the other two where they cross the lines *db* and *de* prolonged at *m* and *n*.

Remark. This curve is termed a *half oval*, or a *three centre curve.* The other half of the curve, on the other side of *AB*, can be drawn by setting off a distance *Cg* equal to *Cd*, and by continuing the arcs described from *b* and *e* around to lines drawn from *g*, through *b* and *e*; and by connecting these arcs by another described from *g*, with a radius equal to *Dd*.

Prob. 31. (Pl. III. Fig. 37.) *Having a given line and the perpendicular that bisects it; also two lines drawn through a given point, on the perpendicular, and each making the same angle with it; to construct a curve formed of four arcs of circles, two of these arcs to have equal given radii, and their centres to lie on the given line, and at equal distances from its extremities; each of the other arcs to have equal radii, and to be tangent respectively to one of the given lines where it crosses the perpendicular and also to one of the first arcs.*

Let *CD* be the given line; *B* the given point on the bisecting perpendicular; and *Bm*, *Bn*, the two lines, drawn through *B*, making the same angle with the perpendicular.

1st. From *C* and *D*, set off the same distance to *b* and *a*, for the given radii of the two first arcs; which distance must, in all cases, be taken *less than the perpendicular distance from the point b* or *a*, *to one of the given lines through B.*

2d. At *B* draw a perpendicular to the line *Bm*.

3d. Set off from *B*, along this perpendicular, a distance *Bd* equal *Cb*.

4th. Draw a line through *bd*, and bisect this distance by a perpendicular.

5th. Having marked the point *c*, where this last perpendicular crosses the one at *B*, draw through *cb* a line, and prolong it beyond *b*.

6th. From *b*, with the distance *bC*, describe an arc, which prolong to the line through *bc*; this is one of the first required arcs.

7th. From *c*, with a distance *cB*, describe an arc. This is one of the second required arcs.

8th. Through *a*, and the point *f*, where *bc* crosses the perpendicular *BA* prolonged, draw a line.

9th. From *a*, set off *ae* equal to *bc*.

10th. From *a* and *e*, with radii respectively equal to *bC*, and *aB*, describe arcs. These are the others required; and *CBD* the required curve.

Remark. If the construction is accurate, the perpendicular through *BA* will bisect the distance *ec*.

This curve is termed a *four centre obtuse* or *pointed* curve, according as the distance *AB* is less or greater than *AC*.

Prob. 32. (Pl. III. Fig. 88.) *Having a line, and the perpendicular which bisects it, and a given point on the perpendicular; to construct a curve formed of five arcs of circles, the consecutive arcs to be tangent; the centres of two of the arcs to be on the given line, and at equal distances from its extremities; the radii of the two arcs, respectively tangent to these two, to be equal, and of a given length; and the centre of the fifth arc, which is to be tangent to these two last, to lie on the given perpendicular.*

Let *AB* be the given line, and *C* the point on its bisecting perpendicular *LC*.

1st. Take any distance, *less than LC*, and set it off from *B* to *D*, and from *A* to *f*.

2d. From *C* set off *CG* equal to *BD*, and draw a line from *G* to *D*.

3d. Bisect the distance *DG* by a perpendicular; and mark the point *E*, where this perpendicular crosses the perpendicular *LC* prolonged.

4th. Draw a line from *E* to *D*.

5th. Take any distance, *less than CE*, equal to the given radius of the second arc, and set it off from *C* to *F*.

6th. Through *F* draw a line *FH* parallel to *AB*.

7th. Take off *GF*, the difference between *CF* and *CG*, and with it describe an arc from *D*; and mark the points *a* and *b* where it crosses the lines *DE* and *FH*.

8th. Take any point *c* on this arc, between the points *a* and *b*, and draw from it a line to *F*.

9th. Bisect the line *cF* by a perpendicular, and mark the point *I* where it crosses the perpendicular *CL* prolonged.

10th. From *c* draw a line through *D* and prolong it; and another from *I* prolonged through *c*.

11th. From *c* draw a perpendicular to *CI*; and from *d*, where it crosses *CI*, set off *dg* equal to *cd*, and mark the point *g*.

12th. From *I* draw a line through *g* and prolong it; and one from *g* prolonged through *f*.

13. From *D* and *f*, with the distance *BD*, describe the arcs *Bm*, and *Ap*; from *c* and *g*, with the distance *cm*, or *gp*, describe the arcs *mn*, and *po*; and from *I* with the distance *IC*, describe the arc *no*. The curve *BCA* is the one required.

Remarks. This curve is also termed a semi oval; and, from the number of arcs of which it is composed, a *curve of five centres.*

Prob. 33. (Pl. III. Fig. 39.) *Having two parallel lines, to construct a curve of three centres which shall be tangent to the two parallels at their extremities.*

Let *AB* and *CD* be the given parallels; and *B* and *D* the points at which the required curve is to be drawn tangent.

1st. From *B* construct a perpendicular to *AB*, and mark the point *b* where it crosses *CD*; and also a perpendicular at *D* to *CD*.

2d. From *B*, set off any distance *Bc less than the half of Bb*; and through *c* draw a line parallel to *AB*, and mark the point *d* where it crosses the perpendicular to *CD*.

3d. From *c*, set off, along *cd* prolonged, the distance *ca* equal to *cB*.

4th. Taking *ca*, as the radius of the first arc, construct a quarter oval by *Prob.* 30 through the points *a* and *D*.

5th. Prolong the arc described from *c* to the point *B*. The curve *BaD* is the one required.

Remark. This curve is termed a *scotia* of two centres.

Prob. 34. (Pl. III. Fig. 40.) *Having two parallels, to construct a quarter of a curve of five centres tangent to them at their extremities.*

Let *AB* and *CD* be the given parallels, and *B* and *D* their extremities.

1st. Proceed, as in the last case, to draw the perpendiculars

at B, and D, and a parallel to AB through a point c, taken on the first perpendicular, at a distance from B less than the half of Bl.

2d. Set off from c a distance ca equal to cB; and on ac and Dd describe the quarter oval by *Prob.* 32.

3d. Prolong the first arc from a to B, which will complete the required curve.

Remark. This curve is termed a *scotia* of three centres.

Prob. 35. (Pl. III. Fig. 41.) *Having two parallels and a given point on each, to construct two equal arcs which shall be tangent to each other and respectively tangent to the parallels at the given points.*

Let AB and CD be the two parallels; B and D the given points.

1st. Draw a line through BD, and bisect the distance BD.

2d. Bisect each half BE, and ED by perpendiculars.

3d. From B, and D draw perpendiculars to AB and CD, and mark the points a, and b, where they cross the bisecting perpendiculars.

4th. From a, with the distance aE, describe an arc to B; and from b, with the same distance, an arc ED. These are the required arcs.

Prob. 36. (Pl. III. Fig. 42.) *Having two parallels, and a point on each, to construct two equal arcs which shall be tangent to each other, have their centres respectively on the parallels, and pass through the given points.*

Let AB and CD be the parallels, B and D the given points.

1st. Join BD by a line and bisect it.

2d. Bisect each half BE, and ED by a perpendicular; and mark the points a and b, where the perpendiculars cross the parallels.

3d. From a, with aB, describe the arc BE; and from b, with the same distance, the arc DE. These are the required arcs.

Construction of Problems of Circles and Rectilineal Figures.

Prob. 37. (Pl. III. Fig. 43.) *Having the sides of a triangle to construct the figure.*

Let AC, BC, and AB be the lengths of the given sides.

1st. Draw a line, and set off upon it the longest side AB.

2d. From the point A, with a radius equal to AC, one of the remaining sides, describe an arc.

3d. From the point B, with the third side BC, describe a second arc, and mark the point C where the arcs cross.

4th. Draw lines from C, to A and B. The figure ACB is the one required.

Remark. The side AC might have been set off from B, and BC from A; this would have given an equal triangle to the one constructed, but its vertex would have been placed differently.

Remark. This construction is also used to find the position of a point when its distances from two other given points are given. We proceed to make the construction in this case like the preceding. It will be seen, that the required point can take four different positions with respect to the two others. Two of them, like the vertex of the triangle, will lie on one side of the line joining the given points, and the other two on the other side of the line.

Prob. 38. (Pl. III. Fig. 44.) *Having the side of a square to construct the figure.*

Let AB be the given side.

1st. Draw a line, and set off AB upon it.

2d. Construct perpendiculars at A, and B, to AB.

3d. From A and B, set off the given side on these perpendiculars to C and D; and draw a line from C to D. The figure $ABCD$ is the one required.

Prob. 39. (Pl. III. Fig. 45.) *Having the two sides of a parallelogram, and the angle contained by them, to construct the figure.*

Let AB, and AC be the given sides; and E the given angle.

1st. Draw a line, and set off AB upon it.

2d Construct at A an angle equal to the given one by *Prob.* 13.

3d. Set off, along the side of this angle, from A, the other given line AC.

4th. From C, with the distance AB describe an arc, and from B with the distance AC describe another arc.

5th. From the point D, where the arcs cross, draw lines to C, and B. The figure $ABDC$ is the one required.

Prob. 40. (Pl. III. Fig. 46.) *To circumscribe a given triangle by a circle.*

Let ABC be the given triangle.

As the circumference of the required circle must be described through the three given points A, B and C, its centre and radius will be found precisely as in *Prob.* 19.

Prob. 41. (Pl. III. Fig. 47.) *In a given triangle to inscribe a circle.*

Let ABC be the given triangle.

1st. By *Prob.* 16 construct the lines bisecting the angles A, and C; and mark the point D where these lines cross.

2d. From D by *Prob.* 8 construct a perpendicular DE, to AC.

3d. From D, with the distance DE, describe a circle. This is the one required.

Prob. 42. (Pl. IV. Fig. 48.) *In a given circle to inscribe a square.*

Let O be the centre of the given circle.

1st. Through O draw a diameter AB, and a second diameter CD perpendicular to it.

2d. Draw the lines AC, CB, BD, and DA. The figure $ADBC$ is the one required.

Prob. 43. (Pl. IV. Fig. 48.) *In a given circle to inscribe a regular octagon.*

1st. Having inscribed a square in the circle bisect each of its sides; and through the bisecting points and the centre O draw radii.

2d. Draw lines from the points d, b, a, c, where these radii meet the circumference, to the adjacent points D, A, &c. The figure $dAbC$ &c. is the one required.

Remark. By bisecting the sides of the octagon, and drawing radii through the points of bisection, and then drawing lines from the points where these radii meet the circumference to the adjacent points of the octagon, a figure of sixteen equal sides can be inscribed, and in like manner one of 32 sides, &c.

Prob. 44. (Pl. IV. Fig. 49.) *To inscribe in a given circle a regular hexagon.*

Let *O* be the centre of the given circle.

1st. Having taken off the radius *OA*, commence at *A*, and set it off from *A* to *B*, and from *A* to *F*, on the circumference.

2d. From *B* set off the same distance to *C*; and from *C* to *D*, and so on to *F*.

3d. Draw lines between the adjacent points. The figure *ABC* &c. is the one required.

Remark. By a process similar to the one employed for constructing an octagon from a square, we can, from the hexagon, construct a figure of 12 sides; then one of 24; and so on doubling the number of sides.

Prob. 45. (Pl. IV. Fig. 49.) *To inscribe in a given circle an equilateral triangle.*

Having, as in the last problem, constructed a regular hexagon, draw lines between the alternate angles, as *AC*, *CE*, and *EA*; the figure thus formed is the one required.

Prob. 46. (Pl. IV. Fig. 50.) *To inscribe in a given circle a regular pentagon.*

Let *O* be the centre of the given circle.

1st. Draw a diameter of the circle *AB*, and a second one *CD* perpendicular to it.

2d. Bisect the radius *OB*, and from the point of bisection *a* set off the distance *aC*, to *b*, along *AB*.

3d. From *C*, with the radius *Cb*, describe an arc, and mark the points *H*, and *I*, where it crosses the circumference of the given circle.

4th. From *H*, and *I*, set off the same distance to *G* and *K* on the circumference.

5th. Draw the lines *CH*, *HG*, *GK*, *KI*, and *IC*. The figure *CHGKI* is the one required.

Prob. 47. *To construct a regular figure, the sides of which shall be respectively equal to a given line.*

Let *AB* be the given line.

First Method. (Pl. IV. Fig. 50.)

1st. Construct any circle, and inscribe within it a regular figure, by one of the preceding *Probs.* of the same number of sides as the one required.

Let us suppose for example that the one required is a pentagon.

2d. Having constructed this inscribed figure, draw from the centre of the circle, through the angular points of the figure, lines; and prolong them outwards, if the side of the inscribed figure is less than the given line.

3d. Prolong any one of the sides, as *CI*, of the inscribed figure, and set off along it, from the angular point *C*, a distance *Cm* equal to the given line.

4th. Through *m*, draw a line parallel to the line drawn from *O* through *C*, and mark the point *n*, where it crosses the line drawn from *O* through *I*.

5th. Through *n*, draw a line parallel to *CI*, and mark the point *o*, where it crosses the line *OC* prolonged.

6th. From *O*, set off, along the other lines drawn from *C* through the other angular points, the distances *Op*, *Oq*, and *Or*, each equal to *Om*, or *On*.

7th. The points *o*, *p*, *r*, and *n* being joined by lines; the figure *opqrn* is the one required.

Second Method. (Pl. IV. Fig. 51.)

1st. Draw a line and set off the given line *AB* upon it.

2d. At *B* construct a perpendicular to *AB*.

3d. From *B*, with *BA*, describe an arc *Aa*.

4th. Divide this arc into as many equal parts as number of sides in the required figure; and mark the points of division from *a*, 1, 2, 3, &c.

5th. From *A*, with *AB*, describe an arc, and mark the point *c* where it crosses the arc *Aa*.

6th From *B* draw a line through the division point 2.

7th. From *c*, set off the distance *c*2. to *b*, on the arc *Bc*.

8th. From *A*, draw a line through *b*, and mark the point *O* where it crosses *B*2.

9th. From *O*, with the distance *OA*, or *OB*, describe a circle.

10th. Set off the distance *AB* to *C*, *D*, &c., on the circumference.

11th. Draw the lines *BC*, *CD*, *DE*, &c. This is the required figure.

Remarks. The figure taken to illustrate this case is the pentagon, for the purpose of comparing the two methods.

Prob. 48. (Pl. IV, Fig. 51.) *To circumscribe a given circle by a regular figure.*

1st. Inscribe in the circle a regular figure of the same number of sides as the one to be circumscribed.

2d. At the angular points of the inscribed figure, draw tangents to the given circle, and mark the points where the tangents cross. These points are the angular points of the required figure, and the portions of the tangents between them are its sides.

Remarks. The figure taken to illustrate this, is the circumscribed regular pentagon *bdef*.

Prob. 49. (Pl. IV, Fig. 49.) *To inscribe a circle in a given regular figure.*

1st. Bisect any two adjacent sides of the figure by perpendiculars, and mark the point where they cross.

2d. From this point, with the distance to the side bisected, describe a circle. This is the one required.

Remarks. The figure taken to illustrate this case is the regular hexagon; *ma* and *na* are the adjacent sides bisected by the perpendiculars to them [illegible], and [illegible] is the centre of the required circle, and [illegible] its radius.

Prob. 50. (Pl. IV, Fig. 52.) *To inscribe, in a given circle, a given number of equal circles which shall be tangent to the given circle, and to each other.*

Let *O* be the centre of the given circle.

1st. Divide the circumference into as many equal parts, by lines drawn from *O*, as the number of circles to be inscribed. Let us take, for illustration, six as the required number

2d. Bisect the angle, as DOB, between any two of these lines of division, and prolong out the bisecting line.

3d. Construct a tangent to the given circle at either B, or D, and mark the point a where this tangent crosses the bisecting line.

4th. From a, set off aB to b, along the bisecting line.

5th. At b construct a perpendicular to Oa, and mark the point c where it crosses OB.

6th. From c, with the distance cB, describe a circle. This is one of the required circles.

7th. From the other points of division, D, &c., set off the same distance Bc, and from the points thus set off with this distance describe circles. These are the other required circles.

Prob. 51. (Pl. IV. Fig. 52.) *To circumscribe a given circle by a given number of circles tangent to it, and to each other.*

1st. Having divided the given circle into a number of equal parts, the same as the given number of required circles: bisect, in the same way, the angle between any two adjacent lines of division.

Let us take for illustration six as the number of required circles.

2d. Prolong outwards one of the lines of division, as OD', and also the line, as Od, that bisects the angle between it and the adjacent line of division Oa. Construct a tangent at D' to the given circle; and mark the point f where it crosses the bisecting line.

3d. From f, set off fD' to d, along the bisecting line; and at d, construct a perpendicular to this line, and mark the point g where it crosses the line OD'.

4th. From g, with the distance gD', or gd, describe a circle. This is one of the required circles.

5th. Prolong outwards the other lines of division; and set off along them, from the points where they cross the circumference, the distance $D'g$; and from these points with this distance describe circles. These are the remaining required circles.

CONSTRUCTION OF PROPORTIONAL LINES AND FIGURES.

Prob. 52. (Pl. IV. Fig. 53.) *To divide a given line into parts which shall be proportional to two other given lines.*

Let AB be the given line to be divided; ac and cb the other given lines.

1st. Through A draw any line making an angle with AB.

2d. From A set off Ac equal to ac: and from c the other line cb.

3d. Draw a line through B, b; and through c a parallel to Bb, and mark the point C where it crosses AB. This is the required point of division; and AC is to CB as ac is to cb.

Prob. 53. (Pl. IV. Fig. 54.) *To divide a line into any number of parts which shall be in any given proportion to each other, or to the same number of given lines.*

Let AB be the given line, and let the number of proportional parts for example into which it is to be divided be four, these parts being to each other as the numbers 3, 5, 7, and 2, or lines of these lengths.

1st. Through A draw any line making an angle with AB.

2d. From any scale of equal parts take off three divisions, and set this distance off from A to 3; from 3 set off five of the same divisions to 5; from 5 set off seven to 7; and from 7 two to 2.

3d. Draw a line through $B2$, and parallels to it through tne points 7, 5, and 3, and mark the points d, c, and b where the parallels cross AB. The distances Ab, bc, cd, and dB are those required.

Remark. Any distance from a point, as A for example, on AB, to any other point as d, is to the distance from this point to any other, as Ab for example, as is the corresponding distance $A7$ to $A3$, on the line $A2$.

Prob. 54. (Pl. IV. Fig. 55.) *To find a fourth proportional to three given lines.*

Let ab, bc, and ad be the three given lines to which it is required to find a fourth proportional which shall be to *ad* as *ab* is to *ac*.

1st. Draw a line, and, from a point *A*, set off *AB* equal to *ab*; and *BC* equal to *bc*.

2d. Through *A* draw any line, and set off upon it *AD*, equal to *ad*.

3d. Draw a line through *DB*, and a parallel to *DB* through *C*, and mark the point *E* where this crosses the line drawn through *A*. The distance *DE* is the required fourth proportional.

Prob. 55. (Pl. IV. Fig. 56.) *To find the line which is a mean proportional to two given lines.*

Let *ab* and *bc* be the given lines.

1st. Draw a line, and set off on it *AB*, and *BC*, equal respectively to *ab*, and *bc*.

2d. Bisect the distance *AC*, and, from the bisecting point *O*, describe a semicircle with the radius *OC*.

3d. At *B* construct a perpendicular to *AC*; and mark the point *D* where it crosses the circumference. The distance *BD* is the line required; and *ab* is to *BD* as *BD* is to *bc*.

Prob. 56. (Pl. IV. Fig. 57.) *To divide a given line into two parts, such that the entire line shall be to one of the parts, as this part is to the other.*

Let *ab* be the given line.

1st. Draw a line, and set off *AB* equal to *ab*; and at *B* construct a perpendicular to *AB*.

2d. Set off on the perpendicular *BD* equal to the half of *AB*, and draw a line through *AD*.

3d. From *D*, with *DB*, describe an arc, and mark the point *C*, where it crosses *AD*.

4th. From *A*, with *AC*, describe an arc, and mark the point *E*, where it crosses *AB*. The point *E* is the one required; and *AB* is to *AE*, as *AE* is to *EB*.

Remark. This construction is used for inscribing a regular decagon in a given circle. To do this divide the radius of the given circle in the manner just described. The larger portion is the side of the required regular decagon.

Having described the regular decagon, the regular pen

tagon can be formed, by drawing lines through the alternate angles of the decagon.

Prob. 57. (Pl. IV. Fig. 58.) *Having any given figure, to construct another, the angles of which shall be the same as the angles of the given figure, and the sides shall be in a given proportion to its sides.*

Let *ABCDEF* be the given figure.

1st. Prolong any two of the adjacent sides of the given figure, as *AB*, and *AF*, if the one required is to be greater than the given one; and, from *A*, draw lines through the other angular points *C*, *D*, and *E*.

2d. From *A* set off a distance *Ab*, which is in the same proportion to *AB*, as the side of the required figure corresponding to *BC*, is to *BC*; or, in other words, *AB* must be contained as many times in *Ab* as *BC* is in the corresponding side of the required figure.

3d. From *b* draw a line parallel to *BC*, and mark the point *c*, where it crosses *AC* prolonged; from *c* draw a parallel to *CD*, and mark the point where it crosses *AD* prolonged; and so on for each required side. The figure *Abcdef* is the one required.

Construction of Equivalent Figures.

Prob. 58. (Pl. IV. Fig. 59.) *To construct a triangle which shall be equivalent to a given parallelogram.*

Let *ABCD* be the given parallelogram.

1st. Prolong the base *AB*, and set off *BE* equal to *AB*.

2d. Draw lines from *C*, to *A* and *E*. The triangle *ACE* is the one required.

Prob. 59. (Pl. IV. Fig. 60.) *To construct a triangle which shall be equivalent to a given quadrilateral.*

Let *ABCD* be the given quadrilateral.

1st. Draw a diagonal, as *AC*.

2d. From *B* the adjacent angle to *C*, to which the diagonal is drawn, draw a line parallel to *AC*, prolong the side *AB* opposite to *BC*, and mark the point *F*, where it crosses the parallel to *AC*.

3d. Draw a line from *C* to *F*. The triangle *FCD* is the one required.

Prob. 60. (Pl. IV. Fig. 61.) *To construct a triangle equivalent to any given polygon.*

Let *ABCDEFG* be the given polygon.

1st. Take any side, as *AB*, as a base, and, from *A* and *B*, draw the diagonals *AF* and *BD* to the alternate angles to *A* and *B*.

2d. From *G* and *C*, the adjacent angles, draw *Ga* parallel to *FA*, and *Cb* to *DB*.

3d. From the alternate angles *F* and *D*, draw the lines *Fa* and *Db*. A figure *abDEF* is thus formed, which is equivalent to the given one, and having two sides less than it.

4th. From the angles *a* and *b*, at the base of this new figure, draw diagonals to the alternate angles, to *a* and *b* (in the Fig. this is the angle *E*), and proceed, precisely as in the 3d operation, to form another figure equivalent to the last formed, and having two sides less than it. Proceed in this way until a quadrilateral or pentagon is formed equivalent to the given figure, and convert this last into its equivalent triangle, which will be the one required. The case taken for illustration is a heptagon, and *HEI* is the equivalent triangle.

Prob. 61. *To construct a triangle equivalent to any regular polygon.*

1st. By *Prob.* 49 find the radius of the circle inscribed in the polygon.

2d. Set off on a right line a distance equal to half the sum of the sides of the polygon. This distance will be the base of the equivalent triangle, and the radius of the inscribed circle its perpendicular or altitude.

CONSTRUCTION OF CURVED LINES BY POINTS.

Prob. 62. (Pl. IV. Fig. 62.) *To construct an ellipse on given transverse and conjugate diameters.*

Definitions. An ellipse is an oval-shaped curve. The line

A—B that divides it into two equal and symmetrical parts is termed the *transverse axis*. The line C—D, perpendicular to the transverse at its centre point, is termed the *conjugate* axis. The points A and B are termed the *vertices* of the curve. The points E and F, on the transverse axis, which are at a distance from the points C and D, the extremities of the conjugate, equal to the semi-transverse O—A, are termed the *foci* of the ellipse.

The ellipse has the characteristic feature that the sum of any two lines, as m—E and m—F, drawn from a point, as m, on the curve to the foci, is equal to the transverse axis. It is this characteristic property that is used in constructing the curve by points.

First Method.

Let ab be the length of the transverse, and cd that of the conjugate diameter.

1st. Set off ab, from A to B, on any line, bisect AB by a perpendicular, and set off on this perpendicular the equal distances OC, and OD, each equal to the half of cd.

2d. From C, with the radius OA, describe an arc, and mark carefully the points E and F, where it crosses AB.

3d. From A, take off any distance Ab, and mark the point b.

4th. With the distance Ab describe an arc from E, and a like one from F.

5th. Take off the remaining portion bB of AB; and with it describe from the points E and F arcs, and mark the points m, n, o, p, where these arcs cross. These are four points of the required ellipse.

6th. To obtain other points of the curve take any other point on AB, as c; and with the distances Ac and cB, describe arcs from E and F, as before. The points where these cross are four more points; and so on for as many as may be required.

Second Method.

Having cut a narrow strip of stiff paper, so that one of its edges shall be a straight line, mark off from the end of this strip, along the straight edge, a distance *rt* equal to *AO*, half the transverse axis of the ellipse; and from the same point *s* distance *rs* equal to *OC*, half the conjugate axis.

1st. Place the strip thus prepared so as to bring the point *s* on the line *AB* of the transverse axis, and the point *t* on the line *CD*; having the strip in this position, mark on the drawing the position of the point *r*; this is one point of the required curve.

2d. Shift the strip of paper to a new position, to the right or left of the first, and having fixed it so that the point *s* is on *AB*, and the point *t* on *CD*, mark the second position of the point *r*; this is the second point of the curve.

By placing the strip so that the first point marked may be near *A*, and gradually shifting it towards *C*, as many points may be marked as may be wanted; and so on for the remainder of the curve.

3d. Through the points thus marked draw a curved line. It will be the required ellipse.

Remark. The accuracy of the curve when completed will depend upon the steadiness of hand and correctness of eye of the draftsman. When the points of the curve have been obtained by the first method, the accuracy of their position may be tested as follows:—Joining the corresponding points, as *m* and *n*, or *o* and *p*, above and below the line *AB*, by right lines, these lines *mn* and *op* will be perpendicular to *AB*, and be bisected by it if the construction is correct.

Prob. 68. (Pl. V. Fig. 68.) *Having the transverse axis of an ellipse, and one point of the curve, to construct the conjugate axis.*

Let *AB* be the transverse axis; and *a* the given point.

1st. Bisect *AB* by a perpendicular; and from the centre point *O*, with a radius *OA*, describe a semicircle.

2d. Construct, from *a*, a perpendicular to *AB*, and mark the point *c* where it crosses the semicircle.

3d. Join *O* and *c*; and from *a* draw a parallel to *AB*, and mark the point *r* where the parallel crosses *Oc*.

4th. From *O*, set off *Or* to *C* on the perpendicular. The distance *OC* is the required semi-conjugate axis.

Remark. Having the semi-conjugate other points of the curve can be found, as in the preceding *Prob.*

Prob. 64. (Pl. V. Fig. 63.) *At a point on the curve of an ellipse to construct a tangent to the curve.*

Let *m* be the point at which the tangent is to be drawn.

1st. With *OA*, as a radius, describe a semicircle on *AB*.

2d. From *m* construct a perpendicular *mq* to *AB*, and mark the point *n*, where it crosses the semicircle.

3d. At *n* construct a tangent to the semicircle, and prolong it to cut the transverse axis prolonged at *p*.

4th. Through *p* and *m* draw a line. This is the required tangent.

Prob. 65. (Pl. V. Fig. 63.) *From a point without an ellipse to construct a tangent to the curve.*

Let *D* be the given point from which the tangent is to be drawn.

1st. Join the point *D* with *O* the centre of the ellipse, and mark the point *e* where this line cuts the ellipse.

2d. From *O*, with the radius *OA*, describe the semicircle *AhB*.

3d. Through *e* draw a perpendicular *eq* to the transverse axis, and mark the point *g* where it cuts the semicircle.

4th. Through the point *D* draw a perpendicular *Df* to the transverse axis, and prolong it towards *d*.

5th. From *O* draw a line through *g*, prolong it to cut the perpendicular *Df*, and mark the point *d* of intersection.

6th. From *d*, by *Prob.* 22, construct a tangent to the semicircle, and mark the point *h* of contact.

7th. From *h* draw a perpendicular *hk* to the transverse axis, and mark the point *i* where it cuts the ellipse.

8th. From *D* the given point draw a line through *i*. This is the required tangent.

Remark. The other tangent from *D* to the ellipse can be readily obtained by constructing the second tangent to the circle, and from it finding the point on the ellipse which corresponds to the one on the circle, in the same manner as the point *i* is found from *h*.

Prob. 66. (Pl. IV. Fig. 64.) *To copy a given curve by points.*

Let *ACD* be the given curve to be copied.

1st. Draw any line as *AB* across the curve.

2d. Commencing at *A* set off along *AB* any number of equal distances as *A*1, 1—2, 2—3, &c.

3d. Through the points 1, 2, 3, &c., construct perpendiculars to *AB*, and prolong them to cut the curve at *m*, *n*, *o*, *p*, &c.

4th. Having drawn a right line, set off on it the equal distances *A*—1, 1—2, &c., taken off from the line *AB*, and through the points thus set off on the second line draw perpendiculars to it. From the points where these perpendiculars cross the line, commencing at the first, set off the distances 1—*m*, 2—*o*, &c., on the portion of the perpendiculars above the line; and the distances 1—*n*, 2—*p*, &c., below it. The curve drawn through the points thus set off will be a copy of the given one; the accuracy of the copy depending on the skill of the draftsman.

Prob. 67. (Pl. IV. Figs. 65, 66.) *To make a copy of a given curve, so that the lines of the copy shall be greater or smaller than the corresponding lines of the given curve in any given proportion.*

1st. Having drawn a line *AB* across the curve (Fig. 64) set off along it the equal distances *A*—1, 1—2, &c., and through the points 1, 2, &c., construct perpendiculars to *AB*, and prolong them to cut the curve on each side of it.

2d. Draw any line, as *ab* (Fig. 65), on which set off equal distances *a*—1, 1—2, &c., each in the given proportion, take for example that of 1 to 3, to those set off on the given figure, that is, make *a*—1 the one-third of *A*—1, &c., and through the points 1, 2, &c., construct perpendiculars to *ab*.

4th. Set off any given line *cd* (Fig. 66), with the distance *cd* describe two arcs, and join the point *e*, where they cross, with *c*, and *d*.

5th. From *e* set off *ef* and *eg*, each equal to one-third of *cd*, and join *f* and *g*.

6th. From *c* set off *cm*, equal to 1—*M* (Fig. 64); *co* equal

2—o, &c; join c with the points m, o, &c.; and mark the points r, s, &c., where these lines cross fg.

7th. Set off the distance fr from 1 to m (Fig. 65); fs from 2 to o, &c. The points m, o, &c., are points of the required copy. In like manner the distances n, p, &c., below ab, are constructed.

Remark. The method here used (Fig. 66) for constructing the proportional distances fr, fs, &c., to those cm, co, &c., can be used in all like cases, as for example in *Prob.* 17. It furnishes one of the most accurate methods for such cases, as the lines drawn from c cross the line fg so as to mark the points of crossing r, s, &c., with great accuracy.

Prob. 68. (Pl. V. Fig. 67.) *Through three given points to describe an arc of a circle by points.*

Let A, B, and C be the given points.

1st. From A, with the radius AC, the distance between the points farthest apart, describe an arc Co; and from C with the same radius an arc Ap.

2d. From A and C, through B, draw lines, and prolong them to a and b on the arcs.

3d. From b, set off any number of equal arcs b—1, 1—2, &c., above b; and from a the same number of equal arcs below a.

4th. From C, draw lines C—1, C—2, &c., to the points above b; and from A lines A—1, &c., to the corresponding points below a.

5th. Mark the points, as m, &c., where the corresponding lines A—1 and C—1, &c., cross. These are points of the curve.

6th. Having set off equal arcs below b, and like arcs above a, join the corresponding points with A and C. The points n, &c., to the left of B, are points of the required curve.

Remark. This construction is only useful when, from the position of the given points, the centre of the circle which would pass through them cannot be constructed.

Prob. 69. (Pl. V. Fig. 68.) *Having given the axis, the vertex, and a point of a parabola, to find other points of the curve and describe it.*

Let AB be the axis; A the vertex; and C the given point.

1st. From C draw a perpendicular to AB, and mark the point d where it crosses AB.

2d. At A construct a perpendicular to AB, and from C a parallel to AB, and mark the point F where these two lines cross.

3d. Divide Cd and CF respectively into the same number of equal parts, say four for example.

4th. From the points of division 1, 2, 3, on Cd draw parallels to AB; and from the point A lines to the points 1, 2, 3 on CF.

5th. Mark the points x, y, z, where the lines from A cross the corresponding parallels to AB. These will be the required points through which the curve is traced.

6th. Through the points x, y, z, drawing perpendiculars to AB, and from the points a, b, c, where they cross it, setting off distances ax', by', and cz' respectively equal to ax, &c.; the points x', y', z' will be the portion AD of the curve below AB.

Prob. 70. (Pl. V. Fig. 69.) *Having given the diameter of a circle, to construct a right line which shall be equal in length to its circumference.*

Let AM be the given diameter.

1st. Draw a right line, and having, from any convenient scale of equal parts, taken off a distance greater than the given diameter, and equal to 113 of these equal parts, set it off from a to b.

2d. From a and b, with the distance ab, describe arcs, and from the point c, where they cross each other, draw lines through a and b.

3d. Take off from the scale a distance equal to 355 equal parts, and set it off from c, to d, and e, on the lines drawn through a and b; and join the points d and e.

4th. From a, set off on ab, the distance am, equal to the given diameter AM; and from c, draw a line through m, and prolong it to cross de at n. The distance dn is the required length of the circumference.

CHAPTER IV.

TINTING AND SHADING.

Line Shading.

1. ***Flat tints.*** It is often necessary to cover a surface with equi-distant parallel lines. This is good practice for the eye, as well as the hand, as the distance between the lines should be obtained by the eye alone; use the triangles for this, sliding one along the other or, better, against the square.

When the spacing is uniform and the lines smooth, it gives the effect of a flat tint. If, while doing this, you should happen to make a space larger, or smaller, than the preceding, do not make the next line at the regular distance from the last, as this would make the break in the spacing more noticeable, but gradually reduce, or increase this distance until the regular space is reached, and then continue with that.

These irregularities in spacing are less noticeable where the spacing is coarse; so that it is well in beginning to make the lines at least $\frac{1}{16}$ of an inch apart. With practice this can be reduced; the fineness of the spacing should have some reference to the size of the figure.

This kind of shading is used mostly for sections, as shown in Fig. 156. Pl. XVII.; it being customary to run the lines 45° in either direction. Where the sections of two bodies join, as in Fig. 3. Pl. I.* let the lines run in opposite directions; where there are more than two bodies, try to arrange so that on no two adjacent ones the lines run in the same direction; if necessary change the angle.

For practice take four rectangles and cover with lines, as shown in Fig. 2. Pl. I*. Afterwards try Figs. 3, 4, 5, using finer spacing. The student can easily vary these figures.

2. *Graduated tints.* There are two methods by which a graduated tint may be obtained; first, by varying the distances without changing the size of the line (Pl. I*. Fig. 6), or second, by changing the size of the lines as well as the distances (Pl. I.* Fig. 7). The effect of the last method is the best; always shade from the dark line to the light. Try shading a rectangle by each method.

For further practice try the shading of an hexagonal prism and cylinder; as seen in Figs. 8 and 9, Pl. I.*, the shading on these surfaces is made up of flat and graduated tints. When shading the cylinder make the darkest line first, and shade both ways from it; the shade on the left-hand side should be made from left to right.

Figs. 10 and 11, Pl. I.* give practice with the compasses in producing graduated tints. In the first (fig. 10), each circle is to be completed with a uniform line, the shade being lightest towards the centre; in the second (fig. 11), each circle is made with tapering lines.

It requires some practice to make a tapering line with the compasses; when the circle is to be complete, set the pen to the size of the finest part and describe the circle; then separate the points of the pen a little, and sweep over the heaviest part of the circle; if the pen is brought in contact with the paper, and also taken from it while it is being turned, and the pressure upon the paper is varied, making it greatest at the darkest part of the circle, a very good taper can be given to the line. It would be well to protect the centre in making these figures.

The rules for locating the dark and light parts on the solids just mentioned, are given in the chapter on shading; they are introduced here merely for practice, and the examples given will be sufficient guides.

India Ink Shading.

3. *Flat tints.* Tinting with India ink is a quicker and easier method of shading than by the use of lines.

For tinting one needs to have at hand a tumbler of clean water and two or three brushes of different sizes; those with

[illegible]
[illegible]
[illegible]

[illegible]
[illegible]
[illegible]

[illegible]
[illegible]
[illegible]
[illegible]
[illegible]
[illegible]
[illegible]

[illegible]
[illegible]
[illegible]
[illegible]
[illegible]

large bodies and fine points are best, as they will hold considerable tint. To prepare the tint, rub the cake of ink upon the tile and then take from that with a brush, and mix with the water in the tumbler, until the desired shade is obtained. Care should be taken that the brush and tumbler are perfectly clean, and it is well to keep the tumbler covered after the tint is prepared. Do not make the tint as dark as you wish it upon the drawing, when finished; it is much easier to lay a light tint smoothly, than a dark one, so that it is better to get the depth of shade required by successive washes; let each wash dry before laying another.

As a rule, it is better to go over the surface to be tinted first with clean water, as the first wash will lay smoother; and if the first wash is spotted, it will show through all the rest; this damping is especially necessary if the tint used is dark, or the surface large; when the surface is small, and some skill has been acquired, the damping may be omitted.

Do not use India rubber upon the surface to be tinted, as it is difficult to lay a smooth tint afterwards; avoid also resting the hands upon the surface, as any moisture from them will affect the flow of the tint.

For practice try laying flat tints upon rectangles of different sizes, commencing with small ones. When doing this, commence at the top and work down, keeping the advancing edge nearly horizontal and always wet; let the board be inclined a little, so that the tint will follow the brush; upon reaching the bottom of the rectangle, if there is any surplus tint upon the paper, it should be removed with the brush, having first wiped it dry.

Try next some surface where it is necessary to watch two or more edges, to see that they do not get dry; the space between two concentric circles will do, or trace the outlines of the irregular curve upon paper, and either tint the curve or else tint around the curve, leaving that white. Let the outlines of surfaces to be tinted be fine hard pencil lines; with care in laying the tints, they make the best finish for the edge, but where the edge has become uneven, a fine light line of ink will improve it.

4. *Graduated tints.* Having acquired some skill in laying

flat tints, try next a graduated tint. There are several methods of doing this, one of which is by

Flat tints. When it is desired to tint a rectangle so that it shall be darkest at the top, and shade off lighter towards the bottom, divide the sides into any number of equal parts with pencil marks (Pl. I.* Fig. 12.); commencing at the top, lay a flat tint upon the first space; when this is dry, commence at the top and lay a flat tint over the first two spaces. Proceed in this way, commencing at the top each time, until the whole rectangle is covered; by making the divisions of the rectangle quite small, the effect is more pleasing. See that the lower edges of the flat tints are as straight as possible, for they show through the succeeding tints, and detract much from the appearance when irregular; it is not well to make the division marks across the surface, as they would be likely to show.

There must be sufficient time between the tints to allow the top space to dry, else some of its tint will be washed to the spaces below, and when completed, the upper spaces of the rectangle will have the same tint.

It is better to follow the order given, instead of going over the whole surface for the first tint, and reducing the surface, by one space, for each succeeding tint; by the first method the edges are covered by the over-laying tints, and a softer appearance is given than would be obtained by the second method. Figs. 11, 12, Pl. I.**, give examples of shading with flat tints.

5 *Softened tints.* This gives a much smoother appearance than the last method. Divide the rectangle as before, and tint the first space; but instead of letting the edge dry, as a line, wash it out with clean water; wash out the edge of each tint in the same way; and when finished, there will not be any abrupt changes from one tint to another, as in the last method.

6. *Dry shading.* First tint the rectangle by the method of flat tints; then keeping the brush pretty dry, so that the strokes disappear about as fast as made, use it as you would a pencil, and shade between the edges until they disappear; keep the point of the brush pretty fine, and make the strokes short and parallel to the edges.

This takes considerable time, but gives a very good result; not as smooth as by softened tints, but full as pleasant to the eye.

When the surface to be shaded is quite small, the flat tints might be omitted, and the tint applied with short strokes of the brush, wherever needed.

For practice, try the different methods upon rectangles about 2 by 4 inches. Let the shade be darkest at the top, or bottom; let the shade be darkest along the right or left hand edges; let it be darkest through the centre, either horizontally or vertically; in the last case the centre space is the first one tinted, and the second wash covers the centre and two adjacent spaces.

7. *Colors.* The directions previously given will apply to the use of colors in forming flat or graduated tints; another method may be used for graduated tints, and that is to shade the surface first with India ink, and then cover it with a flat tint of the color.

CHAPTER V.

CONVENTIONAL MODES OF REPRESENTING DIFFERENT MATERIALS.

1. In mechanical drawing different materials may be represented by appropriate conventional coloring, which is usually done in finished drawings; or else by simply drawing the outlines of the parts in projection, and drawing lines across them according to some rule agreed upon, to represent stone, wood, iron, etc. Although there is no uniformity in the use of conventional tints, the following will be found convenient for this purpose:

Cast iron,	Payne's grey.
Wrought iron,	Prussian blue.
Steel,	Prussian blue and carmine.
Brass,	Gamboge.
Copper,	Gamboge and carmine.
Stone,	Sepia and yellow ochre.
Brick,	Light red.
Wood,	Burnt Sienna.
Earth,	Burnt Umber.

For stone a light tint of India ink might be used instead of the colors given above; if a little carmine be added to the light red, when used to represent brick, it will make a brighter color; raw sienna might be used instead of burnt sienna for wood.

2. *Wood.* When the drawing is on a small scale, the outlines only of a beam of timber are drawn in projection, when the sides are the parts projected, Pl. VII. Fig. 88; when the end is the part projected, the two diagonals of the figure are drawn on the projection.

If a longitudinal section of the beam is to be shown, Pl. VII. Fig. 89, fine parallel lines are drawn lengthwise. In a cross section, fine parallel lines diagonally.

Where the scale is sufficiently large to admit of some resemblance to the actual appearance of the object being attempted, lines may be drawn on the projection of the side of the beam, Pl. VII. Fig. 90, to represent the appearance of the fibres of the wood; and the same on the ends.

In longitudinal sections the appearance of the fibres may be expressed, Pl. VII. Fig. 91, with fine parallel lines drawn over them lengthwise. In cross sections the grain may be shown, as in the projection of the ends, with fine parallel lines diagonally.

Figs. 13, 14, 15, Pl. I.*, give additional examples of the method of representing wood in line drawings. Before attempting to represent graining, it would be well to examine the graining of wood in the material itself, and to have a piece at hand to imitate; in the floor of the drawing-room may often be found good examples.

In beginning to grain a timber, make the knots first, and then fill in the remaining space with lines, arranging so as to enclose the knots; until some practice has been acquired, it would be well to pencil the graining before inking. The size of the knots should have some reference to the size of the timber; let the graining lines be made with a fine steel pen, using light ink; where the wood is to be colored, apply the tint before graining.

When the timber is large, use a brush to make the graining; if it is to be colored, use a dark tint of burnt sienna for the lines, and wash over with a lighter tint of the same; when using the brush for graining, make the points of the knots widest, as in Fig. 15, Pl. I.*; it would add also to the looks of graining made with a pen to widen the ends of the knots with the brush.

Fig. 14, Pl. I.*, differs from Fig. 13 only in having a series of short marks introduced in the graining; if desired to distinguish between soft and hard wood, let Fig. 13 represent soft, and Fig. 14 hard wood.

In Fig. 15, Pl. I.*, the graining is made up of a series of short hatches; when done nicely, this gives a very good effect. This style may also be used to represent hard wood.

The cross sections, Figs. 13, 14, 15, Pl. I.*, are shown by a series of concentric circles, with a few lines radiating from the centre, representing cracks; use the bow compasses to describe the circles, from a centre either within or without the section. When the section is narrow, as at *a*, Fig. 13, Pl. I.*, parallel straight lines are sufficient.

To represent the end of the timber as broken, let the line be made up of a series of sharp points. Where a number of adjoining planks are represented as broken along nearly the same line, let the end of each be distinct, as in Fig. 1, Pl. I.*

3. *Masonry*. In drawings on a small scale, the outlines of the principal parts are alone put down on the projections; and on the parts cut, fine parallel wavy lines, drawn either vertically or horizontally across, are put in.

In drawings to a scale sufficiently large to exhibit the details of the parts, lines may be drawn on the elevations, Pl. VII. Fig. 92, to show either the general character of the combination of the parts, or else the outline of each part in detail, as the case may require. In like manner in section, the outline of each part, Pl. VII. Fig. 93, in detail, or else lines showing the general arrangement, may be drawn, and over these fine parallel lines.

Figs. 16-23, Pl. I.*, give additional examples of stone work. In Figs. 16, 17 there is a ledge cut around each stone, and sunk below the face. The face may be dressed with a pick, Fig. 17, or it might be left rough, and represented as in Figs. 21-23, Pl. I.*. Fig. 16 would be the method of representing such stone work in a line drawing; the lower and right-hand lines of the inner rectangle should be heavy.

Fig. 18, Pl. I.*, represents the surface of the stone as finished; where a number of stones come together, leave a narrow line of light at the top and left-hand edges of each.

In Figs. 19, 20, Pl. I.*, the edges of the stones are bevelled, and the surfaces finished. Fig. 19 is the method of representing in a line drawing. For a finished shaded drawing, Fig. 20 would do, shaded with the stone tint alone, or with India ink first, and then a flat stone tint; the depth of shade upon each face of the stone is shown in the example given.

Figs. 21-23, Pl. I.*, give different methods of representin

stone where the joints only are dressed, and the faces left rough.

4. *Metals.* The conventional colors for the different metals have already been given.

To represent metal as broken, the line should be somewhat irregular, but not as much so as for the breaking of wood; Fig. 1′. Pl. I.* gives examples of the customary method of showing the broken ends of rods, bars, etc.; the parallel lines may be either black or the conventional color.

5. *Earth.* In vertical sections extending below the level of the ground it may be necessary to show the section of the earth, etc., around the foundations. If the soil is common earth this may be done, as shown in Pl. VIII. Fig. 94. If sand, as in Pl. VIII. Fig. 95. If stony, as in Pl. VIII. Fig. 96. If solid rock, as in Pl. VIII. Fig. 97. Where the earth is embanked its section may be shown, as in Pl. VIII. Fig. 98.

If it is desired to color the sections of earth, let a flat tint of burnt umber be laid first, the lower edge being washed out, then when dry the lines may be drawn over it with a pen; or, after laying the flat tint of burnt umber, with the brush, make a series of short horizontal strokes over the wash already laid, varying the shade of the tint for the strokes, some being quite dark.

6. *Water.* This is represented as in Fig. 24. Pl. I.* by horizontal lines; for colored drawings make the lines blue.

Fig. 24. Pl. I.* represents a section of a canal; for practice let this be drawn and finished in colors.

CHAPTER VI.

CONSTRUCTION OF REGULAR FIGURES.

1. The following figures are valuable as exercises in construction. Simple as they may seem, one trial will convince that care is necessary in every step to secure a good result; let the construction lines be fine and light and the intersections good. These figures afford further practice for tinting both with lines and colors; use different shades of the same color, or different colors, laying the lightest first. The arrangement indicated upon the figures may be followed, or changed to suit the taste.

2. *To represent a pavement made up of squares.* (Pl. I.** Fig. 1.) Divide the lower side into any number of equal parts, and through the points of division draw lines 45° both ways; if through the points where these diagonals meet the sides, diagonal lines be drawn, they will complete the figure.

3. *To represent a pavement of equilateral triangles.* (Pl. I.** Fig. 2.) Divide the lower side into any number of equal parts, and through these points draw lines 60° each way; through the points in which these intersect, draw horizontal lines.

4. *To represent a pavement of hexagons.* (Pl. I.** Fig. 3.) Having given the side of the hexagon, lay it off any number of times upon the side, and draw lines 60° through these points; the method of completing the figure will then be apparent; *a c* is equal to half the side of the hexagon.

5. *To represent a pavement made up of octagons and squares.* (Pl. I.** Fig. 4.) Divide the surface first into squares; then construct an octagon in one of these; if it is desired to have a regular octagon, it may be done by taking half of the diagonal of the square as a radius and describing arcs from each corner of the square as a centre, until they in-

tersect the sides; this is indicated in one of the squares of the figure. After constructing one octagon, the others may be obtained from it by projecting, as shown by the dotted lines.

6. *To represent a pavement made up of isosceles triangles.* (Pl. I.** Fig. 5.) Divide the lower side into any number of equal parts, and through the points of division draw vertical lines; through every other point of division draw lines at 30° and 60°; draw horizontal lines through the points in which the lines at 60° intersect. If the lines at 60° are left out, the surface will be covered with rhombuses.

7. In Fig. 6. Pl. I.**, the surface is covered with intersecting and tangent circles. First divide into squares, as shown by the dotted lines; then describe the large circles, and next the small ones tangent.

8. Figs. 7–10. Pl. I.**, are examples of architectural ornament. The method of constructing will be evident from the figures. In Fig. 7, for a change, the dark part might be left white and the rest shaded.

CHAPTER VII.

PROJECTIONS.

By the methods given in the preceding problems, we are enabled to construct most of the geometrical figures that can be traced, or drawn on a plane surface, according to geometrical principles, and with the ordinary mathematical instruments; and if, in a practical point of view, our object was simply to obtain the shape and dimensions of such forms as could be cut from a sheet of paper, a thin board, or a block of wood of uniform thickness, these problems would be sufficient for the purpose; for it would be only necessary to construct the required figure on one side, or end of the board, or block, and then cut away the other parts exterior to the outline of the figure. Here then we have an example, in which the form and dimensions of one side, or end of a body, being given, the body itself can be shaped by means of this one view; and this is applicable to all cases where the thickness of the body is the same throughout, and where the opposite sides, or ends, are figures precisely alike in shape and dimensions. This method is applicable to a numerous class of bodies to be met with in the industrial arts; particular cases will readily occur to any one. Among the most simple, the common brick may be taken as an example; the thickness in this case is uniform, and the opposite sides are equal rectangles; hence taking a board of the same thickness as the brick, marking out on its surface the rectangle of the side, and then cutting away the portion of the board exterior to this outline, a solid will be obtained of the same form and dimensions as the brick.

But it is evident that a drawing of the rectangle that represents the side would not be sufficient to determine the form of the entire brick, if we did not know its thickness. In order that the drawing shall represent the forms and dimensions of all the faces of the brick, it is obvious that some means must be resorted to by which these parts can also be represented.

The necessity for this will be still more apparent when we desire to represent the forms and dimensions of bodies, which, although of uniform thickness, have their opposite faces of different forms and dimensions; and more especially in the more complicated cases, where the surface of the body is formed of figures differing both in forms and dimensions from each other. The means by which we effect this is termed *the method of projections*. By it we are enabled to represent the forms and dimensions of all the parts of a body, however complicated, provided they can be constructed by geometrical principles.

Principles.

If through a given point, *A* (Fig. 19), in space a line be drawn perpendicular to any plane, *M N*, the point *a* in which

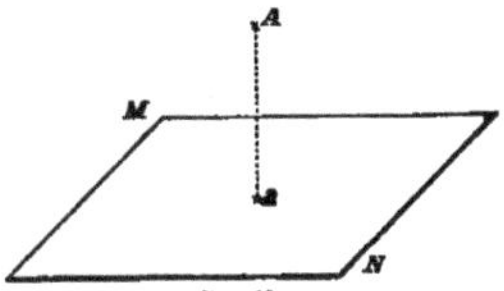

FIG. 19.

the line pierces the plane is called the projection of the point *A* upon that plane.

The projection of a right line is obtained by joining the projections of any two of its points; for example, given the

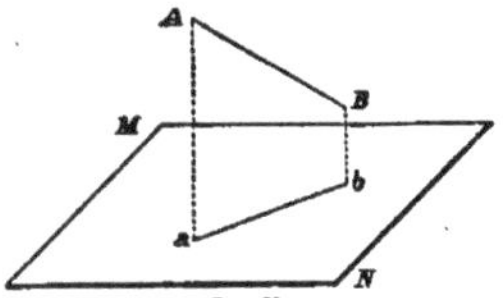

FIG. 20.

line *A B* (Fig. 20), in space, *a* is the projection of *A*, and *b* of *B*; joining *a b* we have the projection of *A B*.

If the given line be curved instead of straight, we have to find the projections of more of its points and join them; the more points found the more accurate the projection. Fig. 21 illustrates this, where $a\,h$, the projection of $A\,H$, is found by joining the projections of its different points.

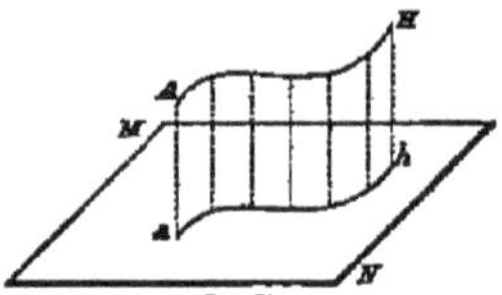

FIG. 21.

A solid being given to find its projection, it will be obtained by joining the projections of its bounding edges.

It is evident in these examples given, that it is impossible to determine from the projections alone, the distance of the points in space from the plane; in other words, the position of the points in space is not fixed.

Having seen that one projection is not sufficient to locate a point in space, and as there can be only one projection of a point on any plane, suppose we take two planes at right angles o each other, and find the projections of a point upon each :f these.

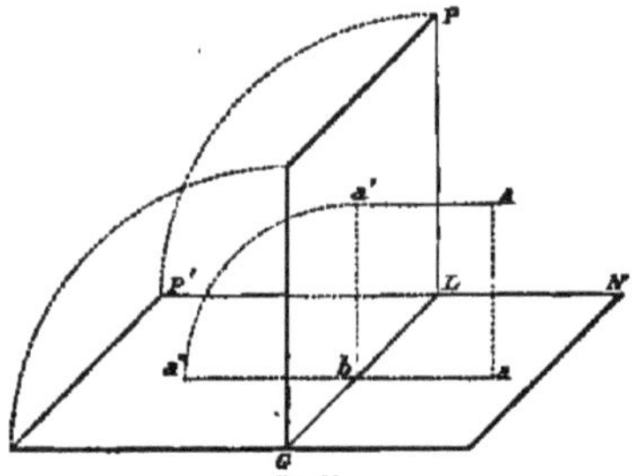

FIG. 22

Fig. 22 shows pictorially the two planes $G\,N$ and $G\,P$ at right angles; A is a point in space, a and a' are its projections on either plane; the distance of A from the plane $G\,N$, or $A\,a$, is equal to the distance $a'b$, and the distance of A from the plane $G\,P$, or $A\,a'$, is equal to $a\,b$. If at the points a and a' perpendiculars should be erected to each plane, we see that these must intersect at the point A in space; and as these perpendiculars can intersect in only one point, it follows that there is only one point in space that can be projected in a and a'.

Thus we see, *if the projections of a point are found upon two planes at right angles, its position in space is fixed*, and can be determined from the projections.

If the projections of two or more points are found upon these same planes, we should not only be able to determine their positions respecting the planes, but also their relative position; hence, it follows, if a solid be projected upon these two planes, we can determine its dimensions from the projections.

We have found, then, that two planes, at right angles, are necessary in projections; these are called, respectively, the horizontal and vertical planes of projection.

The line of intersection, $G\,L$ (Fig. 22), is called the *ground line*. The point a is called the horizontal projection of A, and a' the vertical projection. The horizontal projection of an object is often called the *plan*, and the vertical projection the *elevation*.

The perpendiculars through A are called the projecting lines; the plane of the two is perpendicular to both planes of projection, and also the ground line, and intersects both planes in right lines, perpendicular to the ground line at the same point.

Since it is impracticable to draw upon two planes at right angles, the vertical plane is considered as revolved back, about the ground line, until it forms one and the same surface with the horizontal plane. By this revolution the relative position of points in the vertical plane is not affected; every point remains at the same distance from the ground line after revolution as before. This is shown in Fig. 22, where the vertical plane $G\,P$ is represented as revolved back to the horizontal position $G\,P'$; a' revolves to a''; $a''\,b$ is equal to $a'b$; the line joining $a\,a''$ is perpendicular to $G\,L$

Remark. The preceding figures are pictorial representations; in the remaining figures a horizontal line is used to separate the planes of projection, the part above the line being the vertical plane, and the part below the horizontal.

It is important, then, to note, 1*st*, *that the perpendicular distance from the horizontal projection of a point to the ground line shows how far the point itself is from the vertical plane of projection.*

2*d*, *that, in like manner, the perpendicular distance from its vertical projection to the ground line shows its height above the horizontal plane.*

3*d*, *that the horizontal and vertical projections of a point lie on the right line drawn from one to the other, and perpendicular to the ground line.*

4*th*, *that the distance, measured horizontally, between two points, is that between their horizontal projections.*

5*th*, *that their distance apart vertically, or the height the one is above the other, is measured by the difference between the respective distances of their vertical projections from the ground line.*

6*th*, *that the actual distance between two points, or the length of a right line connecting them; is equal to the hypothenuse of a right angled triangle, the base of which is equal to the distance between the horizontal projections of the points, and the altitude is the difference between the distances of their vertical projections from the ground line.*

For example (Pl. V. Fig. 72), the line $G\,L$ is the ground line. The point a being the horizontal, and the point a' the vertical projection of a point, these two points lie on the right line $a\,x\,a'$ joining them, and perpendicular to $G\,L$. The point itself is at a distance in front of the vertical plane measured by the line $a\,x$; and at a height from the horizontal plane measured by $x\,a'$.

In like manner $b\,b'$, and $c\,c'$, are the projections of two points, the horizontal distance between which is $b\,c$, the distance apart of their horizontal projections; and the vertical distance is $c'y$, equal to the difference between $c'x'$ and $b'x$, their respective heights from the horizontal plane. The actual distance between these points, or the length of the line drawn from one to the other, may be found by constructing a right angled triangle, *m o n*; the base of which, *o m*, being equal to *b c*, and its altitude, *o n*, equal to *c'y*, its hypothenuse, *m n*, will be the distance required.

In making the projections of an object, when it is desirable to designate the projections that correspond to the same point, they are joined by a light broken line; and if the projections are those of an isolated point, either the projections are made with a large round dot, or by a small dot surrounded by a small circle. When the projections of two points are those of the extremities of a right line, a full line is drawn on each plane of projection between the points, as *b c* and *b'c'*; and a broken line is drawn between the projections of the corresponding extremities.

Notation.

Small letters are used to designate the projections of a point, the same letter being used for both projections; to distinguish between them, the vertical is accented. The point *a a'* is also spoken of as the point *A*.

Lines are similarly treated, as the line *ab—a'b'*, or the line *A B*.

The letters *H* and *V* are used to designate the planes of projection.

G L stands for the ground line.

Shade lines.

Shade lines upon outline drawings add very much to their appearance; when properly placed, they give relief to the drawing, and are of assistance in reading it.

In mechanical drawing the light is generally assumed to come in such a direction that its projections shall make angles of 45° with the ground line; the arrows in Figs. 23 and 24 indicate the direction of light.

Those edges should be heavy which separate light from dark surfaces.

In the case of the cube (Fig. 23), we see that the top, front, and left-hand faces must be in the light, while the remaining faces would be in the shade. In the elevation the only visible edges separating light from dark faces are those upon the right and lower sides ($a'b'$ and $b'c'$), while in the plan the shaded edges are upon the right and upper sides (af and fe).

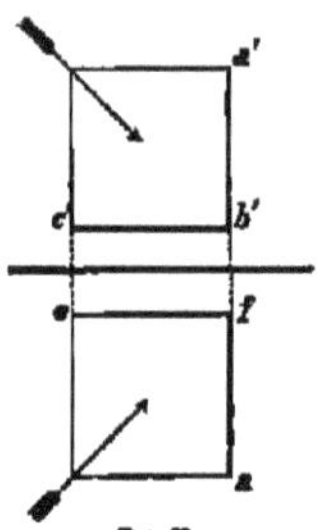

Fig. 23.

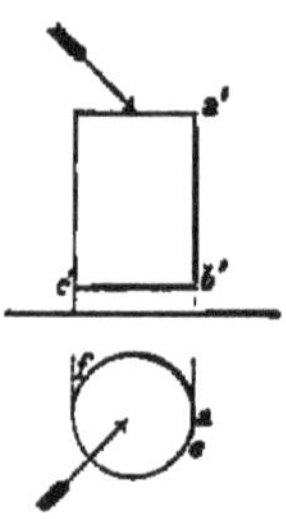

Fig. 24.

In case of a curved surface like the cylinder (Fig. 24), the line $a'b'$ does not separate the light from the dark surface, yet it is well to make it a trifle darker than the left-hand edge, but not as dark as the bottom line $c'b'$. In the plan the circle is made darkest upon the upper and right-hand side, tapering to the points of tangency (e, f) of rays of light.

Shade lines of sections follow the above rules, as shown in Fig. 33. Pl. VI.

Draw the shade lines with their breadth outside the outline.

In colored drawings draw the shade lines last.

In shaded drawings omit the shade lines altogether.

Profiles and *Sections*. The projections of an object give only the forms and dimensions of its exterior, and the positions of points, &c., on its surface. To show the thickness of its solid parts, and the form and dimensions of its interior, intersecting-planes are used. Taking a house as a model, let us conceive it to be cut, or sawed through, at some point between its two ends, in the direction of a vertical plane parallel to the ends. Setting aside one portion, let us imagine a pane of glass placed against the sawed surface of the other, and let an accurate outline of the parts thus cut through be traced on the pane. This outline is termed a *profile*. On it, to distinguish the solid parts cut through from the voids, or hollow parts, we cover them entirely with ink, or some other color, or else simply draw parallel lines close together across them. If, besides tracing the outline of the parts resting against the pane, we were to trace the projections of all the parts, both within and without the outline of the profile, that could be seen through the pane by a person standing in front of it, the profile with these additional outlines is termed a *section*. A section moreover differs from a profile in this, that it may be made in any direction, whereas the profile is made by cutting vertically, and in objects, like a house, bounded by plane surfaces, in a direction perpendicular to the surface.

To show the direction in which the section is made, it is usual to draw a broken and dotted line on the plan and elevation of the object, marking the position of the saw-cut on the surface of the object; and, to indicate the position to which the section corresponds, letters of reference are placed at the extremities of each of these lines, and the figure of the section is designated as *vertical*, or *oblique section on A—B*, *C—D*, &c., according as the section is in a plane perpendicular, or oblique to the horizontal plane of projection.

The sections in most general use are those made by vertical and horizontal planes. A horizontal section is made in the same manner as a vertical one, by conceiving the object cut through at some point above the horizontal plane of projection, and parallel to it, and, having removed the portion above the plane of section, by making such a representation of the lower portion as would be represented by tracing on a pane of glass, laid on it, the outline of the parts in contact with the pane, with the outline of the projection of the parts on the pane that can be seen through it, whether on the exterior, or interior of the object.

The solid parts in contact with the pane are represented in the same way as in other sections. The projected parts are represented only by their outlines. A broken and dotted line, with letters of reference at its extremities, is drawn on the elevation to show where the section is taken; and the section is designated by a title, as, *horizontal section* on *A—B*, &c.

As the broken and dotted lines that indicate the position of the planes of section are drawn on the planes of projection, and are in fact the lines in which the planes of section would cut these two planes, they are termed the *vertical* or *horizontal traces* of the planes of section, according as the lines are traced on the vertical or horizontal plane of projection.

It will be well to note particularly that the planes of section are usually taken in front of, or above the object, that portion of it which is cut by the plane being supposed in contact with the plane; whereas the planes of projection may be placed either behind, or in front of the object, and above or below it, as may best suit the purpose of the draftsman; the position of the ground line therefore will always indicate on which side of the object, and whether above, or below it, the planes of projection are placed. The usual method is to place the horizontal plane of projection below the object represented and the vertical plane behind it. The more usual method also is to represent the object as resting on the horizontal plane; its position with respect to the vertical plane, or that of the vertical plane with respect to it, being so taken as to give the desired elevation to suit the views of the draftsman. In the case of the ordinary house, for example, the elevations of the four sides may be obtained either by supposing one vertical plane, and the four sides successively presented to it; or by supposing the vertical plane shifted so as to be brought behind each of the sides in succession.

Projections of Points and *Right Lines.* The method of projections presents two problems. The one is having given the forms and dimensions of an object, to construct its projections; the other, having the projections of an object, to construct its forms and dimensions. A correct understanding of the manner of projecting points and right lines, and determining their relative positions with respect to each other, is an indispensable foundation for the solution of these two questions.

The methods of projecting a single point, and of obtaining its distance from the planes of projection, also of two points, and determining their distance apart, have already been given. The same process would evidently be followed in projecting any number of points; or, in determining their relative positions, having their projections. But, besides these general methods, there are some particular cases with which it will be well to become familiarised at the outset, as a knowledge of them will materially aid in showing, by a glance at the projections, the relative positions of the lines joining the points to the planes of projection; that is, whether these lines are parallel, oblique, or perpendicular to one, or both of these planes.

Case 1. (Pl. V. Fig. 73.) Let aa' and bb' be the projections of two points, the distances of their vertical projections $a'x$ and $b'x'$ from the ground line being equal, those of their horizontal projections ax and bx' being unequal. The points themselves will be at the same height above the horizontal plane of projection but at unequal distances from the vertical plane. The vertical projection of the line joining the two points $a'b'$ will be parallel to the ground line, and its horizontal projection ab will be oblique to it.

From this we observe, that when two points of a right line are at the same height above the horizontal plane of projection, and at unequal distances from the vertical plane, the vertical projection of the line will be parallel to the ground line, and its horizontal projection oblique to this line.

Finding then the two projections of a right line in these positions with respect to the ground line, we conclude that the line itself is at the same height throughout above the horizontal plane of projection, or parallel to this plane, but oblique to the vertical plane.

Case 2. (Pl. V. Fig. 74.) In like manner, when we find the horizontal projections of two points a and b at the same distance from the ground line, and the vertical projections a' and b' at unequal heights from it, we conclude that the line joining the points is parallel to the vertical plane but oblique to the horizontal.

Case 3. (Pl. V. Fig. 75.) When the horizontal projections of two points are at the same distance from ground line, and the vertical projections also at equal distances from it, we conclude that the line itself is parallel to both planes of projection.

When a line therefore is parallel to one plane of projection, alone, its projection on the other will be parallel to the ground line, and its projection on the plane to which it is parallel will be oblique to the ground line.

When the line is parallel to both planes its two projections will be parallel to the ground line.

Case 4. (Pl. V. Fig. 76.) Suppose two points as *a* and *b* to lie in the horizontal plane of projection, where are their vertical projections? From what has been already shown, these last projections must lie on the perpendiculars, from the horizontal projections *a* and *b* to the ground line; but as the points are in the horizontal plane their projections cannot lie above the ground line. *The vertical projections of a and b therefore must be at a′ and b′ on the ground line, where the perpendiculars from a and b cut it. For a like reason the vertical projection of a line as a—b in the horizontal plane will be as a′—b′ in the ground line.*

In like manner the horizontal projections of points and lines lying in the vertical plane of projection will be also in the ground line.

Case 5. (Pl. V. Fig. 77.) *If a line is vertical, or perpendicular to the horizontal plane of projection, its projection on that plane will be a point simply, as a.* For, the line being vertical, if a plumb line were applied along it the two lines would coincide, and the point of the bob of the plumb line would indicate only one point as the projection of the entire line. *Now as a is the horizontal projection of all the points of the line, their vertical projections must lie in the line from a perpendicular to the ground line, so that the vertical projections of any two points of the vertical line at the given heights b′x, and a′x above the horizontal plane of projection, would be projected on the perpendicular from a to the ground line, and at the given distances b′x and a′x above the ground line.*

In like manner it can be shown, that a line perpendicular to the vertical plane is projected into a point, as *a′*, and its horizontal projection will lie on the perpendicular to the ground line from *a′*, as *a—b*, in which the distances of the points *a* and *b* from the ground line show the distances of the ends of the line from the vertical plane.

The above comprise all of the cases, but one, of the projections of points and right lines; and they give the means of finding the positions of these elements from their projections; or of making their projections when their positions are known.

Prob. II. (Pl. VI. Fig. 73.) *To construct the projections of a regular right pyramid, with its base resting on the horizontal plane of projection.*

1st. Having drawn the ground line $G—L$, construct, at any convenient distance from it, the regular polygon, in this case the pentagon *abcde*, which is the base of the given pyramid; and the point *o* the centre of the polygon. As the vertex of a regular right pyramid is on the perpendicular to its base drawn from the centre of the base, the point *o* will be the horizontal projection of the vertex.

2d. Having drawn a perpendicular from *o* to the ground line, set off upon it the distance *ov*, the height of the vertex above the base; the point *v* will be the vertical projection of the vertex.

3d. Project the points of the base *abc*, &c., upon the vertical plane, at *a' b' c'*, &c., since these points are on the horizontal plane of projection; the line *a'—e'* will be the vertical projection of the base.

4th. Join the points *a' b' c'*, &c., with the point *o'*; the lines *o'—a'*, *o'—b'*, &c., so obtained, will be the vertical projections of the edges of the pyramid.

5th. Join the points *a*, *b*, *c*, &c., with *o*. These lines are the horizontal projections of the same edges.

Remark. In drawing in ink the outline of a solid, it is usual to represent by *dotted lines* the outlines of those parts which could not be seen by a spectator so placed as to bring the object directly between him and the plane of projection, when placed far from the object. Suppose for example the spectator placed at some distant point, *S*, from the pyramid, and on the line drawn from *o* perpendicular to *GL*. In this distant position, the lines drawn from *S* through the various points of the object, as *a*, *b*, *o*, &c., may all be regarded as parallel to *So*; and in this position therefore the spectator would only see the edges of the pyramid drawn from the vertex to the points *a*, *b*, and *c* of the base, the other edges would be hidden. The vertical projections $o'c'$, $o'd'$ of the last will be drawn with dotted lines, and the others in full lines.

In like manner, supposing the spectator placed at a great height above the horizontal plane, and in the direction of the line drawn through the vertex and centre of the base of the pyramid, he would see in this position all the edges of the pyramid, their horizontal projections oa, ob, &c., are therefore drawn in full lines.

Prob. 72. (Pl. VI. Fig. 79.) *Having the projections of a regular right pyramid, as in the last case, to construct the lengths of its edges and the dimensions of its faces.*

The horizontal projection of the edge drawn from a to the vertex is ao, and its vertical projection $a'o'$. The length of this edge therefore will be found by constructing the hypothenuse of a right angled triangle, of which ao is the base, and ao', the vertical distance between the top and bottom points of the edge, is the perpendicular. In like manner the lengths of the other edges can be found.

To construct the face bounded by the two edges drawn from the vertex o to the points a and b, and the edge ab of the base; we must construct a triangle of which the line a—b is the base, and the two edges just found are the other two sides; this triangle will be the required face, and as the pyramid is regular all the other faces will be equal to this.

Remark. It is evident that having found the faces and having the base, a model of the pyramid corresponding to the size of the drawing could be cut from stiff paper, or pasteboard, and put together.

Prob. 73. (Pl. VI. Fig. 80.) *To construct the projections of an oblique pyramid with an irregular base.*

Let the base of the pyramid be any irregular quadrilateral, $abcd$, for example, resting on the horizontal plane of projection.

1st. Having drawn the ground line, construct the base at any convenient distance from it, and set off the position, o, of the horizontal projection of the vertex, which is also supposed to be given with respect to the points of the base.

2d. Construct the vertical projections $a'b'c'd'$ of the points of the base, and o' of the vertex.

3d. Draw lines from o' to the points $a'b'c'd'$.

Remarks. The line $o'd'$ in vertical projection, and the line oc, according to what has been laid down, should be dotted.

Having the projections of a like pyramid we would proceed, as in the last case, to construct its edges and faces if required for a model.

Prob. 14. (Pl. VI. Fig. 81.) *To construct the projections of a right prism with a regular hexagonal base.*

Let the base of the prism be supposed to rest on the horizontal plane of projection.

1st. Construct at a convenient distance from the ground line the regular hexagon abc, &c., of the base; taking two of its opposite sides, as $b—c$, and $f—e$, parallel to this line.

2d. Construct the projections $h'l'm'$, &c., of the points abc, &c.

3d. As the edges of the prism are vertical, their vertical projections will be drawn through the points $h'l'$, &c., and perpendicular to the ground line.

4th. Having drawn these lines, set off the equal distances $h'—a'$, $l'—b'$, &c., upon them, and each equal to the height of the prism.

Remarks. As the edges projected in b and c, and f and e, are projected in the vertical lines $l'—b'$ and $m'—c'$ the back edges cannot be represented by dotted lines.

As the top of the prism is parallel to its base it is projected vertically in the line $a'—d'$ equal and parallel to $h'—n'$, the projection of the base.

All the faces of the prism are equal rectangles, and each equal to $b'c'm'l'$ the projection of the face parallel to the vertical plane.

It has been shown, in the projections of right lines, that when a line is parallel to one plane of projection, its projection on that plane is equal to the length of the line, and that its projection on the other plane is parallel to the ground line. In this case we see that the top of the prism, which is a hexagon parallel to the horizontal plane, is projected on that plane into the equal hexagon abc, &c., and on the vertical plane into a line $a'—d'$ parallel to the ground line. In like manner we see that the face of which $b—c$ is the horizontal projection and $b'c'm'l'$ the vertical, is projected on the horizontal plane in a line parallel to the ground line, and on the vertical plane in a rectangle equal to itself. *From this we conclude, that when a plane figure is parallel to one plane of projection it will be projected on that plane in a figure equal to itself, and on the other plane into a line parallel to the ground line.* Moreover since the faces of the prism are plane surfaces perpendicular to the horizontal plane, and are projected respectively into the lines $a—b$, $b—c$, &c., *we conclude that a plane surface perpendicular to one plane of projection is projected on that plane into a right line.* The same is true of the base and top of the prism; the base being in the horizontal plane, which is perpendicular to the vertical plane, is projected into the ground line in $h'—n'$; the top being parallel to the horizontal plane is likewise perpendicular to the vertical plane, and is projected into the line $a'—d'$.

Traces of Planes on the Planes of Projection. The plane surfaces of the prism and pyramids in the preceding problems being of limited extent, we have only had to consider the lines in which they cut the horizontal plane of projection, as $a—b$, $b—c$, &c., the bounding lines of the bases of these solids These lines are therefore properly the traces of these limited plane surfaces on the horizontal plane. But when a plane is of indefinite extent, we may have to consider the lines in which it cuts, or meets both planes of projection. The most usual cases in which we have to consider these lines are in those of profile planes, and planes of section, in which the planes are perpendicular either to the horizontal, or vertical plane, and parallel, or oblique to the other.

The position of the trace of a plane, when parallel to one plane of projection and perpendicular to the other, as has already been shown, is a line parallel to the ground line, and on that plane of projection to which the plane is perpendicular, as the lines $b—c$, and $f—e$, for example, which are the traces on the horizontal plane of the faces of the prism, which are perpendicular to this plane, and parallel to the vertical plane. The same may be said of the line $a'—d'$, which would be the trace of the plane of the top of the prism, if it were produced back to meet the vertical plane.

When the plane is perpendicular to the horizontal plane, but oblique to the vertical, as for example the face of the prism of which a—f, or d—e is the horizontal trace, its vertical trace will be perpendicular to the ground line at the point where the horizontal trace meets this line. To show this, suppose the prism so placed as to have its back face against the vertical plane; then the line a—f, for example, will be oblique to the ground line, the point f of this line being on it, at the point l', whilst the line l'—b', the one in which the oblique face meets the vertical plane, or its trace on this plane, will be perpendicular to the ground line. The same illustration would hold true supposing the prism laid on one of its faces on the horizontal plane, with its base against the vertical plane.

If A—B (Pl. VI. Fig. 82) *therefore represents the horizontal trace of a plane perpendicular to the horizontal plane its vertical trace will be a line B—b, drawn from the point B, where the horizontal trace cuts the ground line, perpendicular to this line. In like manner, if E—F is the vertical trace of a plane perpendicular to the vertical plane and oblique to the horizontal plane, the line F—f perpendicular to the ground line is its horizontal trace.*

Prob. 75. (Pl. VI. Fig. 83.) *To construct the projections and sections of a hollow cube of given dimensions.*

Let us suppose the cube so placed that, its base resting on the horizontal plane of projection in front of the vertical plane, its front and back faces shall be parallel to the vertical plane, and its other two ends perpendicular to this plane.

Having constructed a square *abcd* (Fig. X) of the same dimensions as the base of the given cube, and having its sides *ab* and *cd* parallel to the ground line, and at any convenient distance from it; this square may be taken as the projection of the base of the cube. But as the top of the cube is parallel to the base, and its four faces are also perpendicular to these two parts, the top will be also projected into the square *abcd*, and the four sides respectively into the sides of the square. The square *abcd* will therefore be the horizontal projection of all the exterior faces of the cube.

Having projected the base of the cube into the vertical plane, which projection (Fig. Y) will be a line $h'—l'$, on the ground line, equal to $a—b$, construct the square $a'b'l'h'$ equal to *abcd*. This is the vertical projection of the cube.

As the interior faces of the cube cannot be seen from without, the following method is adopted to represent their projections: within the square *abcd* construct another represented by the dotted lines, having its sides at the same distance from the exterior square as the thickness of the sides of the hollow cube. This square will be the projection of the interior faces; and it is drawn with dotted lines, to show that these faces are not seen from without.

Supposing the top and bottom of the cube of the same thickness as the sides, a like square constructed within $a'b'l'h'$ will be the vertical projection of the two interior faces, which are perpendicular to the vertical plane, and of the interior faces of the top and base.

Having completed the projections of the cube, suppose it is required to construct the figures of the sections cut from it by a horizontal plane, of which $M—N$ is the vertical trace; and by a vertical plane of which $O—P$ is the horizontal trace. The horizontal plane of section will cut from the exterior faces of the cube a square *mopn* (Fig. Z) equal to the one *abcd*, and from the interior faces another square equal to the one in dotted lines, and having its sides parallel to those of *mopn*. The solid portion of the four sides cut by the plane of section would be represented by the shading lines, as in Fig. Z.

The plane of section of which $O—P$ is the trace, being oblique to the sides, will cut from the opposite exterior faces $a—d$, and $b—c$, and the exterior faces of the top and base, a rectangle of which $r—u$ (Figs. X, W) is the base, and $r—r'$ (Fig. W) equal to the height $b'—l'$, is the altitude; in like manner it will cut from the corresponding interior faces a rectangle of which $s—t$ is the base, and $s—s'$, equal to the height of the interior face, is the altitude. The sides of the interior rectangle $stt's'$ will be parallel to those of the one exterior; the distance apart of the vertical sides being equal to the equal distances $r—s$ (Fig. X) and $t—u$; and that of the horizontal sides being the same as the thickness of the top and base of the cube. In other words, as has already been stated, the figure of the vertical section is the same that would be found by tracing the outline of the part of the cube, cut through by the plane of section, on the vertical plane of projection.

Remarks. The manner of representing the interior faces of the hollow cube by dotted lines is generally adopted for all like cases; that is, when it is desired to represent the projections of the outlines of any part of an object which lies between some other part projected and the plane of projection.

Where several points, situated on the same right line, as *r*, *s*, *t*, *u*, on the line *O—P* (Fig. *X*), are to be transferred to another right line, as in the construction of (Fig. *W*), the shortest way of doing it, and, if care be taken, also the most accurate one, is to place the straight edge of a narrow strip of paper along the line, and confining it in this position to mark accurately on it near the edge the positions of the points. Having done this, the points can be transferred from the strip, by a like process, to any other line. The advantage of this method over that of transferring each distance by the dividers will be apparent in some of the succeeding *problems.*

Prob. 76. (Pl. VI. Fig. 84.) *To construct the projections of a regular hollow pyramid truncated by a plane oblique to the horizontal plane and perpendicular to the vertical plane.*

Let us suppose the base of the pyramid a regular pentagon Having constructed this base, and the projections of the different parts of the entire pyramid as in *Prob.* 71, draw a line, *M—N*, oblique to the ground line, as the vertical trace of the assumed truncating plane; the portion of the pyramid lying above this plane being supposed removed.

Now, as the truncating plane cuts all the faces of the pyramid, and as it is itself perpendicular to the vertical plane of projection, all the lines which it cuts from these faces will be projected on the vertical plane of projection in the trace *M—N*. The points *r'*, *s'*, *t'*, *v'*, and *u'*, where the trace *M—N* cuts the projections of the edges of the pyramid, will be the projections of the points in which the truncating plane cuts these edges; and the line r'—v' for example is the projection of the line cut from the exterior face projected in $b'v'c'$.

The horizontal projections of the points of which r', v', &c., are the vertical projections, will be found on the horizontal projections vc, vb, &c., of the edges of which $v'c'$, $v'b'$, &c., are the vertical projections, and will be obtained in the usual way. Joining the corresponding points r, v, s, &c., thus obtained, the figure $rstuv$, will be the horizontal projection of the one cut from the exterior faces of the pyramid by the truncating plane.

Thus far nothing has been said of the projections and sections of the interior faces of the pyramid. To construct these let us take the thickness of the sides of the hollow pyramid to be the same, in which case the interior faces will be parallel to and all at the same distance from the exterior faces. If another pyramid therefore were so formed as to fit exactly the hollow space within the given one, its faces and edges would be parallel to the corresponding exterior faces and edges of the given hollow pyramid, and its vertex would likewise be on the perpendicular from the vertex of the given pyramid to its base. Constructing, therefore, a pentagon, $mnopq$, having its sides parallel to, and at the same distance from those of $abcde$, this figure may be assumed as the base of the interior pyramid. The horizontal projections of its edges will be the lines vm, vn, &c. To find the vertical projections of these lines, which will be parallel to the vertical projections of the corresponding exterior edges, project the points m, n, &c., into the ground line, at m', n', &c., and, from these last points, draw the lines $m'v''$, $n'v''$, parallel to the corresponding ones $a'v'$, $b'v'$, &c.; the lines $m'v''$, &c., will be the required projections.

To obtain the horizontal projection of the figure cut from the interior faces by the plane of section, find the points x, y, z, &c., in horizontal projection, corresponding to the points x', y', &c., in vertical projection, where the trace M—N cuts the lines $m'v''$, $n'v''$, &c.; joining these points the pentagon xyz, &c., will be the required horizontal projection.

Having constructed the projections of the portion of the pyramid below the truncating plane, let it now be required to obtain a section of this portion by a vertical plane of section through the vertex. For this purpose, to avoid the confusion of a number of lines on the same drawing, let us construct (Fig. 85) another figure of the projections of the outlines of the faces, &c. Having drawn the line O—P for the trace of the vertical section through the projection of the vertex, we observe that this plane cuts the base of the hollow pyramid on the left-hand side, in the line a—b, and on the opposite side in the line m—n; setting off the distances (Fig. 86) a'—b', b'—n', and n'—m' on the ground line, respectively equal to a—b, &c., we obtain the line of section cut from the base. Now the plane of section cuts the exterior line of the top (Fig. 85) on the left-hand side, in a point horizontally projected in c, and vertically in c'', the height of which point above the base is the distance c'—c''; in like manner the plane cuts the interior line of the top, on the same side, in the point projected horizontally in d, and vertically in d'', its height above the base being d'—d''. The corresponding points of the top on the opposite side are those projected in o, o''; and p, p''; their corresponding distances above the base being respectively o'—o'' and p'—p''.

Having thus found the horizontal and vertical distances between these points, it is easy to construct their positions in the plane of section. To do this, set off on the ground line (Fig. 86) the distances a'—c', a'—d', m'—o', and m'—p', respectively equal to the equal corresponding distances a—c, &c. (Fig. 85), on O—P. At the points c', d', p', and o' draw perpendiculars to the ground line, on which set off the distances c'—c'', &c., respectively equal to those c'—c'' of Fig. 85. Having drawn the lines a'—c'', c''—d'', and b'—d'', the figure $a'b'd''c''$ is the section of the left-hand side; in like manner $m'n'p''o''$ is the figure cut from the opposite face by the plane of section.

As the (Fig. 86) represents a section, and not a profile of the pyramid, we must draw upon it the lines of the portion of the pyramid which lie behind the plane; that, is the portion of which $aaedm$ is the base. It will be well to remark, in the first place, that removing the portion in front of the plane of section, and supposing this plane transparent, the interior surfaces of the pyramid would be seen, and the exterior hidden, the outlines of the former would therefore be drawn full on the plane of section, whilst those of the latter, if represented, should be in dotted lines.

To construct the projections of these lines on the plane of section, we observe that this plane, being a vertical plane, and *O—P* being its trace on the horizontal plane of projection, this line *O—P* may be considered as the ground line of these two planes; in the same manner as *G—L* is the ground line of the horizontal plane and the original vertical plane of projection. This being considered, it is plain that all the parts of the pyramid should be projected on this new vertical plane of projection, in the same manner as on the original one. Let us take, for example, the interior edge, of which *q—s* is the horizontal projection. The point *q*, being in the horizontal plane, will be projected, in the ground line *O—P*, into *q′*; and the point *s* would be projected by a perpendicular from *s* to *O—P*, at a height above *O—P*, equal to the height of its vertical projection on the original vertical plane above the ground line *G—L*, which is *s′—s″*. To transfer these distances to the section (Fig. 86), take the distance *a—q′*, on *O—P*, and set it off from *a′* to *q′* on the section; this will give the projection of *q′* on the section. Next take the distance *a—s′*, from *O—P*, and set it off from *a′* to *s′* on the section, and at *s′* erect a perpendicular to the ground line; take from (Fig. 85) the distance *s′—s″*, and set it off from *s′* to *s″* on the section; the point *s″* will be the projection of the upper extremity of the interior edge in question on the plane of section; joining therefore the points *q′* and *s″*, thus determined, the line *q′—s″* is the required projection. In like manner, the projections of the other interior and exterior edges of the portion of the pyramid behind the plane of section can be determined and drawn, as shown in the section (Fig. 86).

Remarks. The preceding problems contain the solutions of all cases of the projections and sections of bodies, the outlines of which are right lines, and their surfaces plane figures. As they embrace a very large class of objects in the series, it is very important that these problems should be thoroughly understood. One of the most useful examples under this head is that of the plans, elevations, and sections of an ordinary dwelling, which we shall now proceed to give.

Prob. 77. *Plans, elevations, &c., of a house.* (Pl. VII. Fig. 87.) Let us suppose the house of two stories, with basement and garret rooms. The exterior walls of masonry, either of stone or brick. The interior wall, separating the hall from the rooms, of brick. The partition walls of the parlors and basement of timber frames, filled in with brick; those of the bedrooms and garret of timber frames simply.

It is necessary to observe, in the first place, that the general plans are horizontal sections, taken at some height, say one foot, above the window sills, for the purpose of showing the openings of the windows, &c.; and that the sections are so taken as best to show those portions not shown on the plans, as the stair-ways, roof-framing, &c. In the second place, that in the plans and sections are shown only the skeleton or framework of the more solid parts, as the masonry, or timber framing of the walls, flooring, roof, &c.

Plans. Having drawn a ground line, $G—L$, across the sheet on which the drawings are to be made, in such a position as to leave sufficient space on each side of it for the plans and elevations respectively, commence, by drawing a line $A—B$ parallel to $G—L$, and at a convenient distance from it to leave room for the plan of the first story towards the bottom of the sheet. Take the line $A—B$, as the interior face of the wall, opposite to the one of which the elevation is to be represented. Having set off a distance on $A—B$ equal to the width between the side walls, construct the rectangle $ABCD$, of which the sides $A—D$ and $B—C$ shall be equal to the width within, between the front wall $D—C$ and the back $A—B$. Parallel to these four sides, draw the four sides $a—b$, $b—c$, &c., at the distance of the thickness of the exterior walls from them. The figure thus constructed is the general outline of the plan of the exterior walls.

Next proceed to draw the outline of the partition wall $E—F$ separating the hall from the parlors. Next the walls of the pantries, G and H, between the parlors. Then mark out the openings of the windows w, w, and doors d', d', in the walls. Then the projections of the fire-places, f, in the parlors.

Having drawn the outline of all these parts with a fine ink line, proceed to fill it between the outlines of the solid parts cut through, either with small parallel lines, or by a uniform black tint. Then draw the heavy lines on those parts from which a shadow would be thrown.

As the horizontal section will cut the stairs, it is usual to project on the plan the outlines of the steps below the plane in full lines as in S; and, sometimes, to show the position of the stairway to the story above, to project, in *dotted lines*, the steps above the plane.

If the scale of the drawing is sufficiently great to show the parts distinctly, the sections of the upright timbers that form the framing of the partition walls of the pantries should be distinguished from the solid filling of brick between them, by lines drawn across them in a different direction from those of the brick.

The plan of the second story is drawn in the same manner as that of the first, and is usually placed on one side of it.

Front elevation. The figure of the elevation should be so placed that its parts will correspond with those on that part of the plan to which it belongs; that is, the outlines of its walls, of the doors, windows, &c., should be on the perpendiculars to the ground line, drawn from the corresponding parts of the front wall $D—C$. In most cases the outlines of the principal lines of the cornice are put in, and those of the caps over the windows, if of stone when the wall is of brick, &c.; also the outline of the porch and steps leading to it.

Section. In drawings of a structure of a simple character like this, where the relations of the parts are easily seen, a single section is usually sufficient, and in such cases also it is usual to represent on the same figure parts of two different sections. For example, suppose $O—P$ to be the horizontal trace of the vertical plane of section as far as P, along the hall; and $Q—R$ that of one from the point Q opposite P along the centre line of the parlors. On the first portion will be shown the arrangement of the stairways; and on the other the interior arrangements from Q towards R. With regard to the position for the figure of the section, it may, in some cases, be drawn by taking a ground line parallel to the trace, and arranging the lines of the figure on one side of this ground line in the same relation to the side B—C, of the plan, as the elevation has with respect to the side A—B; but as this method is not always convenient, it is usual to place the section as in the drawing, having the same ground line as the elevation, placing the parts beneath the level of the ground below the ground line.

For the better understanding of the relations of the parts, where the sections of two parts are shown on the same figure, it is well to draw a heavy uneven line from the top to the bottom of the figure, to indicate the separation of the parts, as in T—U; the part here on the left of T—U representing the portion belonging to the hall, that on the right the portion within the parlors. In other words, the figure represents what would be seen by a person standing towards the side A—D of the house, were the portion of it between him and the plane of section removed.

This figure represents the section of the stairs and floors, and the portion of the roof above, and basement beneath of the hall; with a section of the partition walls, floors, roof, &c., of the other portion.

As the relations of the parts are all very simple and easily understood, the parts of the plans as well as of the elevations and vertical section being rectangular, figures of which all the dimensions are put down, the drawings will speak for themselves better than any detailed description. Nothing further need be observed, except that the drawing of the vertical section may be commenced, as in the plans, by drawing the inner lines of the walls, and thence proceeding to put in the principal horizontal and vertical lines.

Remarks. In drawings of this class, where the object is simply to show the general arrangement of the structure, the dimensions of the parts are not usually written on them, but are given by the scale appended to the drawing. Where the object of the drawing is to serve as a guide to the builder, who is to erect the structure, the dimensions of every part should be carefully expressed in numbers, legibly written, and in such a manner that all those written crosswise the plan, for example, may read the same way; and those lengthwise in a similar manner; in order to avoid the inconvenience of having frequently to shift the position of the sheet to read the numbers aright.

Where several numbers are put down, expressing the respective distances of points on the same right line, it is usual to draw a fine broken line, and to write the numbers on the line with an arrow-head at each point, as shown in Pl. XI. Fig. *a*, which is read—5 feet; 7 feet 6 inches; 10 feet 9 inches and 7 tenths of an inch.

Where the whole distance is also required to be set down, it may be done either by writing the sum in numbers over the broken line, as in this case, 23 feet 3 inches and 7 tenths; or, better still, with the numbers expressing the partial distances below the broken line, and the entire distance above it, as in Pl. XI. Fig. *b*. Besides these precautions in writing the numbers, each figure also should be drawn with extreme accuracy to the given scale, and be accompanied by an explanatory heading, or reference table.

On all drawings of this class the scale to which the drawing is made should be constructed below the figs., and be accompanied by an explanatory heading; thus, *scale of inches, of feet to inches, or feet.* In some cases, the draughtsman will find it more convenient to construct a scale on a strip of drawing paper for the drawing to be made, than to use the ivory one; particularly, as with the paper one he can lay down his distances at once, without first taking them off with the dividers, in the same way as points are transferred by a strip of paper. In either case, the scale should be so divided as to aid in reading and setting off readily any required distance. The best mode of division for this purpose is the decimal; and the following manner of constructing the scale the most convenient:—Having drawn a right line, set off accurately, from a point at its left-hand extremity, ten of the units of the required scale, and number these from the left 10, 9, &c., to 0. From the 0 point, set off on the right, as many equal distances, each of the length of the part from 0 to 10, as may be requisite, and number these from 0 to the right 10, 20, &c. From this scale any number of tens and units can be at once set off. This scale should be long enough to set off the longest dimension on the drawing.

See, for example, the scale and its heading at bottom of Pl VII.

Preliminary Problems in Projections.

Before entering upon the drawings of some of the many objects belonging to this class, it will be necessary to show the manner of making the projections of the cone, cylinder, and sphere; that of obtaining their intersections by a plane; and also that of representing their intersections with each other.

Cylinder. (Pl. X, Fig. 107.) If we suppose a rectangle, *ABCD*, cut out of any thin inflexible material, as stiff pasteboard, tin, &c., and on it a line, *O—P*, drawn through its centre, parallel to its side *B—C*, for example; this line being so fixed that the rectangle can be revolved, or turned about *O—P*, it is clear that the sides *A—D*, and *B—C*, will, in every position given to the rectangle, be still parallel to *O—P*, and at the same distance from it. The side *B—C*, or *A—D*, therefore, may be said to describe or generate a surface, in thus revolving about *O—P*, on which right lines can be drawn parallel to *O—P*. It will moreover be observed, that as the points *A* and *B*, with *D* and *C* are, respectively, at the same perpendicular distance (each equal to *O—B*) from the axis *O—P*, they, in revolving round it, will describe the circumferences of circles, the radii of which will also be equal to *O—B*. In like manner, if we draw any other line parallel to *A—B*, or *D—C*, as *a—b*, its point *b*, or *a*, will describe a circumference having for its radius *o—b*, which is also equal to *O—B*.

The surface thus described is termed a *right circular cylinder*, and, from the mode of its generation, the following properties may be noted.—1st, any line drawn on it parallel to the line *O—P*, which last is termed *the axis*, is a right line and is termed a *right line element* of the cylinder; 2d, any plane passed through the axis will cut out of the surface two right line elements opposite to each other; 3d, as the planes of the circumferences described by the points B, b, &c., are perpendicular to the axis, any plane so passed will cut out of the surface a circumference equal to those already described.

Prob. 85. (Pl. X. Fig. 108.) *Projections of the cylinder.* Let us in the first place suppose the cylinder placed on the horizontal plane with its axis vertical. In this position all of its right line elements, being parallel to the axis, will also be vertical and be projected on the horizontal plane in points, at equal distances from the point o, in which the axis is projected. Describing therefore a circle, from the point o, with the radius equal to the distance between the axis and the elements, this circle will be the horizontal projection of the surface of the cylinder.

To construct the vertical projection, let us suppose the generating rectangle placed parallel to the vertical plane; in this position, it will be projected into the diameter a—b of the circle on the horizontal plane, and into the equal rectangle $a'b'c'd'$ on the vertical plane; in which last figure c'—d' will be the projection of circle of the base of the cylinder; the line a'—b' that of its top; and the lines a'—d', and b'—c' those of the two opposite elements. As all the other elements will be projected on the vertical plane between these two last, the rectangle $a'b'c'd'$ will represent the vertical projection of the entire surface of the cylinder. To show this more clearly, let us suppose the generating rectangle brought into a position oblique to the vertical plane, as e—f for example; in this position, the two elements projected in e, and f on the horizontal plane, would be projected respectively into e'—o', and f'—h', on the vertical plane; and as the one projected in f, f'—h', lies behind the cylinder, it would be represented by a dotted line.

All sections of the cylinder parallel to the base, or perpendicular to the axis, being circles, equal to that of the base, will be projected on the horizontal plane into the circle of the base, and on the vertical in lines parallel to c'—d'. All sections through the axis will be equal rectangles; which, in horizontal projection, will be diameters of the circle, as *e—f*; and, in vertical projection, rectangles as *e'f'h'o'*. All sections, as *M—N*, parallel to the axis, will cut out two elements projected respectively in *m*, *m'—p'*; and *n*, *n'—u'*.

Note. The manner of constructing oblique sections will be given farther on.

Prob. 86. (Pl. X. Fig. 109.) *Cone.* If in a triangle, having two equal sides *d'—p'*, and *c'—p'*, we draw a line *p'—o'*, bisecting the base *c'—d'*, and suppose the triangle revolved about this line as an axis, the equal sides will describe the curved surface, and the base the circular base of a body termed a *right cone with a circular base.*

From what has been said on the cylinder, it will readily appear that, in this case, any plane passed through the axis will cut out of the curved surface two right lines like *d'—p'*, and *c'—p'*; and, therefore, that from the point *p'* of the surface, termed the *vertex*, right lines can be drawn to every point of the circumference of the base. These right lines are termed the *right line elements* of the cone. It will also be equally evident that any line, as *a—b*, drawn perpendicular to the axis, will describe a circle parallel to the base, of which *a—b* is the diameter, and, therefore, that every section perpendicular to the axis is a circle.

From these preliminaries, the manner of projecting a right cone with a circular base, and its sections either through the vertex, or perpendicular to the axis, will be readily gathered by reference to the figures.

The horizontal projection of the entire surface will be within the circumference of the base, that of the vertex being at *p*. The vertical projection of the surface will be the triangle *d'p'c'*; as the projection of all the elements must lie within it. Any plane of section through the axis, as *e—f*, will cut from the surface two elements projected horizontally in *p—f* and *p—e*; and vertically in *e'—p'* and *f'—p'*. Any plane passed through the vertex, of which *M—N* is the horizontal trace, will cut from the surface two right line elements, of which *p—m* and *p—n* are the horizontal, and *p'—m* and *p'—n'* the vertical projections. Any plane as *R—S* passed perpendicular to the axis will cut out a circle, of which $a'—b'$ is the vertical, and the circle described from p, with a diameter $a—b$ equal to $a'—b'$, is the horizontal projection.

Prob. 87. *Sphere.* (Pl. X. Fig. 110.) Drawing any diameter, $O—P$, in a circle, and revolving the figure around it, the circumference will describe the surface of a sphere; the diameter $A—B$ perpendicular to the axis will describe a circle equal to the given one; and any chord, as $a—b$, will describe a circle, of which $a—b$ is the diameter. Supposing the sphere to rest on the horizontal plane, having the axis $O—P$ vertical, every section of the sphere perpendicular to this axis will be projected on the horizontal plane in a circle; and, as the section through the centre cuts out the greatest circle, the entire surface will be projected within the circle, the diameter of which, $A—B$, is equal to the diameter of the generating circle. In like manner the vertical projection will be a circle equal to this last. The centre of the sphere will be projected in C and C'; and the vertical axis in C and $O—P$. Any section, as $R—S$, perpendicular to the axis, will cut out a circle of which $a—b$ is the diameter, and also the vertical projection; the horizontal projection will be a circle described from C with a diameter equal to $a—b$. Any section, as $M—N$, by a vertical plane parallel to the vertical plane of projection, will also be a circle projected on the horizontal plane in $m—n$; and on the vertical plane in a circle, described from C' as a centre, and with a diameter equal to $m—n$.

Remarks. The three surfaces just described belong to a class termed *surfaces of revolution*, which comprises a very large number of objects; as for example, all those which are fashioned by the ordinary turner's lathe. They have all certain properties in common, which are—1st, that all sections perpendicular to the axis of revolution are circles; 2d, that all sections through the axis of revolution are equal figures.

Prob. 88. (Pl. X. Fig. 111.) *To construct the section of a right circular cylinder by a plane oblique to its axis, and perpendicular to the vertical plane of projection.*

1st Method. Let *aobh* and $a'b'c'd'$ be the projections of the cylinder, and $M—N$ the vertical trace of the plane of section. This plane will cut the surface of the cylinder in the curve of an ellipse, all the points of which, since the curve is on the surface of the cylinder, will be horizontally projected in the circle [illegible], and vertically in $m'—n'$, since the curve lies also in the plane of section. Now the plane of section cuts the two elements, projected in a, $a'—[illegible]$, and [illegible], in the points projected in [illegible] and m' [illegible] and [illegible] and n'. It cuts the two elements projected in [illegible], and [illegible], and [illegible], in the points projected vertically in [illegible], and horizontally in [illegible] and [illegible]. Taking any other element as the one projected in [illegible], the plane cuts it in a point projected vertically in [illegible], and horizontally in [illegible]. The same projection [illegible] would also correspond to the point in which the element projected in [illegible], is cut by the plane; and so on for any other pair of elements similarly placed, with respect to the line [illegible] in the base.

2d Method. As the plane of section is perpendicular to the vertical plane of projection, its trace on the horizontal plane (Pl. VI. Fig. [illegible]) [illegible] the line $M—N$, perpendicular to the ground line. [illegible] the plane of section was cut by another horizontal plane, as [illegible] of the original horizontal plane was [illegible] the position of the second, [illegible] would become the new ground line, and the line [illegible], the trace of the plane of section on this second horizontal plane. [illegible] the line in which the second horizontal [illegible] the plane of section is projected vertically [illegible] the line $p—p'$, on the first [illegible] the horizontal plane of which [illegible] perpendicular to the axis of [illegible] which is projected [illegible] that since the [illegible] $p—$ [illegible] which $p—p'$ [illegible] the projections of the points [illegible] corresponding construction [illegible] other points, as [illegible]

[illegible] as will [illegible] acquirable, as

requiring more simple constructions; but the 1st is the more suitable for this particular case, as giving the results by the simplest constructions that the problem admits of.

Prob. 89. (Pl. X. Fig. 112.) *To construct the sections of a right cone with a circular base by planes perpendicular to the vertical plane of projection.*

This problem comprises five cases. 1st, where the plane of section is perpendicular to the axis; 2d, where it passes through the vertex of the cone; 3d, where its vertical trace makes a smaller angle with the ground line than the vertical projection of the adjacent element of the cone does; 4th, where the trace makes the same angle as the projection of the adjacent element with the ground line, or, in other words, is parallel to this projection; 5th, where the trace makes a greater angle than this line with the ground line.

Cases 1st and 2d have already been given in the projections of the cone (Pl. X. Fig. 109); the remaining three alone remain to be treated of.

Case 3d. In this case, the angle *NML*, between the trace *M—N* of the plane and the ground line *G—L*, is less than that *o'a'b'*, or that between the same line and the element projected in *o'—a'*; and the curve cut from the surface of the cone will be an ellipse.

From what precedes (*Prob.* 86), if the cone be intersected by a horizontal plane, of which *g—l* is the trace, it will cut from the surface a circle of which *c'—d'* is the diameter, and which will be projected on the horizontal plane in the circumference described from *o* on this diameter; this plane will also cut from the plane of section a right line, projected vertically in *r'*, and horizontally in *r—r''*; and the projections of the points *s* and *u*, in which this line cuts the projection of the circumference, will be two points in the projection of the curve cut from the surface.

Constructing thus any number of horizontal sections, as *g—l*, between the points *m'* and *n'* (the vertical projections of the points in which the plane of section cuts the two elements parallel to the vertical plane), any number of points in the horizontal projection of the curve can be obtained like the two, *s* and *u*, already found.

which these intersect, will be points in the projection of the required curve.

The points m' and n', in which M—N cuts the vertical projection of the sphere, will be the vertical projections of the points in which the plane cuts the circle parallel to the vertical plane, and which is projected in a—b; the horizontal projections of these points will be m, and n, on a—b. The horizontal projections of the points in which the plane cuts the horizontal plane g'—l', through the centre of the sphere, are c and d. The projection of the curve of intersection is an ellipse, of which c—d is the transverse, and m—n the conjugate axis.

Fig. A is the circle cut from the sphere, the diameter of which is m'—n'.

Prob. 92. (Pl. X. Fig. 115.) *To construct the curves of intersection of the planes of section and the surfaces in the preceding problems.*

In each of the preceding problems, the horizontal and vertical projections of the curves cut from the surface have alone been found; the true dimensions of these curves, as they lie in their respective planes of section, remain to be determined.

1*st Method.* An examination of (Figs. 111, 112, 113, 114) will show that as the points vertically projected in m' and n' and horizontally on the lines a—b, are at the same distance from the vertical plane of projection, the line joining them will be vertically projected into its true length m'—n'. In like manner, the lines cut from the plane of section by the horizontal planes, as g—l, and projected horizontally in s—u, are projected in their true length, and they, moreover, lie in the plane of section and are perpendicular to the line m'—n'. If we construct therefore the true positions of these lines, with respect to each other, we shall obtain the true dimensions of the curve. To do this, draw any line, and set off upon it a distance m'—n' equal to m'—n'; from m', set off the distances m'—q', m'—r', m'—p', &c., equal to those on the corresponding projections m'—q', &c.; through the points q', r', &c., draw perpendiculars to m'—n'; and on these last, from the same points, set off each way the equal coincide with the vertical plane. In like manner, ns of the points projected in s and u are found, by hrough the point r', their vertical projection, a ılar to $M—N$, and setting off on it the lengths $r'—u$, equal to the respective lengths $r—s$, and distances of the horizontal projections of the points ground line; and so on for the other points.

:s. A moment's examination of the two methods, ined, will show that their results are identical, the —u, for example, being of the same length and the same position, with respect to the equal lines nd $m'''—n'''$. The second shows the connection ıe different points more clearly than the first, and is, ses, the more convenient one for constructing them. ›e seen farther on, that this principle of finding the ons of points in a plane, with respect to each other, ng the plane around some line in it, selected as an frequent and convenient application in obtaining tions of points.

ions of the right cylinder and right cone in posi- 'e their axes are oblique to either one or both planes ion.

inary Problems. The 2d method employed in the proposition, by which the true positions of any ι plane are found, when their projections are given, ng the plane to coincide with either the vertical or plane of projection, may be used, with great , for constructing the projections of any series of ıtained in a plane, in any *assumed* position of this ın the projections of the same points are known in position of the plane.

4. (Pl. X. Fig. 116.) Let $a'b'c'd'$ be the vertical of a circle, contained in a plane parallel to the ane of projection, of which $O—P$ is the horizontal ι the plane, containing the circle, is perpendicular rizontal plane, all the points of the circle will be horizontally in the trace $O—P$. The points, of and b', for example, are the vertical projections, ected in a and b, &c.

[illegible] the projections of the circle in this position of its [illegible] to find the projections when the [illegible] revolved about any vertical line drawn [illegible] as, for [illegible] the vertical, and [illegible] the [illegible] a position, as [illegible], [illegible] projection.

[illegible] this [illegible] of the [illegible] plane of [illegible] moved in [illegible] a similar [illegible] the surface [illegible] pencil [illegible] same distances [illegible] as they were [illegible] in their [illegible] as a [illegible] of the plane [illegible] the points [illegible] new position [illegible], as in [illegible] projections of [illegible] drawing [illegible] ground line [illegible] the ground [illegible]. Describ- [illegible] corresponding [illegible] vertical pro- [illegible] an ellipse, [illegible] transverse [illegible] diameter [illegible] conjugate axis.

[illegible] circle and the [illegible] the circle [illegible], [illegible] parallel to the [illegible] transverse axis of the ellipse, [illegible] and which, in [illegible] the vertical plane, be- [illegible] conjugate axis [illegible] so that the lines of the circle parallel to c'—d', as m'—m'', remain of the same length in the ellipse, and parallel to c''—d''.

In all oblique positions that can be given to the plane of a circle, with respect to either plane of projection, the projection of the circle, upon that plane of projection to which it is oblique, will be an ellipse; the transverse axis of which will be that diameter of the circle which is parallel to the plane of projection, and the conjugate axis is the projection of that diameter which is perpendicular to the transverse axis. Whenever, therefore, the projections of these two diameters can be found, the curve of the ellipse can be described by the usual methods

Prob. 95. (Pl. X. Fig. 116.) *Having the projections of a figure contained in a plane perpendicular to one plane of projection, but oblique to the other, to find the true dimensions of the figure.*

This problem which is the converse of the preceding is also of frequent application, in finding the projections of points as will be seen further on.

Suppose O—P', the horizontal trace of a plane, perpendicular to the horizontal plane of projection, but oblique to the vertical; and let the points a_1, c_1, b_1, &c., be the horizontal projections, and a'', c'', b'', d'' the vertical projections of the points of a figure contained in this plane. If we suppose the plane to be revolved about any line drawn in it perpendicular to the horizontal plane, as the one of which O, and M—N are the projections, until it is brought parallel to the vertical plane, the horizontal trace, after revolution, will be found in the position O—P, parallel to the ground line; and the points a_1' c_1', &c., in the new positions a, c, &c., on O—P. The vertical projections of these points will be found in a', c', b', d', &c., at the same height above the ground line as in their primitive positions. The new figure, being parallel to the vertical plane, will be projected in one $a'b'c'd'$, &c., equal to itself.

Remarks. This method, it may be well to note, will also serve to find the projections of any points, or of a figure, contained in a plane perpendicular to the horizontal, but oblique to the vertical plane, for any new oblique position of this plane, with respect to the vertical plane, taken up, by revolving it around a line assumed in a like position to the one of which the projections are O, and $M—N$.

Prob. 96. (Pl. X. Fig. 117.) ***To construct the projections of a given right cylinder with a circular base, the cylinder resting on the horizontal plane, with its axis oblique to the vertical plane of projection.***

We have seen (*Prob.* 85) that the axis of a right cylinder is perpendicular to the planes of the circles of its ends; and that, when the axis is parallel to one of the planes of projection, the projection of the cylinder on that plane is a rectangle, the length of which is equal to the length of the axis, and the breadth equal to the diameter of the circles of its ends; constructing, therefore, a rectangle $abcd$, of which the side $b—c$ is equal to the length of the axis, and the side $a—b$ is the diameter of the circle of the ends, this figure will be the horizontal projection of the cylinder; the line $o—p$, drawn bisecting the opposite sides $a—b$, $c—d$, is the projection of the axis.

To make the vertical projection, it will be observed, that the bottom element of the cylinder, being on the horizontal plane, and projected in the line $o—p$, will be projected into the ground line, in the line $o''—p''$; whilst the top element, which is also horizontally projected in $o—p$, will be projected in $o'—p'$, at a height above the ground line equal to the diameter of the cylinder. The line $s'—t'$, parallel to $o''—p''$, and bisecting the opposite sides $o'—o''$, and $p'—p''$, is the vertical projection of the axis.

The planes of the circles of the two ends, being perpendicular to the horizontal plane, but oblique to the vertical, the circles (*Prob.* 94) will be projected into ellipses on the vertical plane; the transverse axes of which will be the lines $o'—o''$, and $p'—p''$, the vertical projections of the diameters of the circles parallel to the vertical plane; and the lines $a'—b'$, and $d'—c'$, the vertical projections of the diameters parallel to the horizontal plane, are the conjugate axes Constructing the two ellipses $a'o''b'o'$, and $d'p''c'p'$, the vertical projection of the cylinder will be completed.

Having the projections of the outlines of the cylinder, the

projections of any element can be readily obtained. Let us take, for example, the element which is horizontally projected in $m—n$. The vertical projections of the points m, and n, will be in the curves of the ellipses; the former either at m, or m''; the latter at n', or n''; drawing, therefore, the lines $m'—n'$, and $m''—n''$, these lines, which will be parallel to $s'—t'$, will be the vertical projections of two elements to which the horizontal projection $m—n$ corresponds.

Prob. 97. (Pl. XI. Fig. 118.) *To construct the projections, as in the last problem, when the axis is parallel to the vertical, but oblique to the horizontal plane; the cylinder being in front of the vertical plane.*

This problem differs from the preceding only in that the position of the cylinder with respect to the planes of projection is reversed; the vertical projection, therefore, in this case, will be a rectangle, having its sides oblique to the ground line; whilst, in horizontal projection, the elements will be projected parallel to the ground line, and the circles of the ends into two equal ellipses.

To make the projections, let us imagine the cylinder resting on a solid, of which the rectangle XY is the horizontal, and the one Z the vertical projection, and touching the horizontal plane at the point of its lower end, of which c and c' are the projections. In this position, the rectangle $c'd'b'a'$, constructed equal to the generating rectangle, will be the vertical projection of the cylinder; the lines $o'—p'$, and $o—p$, the projections of the axis; and the two ellipses $arbt$, and $csdu$, of which $r—t$, and $s—u$, equal to the diameters of the circles of the ends, are the transverse, and $a—b$, and $c—d$, the horizontal projections of the diameters parallel to the vertical plane, are the conjugate axes, the projections of the ends. Any line, as $m'—n'$, drawn parallel to $o'—p'$, will be the vertical projection of two elements, the horizontal projections of which will be the two lines $m—n$, drawn at equal distances from $o—p$, the points m, m, and n, n, on the ellipses, being the horizontal projections of the points of which m', and n' are the vertical projections.

Prob. 98. (Pl. XI. Fig. 119.) *To construct the projec-*

tions, as in the last problem, when the axis of the cylinder is oblique to both planes of projection.

To simplify this case, let us imagine the cylinder, with the solid XY, Z on which it rests, to be shifted round, or revolved, so as to bring them both oblique to the vertical plane of projection, but without changing their position with respect to the horizontal plane. In this new position, since the cylinder maintains the same relative situation to the horizontal plane as at first, it is evident that its horizontal projection will be the same as in the preceding case; the projections of the axis and elements being only oblique instead of parallel to the ground line. Moreover as all the points of the cylinder are at the same height above the horizontal plane in the new as in the former position, their vertical projections will be at the same distance above the ground line in both positions; having the horizontal projection of any point in the new position, it will be easy to find its vertical projection by the usual method, *Prob.* 94. In the vertical projection of the axis $o'—p'$, in the new position, the points o', and p' will be at the same distance above the ground line as in the original one. The vertical projections of the circles of the ends will be the ellipses $a'r'b't'$, and $c's'd'u'$. The vertical projections of the elements, of which the two lines $m—n$ are the horizontal projections, will be the lines $m'—n'$, and $m''—n''$; &c., &c.

Remarks. The preceding problem naturally leads to the method of constructing the projections of any body, upon any vertical plane placed obliquely to the original vertical plane of projection, when the projections on this last plane and the horizontal plane are given. A moment's reflection will show that, whether a body is placed obliquely to the original vertical plane and in that position projected on it, or whether the projection is made on a vertical plane oblique to the original vertical plane, but so placed, with respect to the body, that the latter will hold the same position to the oblique plane that it does to the original vertical plane, the result in both cases will be the same. If, for example, $G'—L'$ be taken as the trace of a vertical plane oblique to the original vertical plane of projection, and such that it makes the same angle, $G'Md$, with the horizontal projection of the axis of the cylinder, as the latter, in its oblique position to the original ground line $G—L$, makes with this line; and the cylinder be thus projected on this new vertical plane, and with reference to the new ground line, $G'—L'$ in the same manner as in its oblique position to the original vertical plane of projection, it is evident that the same results will be obtained in both cases; since the position of the cylinder, with respect to the original vertical plane, is precisely the same as that of the new vertical plane to the cylinder in its original position. If, therefore, perpendiculars be drawn, from the horizontal projections of the points, to the new ground line $G'—L'$, and distances be set off upon them, above this line, equal to the distances of the vertical projections of the same points above $G—L$, the points thus obtained will be the new vertical projections.

By a similar method it will be seen that a vertical projection on any new plane can be obtained when the horizontal and vertical projections on the original planes of projection are known.

Prob. 99. (Pl. XI. Fig. 120.) *To construct the projections of a right cone with a circular base, the cone resting on its sides on the horizontal plane, and having its axis parallel to the vertical plane, and in front of it.*

In this position of the cone, its vertical projection will be equal to its generating isosceles triangle, $a'b'c'$; and the line $c'—o'$ drawn from the projection of the vertex, and bisecting the projection of the base, $a'—b'$, is the projection of the axis.

To construct the horizontal projection, draw a line $b—c$, at any convenient distance from the ground line, for the position of the horizontal projection of the axis; and find on it the horizontal projections c, and o of the points corresponding to those c', and o' of the vertical projection of the axis; through the point o drawing a line $d—e$ perpendicular to $b—c$, and setting off from o the distances $o—d$, and $o—e$, equal to the radius of the circle of the cone's base, the line $d—e$ will be the transverse axis of the ellipse, into which the circle of the base is projected on the horizontal plane. The points b, and a are the horizontal projections of the points of the base of which b' and a' are the vertical projections; and b—a is the conjugate axis of the same ellipse.

To find the horizontal projection of any element, of which c'—m', for example, is the vertical projection, find the horizontal projections m, m corresponding to m' and join them with c; the two lines c—m will be the horizontal projections of the two elements of which c'—m' is the vertical projection.

If it is required to find the horizontal projections of any circle of the cone parallel to the base, of which h'—f', parallel to a'—b', is the vertical projection, find the horizontal projection i of the point corresponding to the projection i' on the axis; and through i draw p—q parallel to d—e; this will give the transverse axis of the ellipse into which the circle is projected on the horizontal plane; the points f, and h, corresponding to f' and h', are the horizontal projections of the extremities of the conjugate axis f—h.

Prob. 100. (Pl. XI. Fig. 121.) *To construct the projections of the cone resting, in the same manner as in the last problem, on the horizontal plane, and having its axis oblique to the vertical plane of projection.*

In this position of the cone its horizontal projection will be the same as in the last problem; the vertical projections of the different points will be found as in the case of the cylinder having its axis oblique to both planes of projections; since the heights of the different points above the horizontal plane remain as they were before the position of the cone was changed with respect to the vertical plane.

Prob. 101. If we imagine the cone so placed, with respect to the vertical plane, that the horizontal projection of its axis is perpendicular to the ground line, then its vertical projection will be as represented in (Pl. XI. Fig. 122), in which the element, or side on which the cone rests, will be projected in the point c'; and the circle of the base into the ellipse $a'b'c'd$, of which a'—d', parallel to the ground line, and equal to the diameter of the circle of the base, is the transverse axis. The projection of any circle parallel to the base will be constructed in a like manner.

Prob. 102. (Pl. XII. Fig. 123.) *To construct the projec*

tions of a right hollow cylinder with a circular base, having its axis parallel to the vertical plane, but oblique to the horizontal plane of projection; the cylinder touching the horizontal and being in front of the vertical plane.

This case differs in no other respect from *Prob.* 97, Fig. 118, than in having for its base a circular ring instead of a circle. The vertical projection of the outer surface of the cylinder will be the rectangle $a'b'c'd'$; that of the interior surface $a''b''c''d''$: and that of the axis the line o'—p', making the same angle with the ground line as the axis itself does with the horizontal plane.

The horizontal projections of the exterior and interior circles of the upper end are the two concentric ellipses $arbt$, and $a'r'b't'$; those of the lower end the two ellipses $csdu$, and $c's'd'u'$; and that of the axis the line o—p.

If we construct the circular ring of the upper base (Pl. XII. Fig. 124), and imagine planes of section so passed through the axis of the cylinder as to divide it into eight equal parts, these planes will cut the ring of the upper end in lines, as r—m, q—p, &c., drawn through the centre o of the exterior and interior circles; and the ring of the lower end also in corresponding lines. The same planes will cut from the exterior surface of the sides corresponding elements, which will be vertically projected in the lines p'—p'', m'—n', &c., of the exterior, and the lines q'—q'', r'—r'', &c., of the interior surface. The corresponding horizontal projections of these lines are m—n, r''—r''', &c.

Prob. 103. (Pl. XII. Fig. 125.) *To construct the projections of the hollow cylinder, as in the last problem, the axis remaining the same with respect to the horizontal, but oblique to the vertical plane.*

This case is the same, in all material respects, as in *Prob.* 98, Fig. 119. The horizontal projection will be the same as in the last case; and the vertical projection also will be determined, from the vertical projection in the last case, in the same manner as in *Prob.* 98. Fig. 119.

Prob. 104. (Pl. XII. Fig. 126.) *To construct the projections of a hollow hemisphere, resting on the horizontal plane and in front of the vertical; the plane of section of the* hemisphere being perpendicular to the vertical plane, but oblique to the horizontal plane.

[illegible]

[illegible] the horizontal projection of the centre [illegible] any convenient distance from the ground line, the diameter of the exterior circle of the ring [illegible] vertically [illegible] will be horizontally projected in the line [illegible] parallel to the ground line; and the diameter vertically projected in [illegible] will be projected in the line [illegible] drawn through [illegible] perpendicular to [illegible]; and as this diameter is parallel to the horizontal plane, it will be projected in a line equal to [illegible] the diameter of the ring. The exterior circle of the ring will therefore be projected into an ellipse, of which the lines [illegible] and [illegible] are the axes. In like manner, the interior circle will be projected into an ellipse of which the line [illegible], the horizontal projection of [illegible], is the conjugate, and [illegible], equal to diameter of the interior circle of the ring, is the transverse axis.

The portion of the surface of the hemisphere on the right, exterior to the ring, is projected in the semicircle [illegible]; the point f' being the vertical projection corresponding to f in horizontal projection.

Prob. [illegible]. Pl. XII. Fig. [illegible]. *To project the hemisphere, as in the last case, the plane of section retaining the same inclination to the horizontal, but being oblique to the vertical plane.*

As the hemisphere has not changed its position with respect to the horizontal plane, its horizontal projection will be the same as in the last case.

The vertical projection will be found, as in similar cases preceding, by finding the vertical projections of the points corresponding to the horizontal projections in the new positions, which will be at the same height above the ground line in the new as in the preceding position.

The exterior surface of the hemisphere will be projected on the vertical plane in the semicircle $g'p'h'$, of which o' is the centre, and o'—p' the radius.

The horizontal projection of the diameter, corresponding to g'—h', is the line g—h, parallel to the ground line.

Intersections of the preceding Surfaces.

The manner of finding the projections of the lines cut from surfaces by planes of section, as well as the true dimensions of these sections, has already been shown (*Probs.* 88, &c.), but in machinery, as well as in other industrial objects, the curved portions are, for the most part, either some one of the preceding surfaces of revolution, or else cylindrical, or conical surfaces, which do not belong to this class: and as these surfaces are frequently so combined as to meet, or intersect each other, it is very important to know how to find the projections of these lines of meeting, or intersection; and, in some cases, even the true dimensions of these lines. The object then of this section will be to give some of the more usual cases under this head.

Prob. 106. (Pl. XI. Fig. 128.) *To construct the projections of the lines of intersection of two circular right cylinders, the axis of the one being perpendicular to the horizontal plane, and of the other parallel both to the vertical and horizontal plane.*

In examining the lines in which any two surfaces, whether plane or curved, meet, it will be seen, as in the cases of *Probs.* 88, &c., if the two surfaces are intersected by any plane of section, through a point of their line of meeting, that this plane will cut from each surface a line; and that the lines, thus cut from them, will meet on the line of intersection of the surfaces, at the point through which the plane of section is passed. From this, it will also be seen that, in order to find the line of intersection of two surfaces, they must be intersected by planes in such a way as to cut lines out of the respective surfaces that will meet; and the points of meeting of the lines, thus found, being joined, will give the lines of meeting of the surfaces. To apply this to the problem now to be solved, let us imagine the surfaces of the two cylinders to be cut by planes of section which will cut right line elements from each, the points of meeting of these elements, in each plane of section, will be points of the required line of meeting of the two surfaces.

Let the circle *abcd* be the horizontal projection, and the rectangle *a'b'l'i'* the vertical projection of the cylinder perpendicular to the horizontal plane; the point *o*, and line *o'—p'* being the projections of its axis. Let the rectangles *fghe*, and *r's's''r''* be the projections of the other cylinder, the lines *r—s* and *g'—h'* being the projections of its axis.

In these positions of the two cylinders, the vertical one intersects the horizontal one on its lower and upper sides; and the two curves of intersection will be evidently in all respects the same. Moreover, as these curves are on the surface of the vertical cylinder, they will be projected on the horizontal plane in the circle *abcd*, in which the surface of the cylinder is projected. The only lines then to be determined are the vertical projections of the curves. To do this, according to the preceding explanation, let us imagine the two cylinders cut by vertical planes of section, parallel to the vertical plane of projection.

Let the line *t—u*, for example, parallel to the ground line, be the trace of one of these planes. This plane will cut from the vertical cylinder two elements, which will be horizontally projected in the points *m* and *n*, where this trace cuts the circle, and vertically in the two lines *m'—x'*, and *n'—s'*. The same plane will cut from the horizontal cylinder two elements, which will both be projected horizontally in the trace *t—u*, and vertically in the two lines *t'—u'*, and *t''—u''*, each at the same distance from the line *g'—h'*; the one above, the other below this line. To find the distance, let a circle *s'u''h''*, &c., be described, having its centre *r'*, on the line

r—s prolonged, and with a radius equal to s—h, that of the base of the horizontal cylinder. This circle may be regarded as the projection of the horizontal cylinder on a vertical plane, taken perpendicular to the axis of the cylinder. In this position of the plane and cylinder, the elements of the cylinder will be projected into the circumference $e'u''h''$, &c., of the circle; and its axis into the point r', the centre of the circle. The two elements cut from the cylinder, by the plane of which t—u is the trace, for example, will be projected in the points u', and u''; each at the equal distances v'—u', and v'—u'' from the horizontal diameter e'—h'', of this circle. Drawing the lines t'—u', and t''—u'', at the same distance from g'—h' as the points u' and u'' are above and below the horizontal diameter e'—h'', they will be the projections on the primitive vertical plane of the same elements, of which u' and u'' are the projections on the vertical plane perpendicular to the axis. The four points x', x', and x'', x'', in which the lines t'—u', and t''—u'' cut the lines m'—x', and n'—z' will be the projections of four points of the curves in which the cylinders intersect. In like manner, the vertical projections of as many points of the curves, in which the cylinders intersect above and below the axis of the horizontal cylinder, may be found, as will be requisite to enable us to draw the outlines of their projections.

The portions of the curves, drawn in full lines, lie in front of the two cylinders; the portions in dotted lines, lie on the other side of the cylinders.

The highest points d, and c of the lower curve will lie on the elements of the vertical cylinder, projected in the points d, and c. The lowest points y, y of the same will lie on the lowest element of the horizontal cylinder, projected in r—s. The corresponding points of the upper curve will hold a reverse position to those of the lower.

Prob. 107. (Pl. XIII. Fig. 129.) *To construct the projections of the curves of intersection of two right cylinders, one of which is vertical, and the other inclined to the horizontal plane, the axes of both being parallel to the vertical plane.*

Let the trapezoid $a'b'k'a'$ be the vertical projection of the *tions of the curves of intersection of a right cone and right cylinder, the axis of the cone being vertical, that of the cylin der horizontal and parallel to the vertical plane.*

Let $abcd$ be the circle of the base of the cone, and o the projection of its axis; $a'o'b'$ the vertical projection of the cone, and $o'—p'$ that of its axis. The rectangles $efgh$ and $r's's''r''$, the projections of the cylinder.

If we intersect these surfaces by horizontal planes, any such plane, as the one of which $t—u$ is the vertical trace, will cut from the cylinder two elements, of which $t—u$ is the vertical projection, and from the cone a circle of which $m—n$ is the vertical projection; the projections of the points, in which the elements of the cylinder cut the circumference of the circle on the cone, will be points in the required projections of the curves. The circle cut from the cone will be the one syx, the radius of which, $o—s$, is equal to $q'—m$. To find the corresponding horizontal projections of the two elements cut from the cylinder, first on the prolongation of $f'—g'$, describe a circle $s''u'f'$, &c. (Pl. XIII, Fig. 132), with a radius $s''—g''$, equal to that of the end of the cylinder, this circle may be regarded as the projection of the cylinder, on a vertical plane perpendicular to the axis of the cylinder; the two elements, cut from the cylinder by the plane of which $t—u$ is the trace, will be projected in the points v', and v'', at equal distances $i—v'$ and $i—v''$ from the vertical diameter $s''—f'$ of the circle. These two elements will be projected on the horizontal plane in the two lines $t—u$, at the equal distances $i—v'$, $i—v''$ from the horizontal projection $n—s$ of the axis. The points y, y and x, x, where these lines cut the circumference of the circle $o—s$, will be the projections of four points of the curve; the points y' and x' are the corresponding vertical projections.

In the positions here chosen for the two surfaces, the cylinder fits, as it were, into a notch cut into the cone. The edges of this notch, on the surface of the cone, are projected vertically into the curvilinear quadrilateral $d'e'c''e'd'c'$; the points e' being the highest, and c'' the lowest of the upper edge; those d' being the lowest and c' the highest of the lower edge.

Fig. 132 represents the projections of the surfaces on a side vertical plane perpendicular to the axis of the cylinder.

The projections of the same curves, when the axis of the cylinder is placed obliquely to the vertical plane, are obtained by the same processes as in the like cases of preceding problems.

Remarks. When the cylinders, in the preceding *Probs.*, have the same diameters, and their axes intersect, the curves of intersection of the surfaces will be ellipses, and will be projected on the vertical plane into right lines, when the axes are parallel to this plane. In like manner, in the intersection of the cone and cylinder, the curves of intersection of the two surfaces will be ellipses, when the axes of the two surfaces intersect, and when the position of the cylinder is such, that the circle, into which it is projected on the vertical plane perpendicular to its axis, is tangent to the two elements that limit the projection of the cone on the same plane. In these positions of the two surfaces, if their axes are parallel to the vertical plane, their curves of intersection also will be projected into right lines.

Prob. 110. (Pl. XIII. Fig 133.) *To construct the projections of the curve of intersection of a circular cylinder and hemisphere, the axis of the cylinder being vertical.*

Let the circle *adbc* be the horizontal, and the rectangle *a'b'z'x'* the vertical projection of the cylinder; *p*, and *p'—q'* the projections of its axis.

Let the semicircles *ghi*, be the horizontal, and *g'h'i'* the vertical projections of the front half of the hemisphere, being that portion alone which the cylinder enters; *o* and *o'* the projections of its centre.

Any horizontal plane will cut from the quarter of the sphere, thus projected, a semicircle, and from the cylinder a circle; and if the plane is so taken that the semicircle and circle, cut from the two surfaces, intersect, the point or points, in which these two curves intersect, will be points in the intersection of the two surfaces. Let *m—n* be the vertical trace of such a horizontal plane; it will cut from the spherical surface a semicircle projected vertically in *m—n*, and horizontally in the semicircle *mxyn*, the diameter of which is equal to $m—n$. This semicircle cuts the circle $adbc$, which is the horizontal projection of the one cut by the same plane from the cylinder, in the two points x and y, which are the horizontal projections of the two points required; their vertical projections are at x' and y', on the line $m—n$. By a like construction, any required number of points may be found.

The highest point of the projection of the required curve will evidently, in this case, lie on that element of the cylinder which is farthest from the centre of the hemisphere; and the lowest point on the element nearest to the same point. Drawing a line, from the projection o of the centre of the hemisphere, through p, that of the axis of the cylinder, the points c and d, where it cuts the circle $abcd$, will give the projections of the two elements in question. The vertical projections of these points will therefore be found at c' and d', on the vertical projections of the semicircles of which $o—c$, and $o—d$ are the respective radii.

The curve traced through the points $c'x'd'y'$, &c., is the vertical, and the circle $adbc$ the horizontal projection required.

Prob. 111. (Pl. XIII. Fig. 134.) *To construct the projections of the curves of intersection of a right circular cone and sphere.*

The processes followed, in this problem, are in all respects the same as in the one preceding. Any horizontal plane will cut from the two surfaces circles, and the points in which the two circles intersect will be points of the required curve.

Let $ghik$ and $g'h'i'k'$ be the projections of the sphere; o and o' those of its centre; $aybc$ and $a'o'b$ the projections of the cone; o, and $o'—p'$ those of its axis.

Let $m'—n'$ be the vertical trace of a horizontal plane. This plane will cut from the sphere a circle of which $m'—n'$, and $mxny$ are the projections; and from the cone one of which $r'—s'$, and $rxsy$ are the projections; the points x and y in horizontal projection, and x' and y' the corresponding vertical projections of the points where the two circles intersect, are projections of the points of the required curve. In like manner, the projections of any number of points may be obtained, both in the lower and upper curves, in which the cone penetrates the sphere.

The highest and lowest points [illegible] the vertical projection of the [illegible] will be at the extremities of the [illegible] farthest from and nearest to the centre of the sphere. [illegible]

[illegible]

The points [illegible] are the projections of the highest points of the lower curve, [illegible]. In like manner, the point [illegible] which is the [illegible] point of the vertical projection of the same curve, may be found; and the points [illegible] of the vertical projections of the highest and lowest points of the other curve.

The curves traced through the horizontal and vertical projections of the points thus obtained will be the required projections of the curves.

Development of Cylindrical and Conical Surfaces.

Cylinders and cones, when laid on their sides on a plane surface, touch the surface throughout a right line element. If, in this position, a cylinder be rolled over upon the plane, until the element, along which it touched the plane in the first position is again brought in contact with the plane, it is evident that, in thus rolling over, the cylinder would mark out on the plane a rectangle, which would be exactly equal in surface to the convex surface of the cylinder. The base of the rectangle being exactly equal in length to the circumference of the circle of the cylinder's base, and its altitude equal to the height of the cylinder, or the length of its elements.

In like manner a cone, laid on its side on a plane, and having its vertex confined to the same point, if rolled over on the plane, until the element on which it first rested is brought again into contact with the plane, would mark out a surface on the plane exactly equal to its convex surface; and this surface would be the sector of a circle, the arc of which would be described from the point where the vertex rested, with a radius equal to the element of the cone; the length of the arc of the sector being equal to the circumference of the base of the cone; and the two sides of the sector being the same as the element in its first and last positions.

Now, any points, or lines, that may have been traced on these surfaces in their primitive state, can be found on their developments, and be so traced, that, if the surfaces were restored to their original state, from the developments, these lines would occupy upon them the same position as at first.

The developments of cylinders and cones are chiefly used in practical applications, to mark out upon objects, having cylindrical or conical surfaces, lines which have been obtained from drawings representing the developed surfaces of the object.

Prob. 112. (Pl. XI. Fig. 135.) *To develop the surface of a right cylinder; and to obtain, on the developed surface, the curved line cut from the cylindrical surface by a plane oblique to the axis of the cylinder.*

Turning to *Prob.* 88, Fig. 111, which is the same as the one of which the development is here required. Draw a right line, on which set off a length *a*—*a*, equal to the circumference *abcd* of the cylinder's base; through the points *a*, construct perpendiculars to *a*—*a*, on which set off the distances *a*—*a'*, equal to the altitude *x'*—*a'* of the cylinder; join *a'*—*a'*; the rectangle *aa'a'a* is the entire developed convex surface of the cylinder. Commencing at the point *a*, on the left, next set off the distances *a*—*e*, *e*—*c*, *c*—*k*, &c., respectively equal to the corresponding portions of the circumference *a*—*e*, &c.; and, at these points, construct perpendiculars to *a*—*a*. To find the developed position of the curve projected vertically in the points *mepn*, &c.; on the perpendiculars at *a*, set off the two distances *a*—*m*, equal each to *a'*—*m*, on the projection of the cylinder; at *e* and *f*, the distances *e*—*e*, and *f*—*e*, each equal to *e'*—*e* on the projection of the cylinder, &c.; and so on for the other points. Through the points *mepn*, &c., on the development, trace a curve; this will be the developed curve required.

To show the practical application of this problem, let us suppose we have a cylinder of any solid material, on the surface of which we wish to mark out the line that an oblique plane would cut from it. We would first make a drawing of the intersection of the cylinder and plane, as in *Prob.* 92, either on the same scale as the given solid, or on a proportional scale; and then the development of the curve. If the drawing is on the same scale as the model, the development may be drawn at once on thick paper, or thin pasteboard; and the paper be very accurately cut off along the developed curve. Then wrapping this portion around the solid, so as to bring the line *a*—*a* to coincide with its base, and the two edges *a*—*a'* to meet accurately, the curve may be accurately traced by moving any sharp pointed instrument carefully along the upper curved edge of the paper.

Prob. 113. (Pl. XI., Fig. 136.) ***To develop the surface of a right cone, and that of the curve cut from the surface by a plane oblique to the axis of the cone.***

Turning to *Prob.* 89 (Fig. 112), take the distance *o'*—*a'*, the length of the element, and from the point *o'* (Fig. 136) describe an arc. Commencing at any point, *a*, of this arc, set off along it a length, *a*—*a*, equal to the circumference *aebf* of the cone's base; next set off on this arc the distances *a*—*e*, *e*—*b*, &c., respectively equal to those *a*—*e*, *e*—*b*, &c., of the cone's base; and through them draw the radii *o'*—*e*, &c. The sector, thus obtained, will be the developed surface of the cone; and the radii on it the positions of the elements drawn, from the vertex, to the points *a*, *e*, *b*, *f* of the circumference of the base, which pass through the points *m'*, *r'*, *n'*, the vertical projections of the curve. The distances *o'*—*m'* and *o'*—*s'*, from the vertex to the points projected in *m'* and *s'*, are projected in their true lengths; setting these off, therefore, on the radii *o'*—*a* and *o'*—*b* from *o'* to *m'* and *s'*, we obtain three points of the developed curve. To obtain the true length of the portion of the elements drawn from the vertex to the points projected in *r'*; draw, through *r'*, the line *x*—*y* parallel to *a'*—*b'*; then *o'*—*x* will be this required length. Setting this length off, along the radii drawn through *c* and *d*, from *o'* to *r'*, we obtain the points corresponding to those of which *r'* is the projection. The curve *m'n'r's'*, &c., traced through these points, will be the developed curve required.

CHAPTER VIII.

SHADOWS.

In finding the shadows of objects, the rays of light are assumed to be parallel straight lines; although the direction of light may be taken in any position, it is customary, as previously stated, to assume such a direction that the projections shall make angles of 45° with the ground line.

The shadow of a point is where a ray of light through the point pierces the surface receiving the shadow.

To find the shadow of a point upon either plane of projection, pass through the point a ray of light; one projection of the ray will generally meet the ground line before the other; through this point of intersection erect a perpendicular to the ground line, and where this perpendicular meets the other projection of the ray will be the shadow of the point.

If the horizontal projection of the ray meets G L first, then the shadow is upon V, and upon H if the vertical projection meets G L first; if both projections meet G L at the same point that will be the shadow.

To illustrate, let it be required to find the shadow of the point A (Fig. 1, Pl. XXX.). Passing the ray of light A B through the point, we find that the vertical projection of the ray meets the ground line first, showing that the shadow is upon H; drawing a perpendicular at b we get b as the shadow. If A had been nearer the ground line than a, the shadow would have been upon V.

To obtain the shadow of a right line, find the shadows of any two points and join.

To obtain the shadow of a curved line, join the shadows of a number of its points.

The shadow of a solid is obtained by finding the shadows of those edges, or lines of the surface, which cast shadows.

Prob. 1. (Pl. XXI. Fig. 2.) *To find the shadow of a cube.* The edges which cast shadows are *a—a'b'*, *ae—a'*, *fe—c'a'*, *f—c'd'*. The shadow of the first must commence at *a*, where the line pierces *H*; joining this point with *o*, the shadow of *A* (*a*, *a'*), we have the shadow of the line *a—a'b'*; *no* is the shadow of *ae—a'*; *mn* of *fe—c'a'*; and *fm* of *f—c'd'*.

Notice that *on* is equal and parallel to *ae—a'*, and *mn* to *fe—c'a'*; whence we derive the principle that,

The shadow of a right line upon a plane is equal and parallel to the line, when the line is parallel to the plane.

Notice also that *ao* and *fm* both correspond with the direction of the projection of light upon *H*; whence the principle that,

The shadow of a right line upon a plane, to which it is perpendicular, has the same direction as the projection of light upon that plane.

Remark. In drawing these problems the shadows might be made with parallel lines, or with a flat tint of India ink.

Prob. 2 (Pl. XXI. Fig. 3.) *To find the shadow of the frustum of a square pyramid.* Find, first, the shadow of the vertex. *VB*, and *VS* are the edges of the pyramid which cast shadows, and *bx* and *sx* are the shadows of those edges. To find the shadow of the point *E* it is sufficient to draw the horizontal projection of the ray through *e* until it meets *bx* at *t*; or it might be found in the regular way; *dt* is the shadow of *he—h'e'*; the shadow of *ho—h'o'* is a parallel through *d*, the intersection of this with *sx* completes the required shadow.

Prob. 3. (Pl. XXI. Fig. 4.) *To find the shadow of a short hexagonal prism.* The edges which cast shadows are *c—c'o'*, *bc—b'c'*, *bd—b'c'*, *de—c'f'*, *e—f'h'*, *ae—h'k'*, *af—h'k'*, and *cf—h'o'*; these are all right lines, and the construction of their shadows is evident from the figure.

Find the shadow when the prism rests with one of its faces in the horizontal plane, and the bases parallel to *V*.

Prob. 4. (Pl. XXI. Fig. 5.) *To find the shadow of a vertical cylinder.* To determine the lines of the convex surface which cast shadows, pass vertical planes of rays tangent to the cylinder; *en* and *tl* are their traces; these are tangent to the cylinder along the elements *e—e'o'*, *t—t'r'*, the lines of the surface which cast shadows; these are called *elements*, or *lines of shade*. On the upper base that part of the circle to the right, and between t and e, casts a shadow.

The elements of shade cast the shadows ee' and tt'.

To find the shadow of the circle, assume points B, P, W, and find their shadows u', m', x'.

Assume a short cylinder in a position similar to that of the prism in Fig. 4, Pl. XXI., and find its shadow on V.

Prob. 5. (Pl. XXI. Fig. 9.) *Shadow of a cylindrical abacus upon an octagonal prism.* That part of the lower base of the abacus nearest the light casts the shadow; to determine how much of it casts the shadow, pass vertical planes of rays tangent to the prism, ax and wx are their traces; these planes intersect the lower base in the points a and w; that part of the circle between these points will cast the shadow.

To find the shadow, assume any vertical plane of rays whose horizontal trace is st; this plane intersects the prism in the vertical line $t—n't'$; it also intersects the circle in the point S; the shadow of S will be at the intersection of the ray through S and the line $t—n't'$, which gives us the point n'. In the same way other points of the shadow may be found: to find the points where the shadow crosses the edges of the prism, proceed in the same way, passing the planes of rays through the edges.

Find the shadow of a square or hexagonal abacus, upon a vertical cylinder.

Prob. 6. (Pl. XXI. Fig. 6.) *Shadow on interior of hollow semi-cylinder.* Suppose the cylinder to be vertical and covered by the board $abcd$, $a'—b'$; the left-hand edge of the cylinder, and the lower front edge of the board are the lines which cast shadows on the interior.

The shadow of the edge of the cylinder is found by passing a plane of rays through it; this intersects the cylinder in the element h, $h'—o'$; h' is the shadow of E. The shadow of the board is found by assuming points, as I, Y, etc., and finding their shadows in the same way that the shadow of E was found.

Find the shadow on the interior when the board is removed.

Prob. 7. (Pl. XXII. Fig 1.) *Shadow on steps.* Let the steps be given as in the figure, there being a wall at one end. It is required to find, first, the shadow of the wall on the steps, and, second, the shadow of the steps upon *H* and *V*.

1st. Shadow of wall on steps. The edges casting shadows are $a—a'b'$, and $an—a'$. As $a—a'b'$ is perpendicular to the top of each step, its shadow upon these surfaces will lie in the direction of the projection of light, as *ao*, the part *ap* being on the top of the 1st step, and *po* on that of the 2d.

As $a—a'b'$ is parallel to the front face of each step, its shadow upon these faces will be parallel to the line itself; therefore $p'q'$, found by projecting up from *p*, will be its shadow upon the front of 2. The shadow of *A* is at *O* on the top of 2.

The shadow of $an—a'$ upon the front faces of the steps will have the same direction as the projection of light; while the shadow upon the upper faces will be parallel to itself; $c'e'$ and $e'o'$ are the shadows upon the faces of 3 and 4; *dc* and *he*, found by projecting down from c' and e', are the shadows on the tops of the same steps.

Remark. In finding the shadow of *A*, there can be no question as to which surface it falls upon, if we remember that both projections of the shadow must lie in the projections of the same surface.

2d. Shadow of steps on H and V. As this problem presents no new principles, let the student, having first determined what edges cast shadows, verify the shadow given The shadow on *H* is not complete in the figure.

Prob. 8. (Pl. XXI. Fig. 10.) *Shadow of framing.* (Fig. 8, Pl. XXIV., shows an isometrical projection of the same framing.) It is required to find the shadow of the brace upon the horizontal timbers and also upon *H*.

The edges of the brace which cast shadows are $cd—c'd'$ and $ae—a'e'$. Assume any point as *M* on $cd—c'd'$ and find its shadow, *k*, on the upper face of the horizontal timbers; in this case *k* is on the plane of the top produced; *dk* is the shadow of $cd—c'd'$ upon the top of the timbers; a parallel line through *e* is the shadow of the other edge.

To obtain the shadow on H, produce the ray through the

point *M* until it pierces H in *i*; draw a line through *i* parallel to *dk* and it will be the shadow of *od—o'd'* upon H. A line through *q* parallel to it would be the shadow of *ae—a'e'* upon H; it does not show in this case. There is another shadow shown in the figure, the construction of which will be evident.

Construct the shadow of the whole framing upon H and V.

Prob. 9. (Pl. XXI. Fig. 8.) *Shadow of timber resting upon the top of a wall.* It is required to find the shadow of the timber upon the wall, and also the shadow of both upon V.

The edges of the timber which cast shadows, whether upon the wall or upon V, are *ae—a'e'*, *ab—a'c'*, *b—b'c'*, *bo—b'o'*, *oe—o'h'*, and *e—h'e'*. The shadow of *ae—a'e'* upon the wall commences at *n'* and *v'n'* is its shadow; *v'g'* is the shadow of *ab—a'c'*; *g'x'*, of *b—b'c'*; the line through *x'* parallel to *v'n'*, is the shadow of *bo—b'o'* upon this face. The line *bo—b'o'* also casts a shadow on the top of the wall which will be parallel to itself through the point *l*.

The construction of the shadow on V, is evident from the figure.

Prob. 10. (Pl. XXII. Fig. 2.) *Shadow of inclined timber upon triangular prism.* The relative position of the pieces is given in the figure, the timber makes an angle of 60° with H, and is parallel to V.

Commencing with *ad—a'd'* which casts the shadow *ds* upon H, we find that this meets the prism at *v*, which will therefore be one point of the shadow upon the nearest inclined face of the prism. To obtain another point, find the shadow of *ad—a'd'* upon an auxiliary horizontal plane through *pq—p'q'*; *p'q'* is its vertical trace; *e* is the shadow of *A* upon this plane, and the line *eo*, parallel to *ds*, is the shadow of *ad—a'd'* upon the same plane; this meets *pq* in the point *o*, which is therefore another point of the shadow of *ad—a'd'* upon the face of the prism; join *o* with *v*, and we have the required shadow.

The shadow of the diagonally opposite edge *cf—c'f'* can be found in the same way, or by drawing *fn* parallel to *ds* and *nz* parallel to *vo*. Part of the shadow of the timber falls on H beyond the prism; *ab—a'* and *bo—a'c'* are the only remaining edges of the timber which cast shadows. There will be no difficulty in finding these as well as the shadow of the prism.

Prob. 11. (Pl. XXII. Fig. 4.) *To find the angle which a ray of light makes with either plane of projection.* Let ab—$a'b'$ be the projections of a ray of light. Now if we consider the vertical projecting plane of the ray to be revolved into V, the ray would take the position $a''b'$; the distance $a'a''$ being equal to oa, the distance of the point A in front of V; the angle $a'b'a''$ is the angle which the ray AB makes with V, and is equal to 35° 16′. As both projections of the ray make the same angle with the ground line, the ray must make the same angle with H that it does with V.

Prob. 12. (Pl. XXII. Fig. 3.) *Shadow on interior of hollow hemisphere.* The shadow is cast by the semicircle tas, and it will be obtained by finding where rays through different points of this semicircle pierce the interior. Suppose the hemisphere projected upon a plane xy, which is parallel to the direction of light and perpendicular to V. To find a point of the shadow, intersect the hemisphere by a vertical plane of rays, av; this cuts the semicircle av—$a'e'v'$ from the hemisphere. Since the plane xy is parallel to the direction of light and perpendicular to V, rays of light will be projected upon it making the same angle with xy that rays of light make with V; that is, at an angle of 35° 16′. Draw a ray through a' at such an angle, and project e', its intersection with $a'e'v'$, to e; this will be one point of the shadow on the interior.

Other points may be found in the same way; the point o is found by using the plane bw. The shadow commences at the points t and s, where the projection of a ray would be tangent to the circle $asvt$.

Remark. The rays $a'e$, $b'o'$, &c., are parallel to $a''b'$ in Fig. 4.

Line of shade. This is the line that separates the light from the dark part of the surface. It is the line also that casts the shadow. This line can often be determined by mere inspection, as in the preceding problems, but in some cases special methods must be resorted to in order to determine it.

The method of finding the line of shade upon a vertical cylinder has been given in *Prob.* 4, the elements *s*—*s'o'* and *t*—*t'r'* being the lines of shade.

Prob. 13. (Pl. XXI., Fig. 7.) *To find the line of shade upon a cone.* If a plane of rays be passed tangent to a cone, the element along which it is tangent, will be the line of shade. As every plane tangent to a cone must contain the vertex, a tangent plane of rays must contain the ray through the vertex, and the shadow of the vertex will be a point of its trace; through *c*, the shadow of the vertex, draw the line *ce* tangent to the base of the cone; this is the trace of the tangent plane, and *ve*—*v'e'* is the element of contact with the cone; *cd* is the trace of another plane tangent on the other side of the cone; *dv*—*d'v'* is its element of contact. The lines *ce* and *cd* are the shadows of *ve*—*v'e'*, and *dv*—*d'v'*, and the space included between them is the shadow of the cone.

Prob. 14. (Pl. XXII. Fig. 5.) *To find the line of shade upon a sphere.* Only the vertical projection of the sphere is used, and the vertical plane is supposed to pass through the centre of the sphere. The line of shade is the circle of contact of a tangent cylinder of rays.

To find points of this curve, assume planes of rays, perpendicular to *V*, whose traces are *dw*, *sv*, &c.; each of these planes will intersect the sphere in a circle, and the point at which a ray is tangent to this circle will be one point of the curve of shade. The plane *sv* intersects the sphere in a circle projected in *sv*; revolve this circle about *sv* until it coincides with V; it will then have the position *vo'z*. To get the point at which a ray will be tangent to this circle, it is necessary to find the position of a ray when revolved in a similar manner to the circle. According to Prob. 11, the revolved position of a ray would make an angle of 35°16′ with *dw*. Now, if a line be drawn at this angle and tangent to the circle *vo'z*, it will give *o'* as the point of tangency; when the circle is revolved back to its original position, *o'* is projected at *o*, and is one point of the curve of shade.

Other points of the curve of shade can be determined in the same way. The curve commences at the points *a* and *b*, where planes of rays, parallel to *dw*, would be tangent to the sphere.

To find the point of the sphere which appears the brightest, revolve the circle *dw* into the position *dbw*; *fc* is the revolved position of a ray passing through the centre; bisect the angle *fcb* at *m'*; when the circle is revolved back *m'* falls at *m*, the lightest point.

CHAPTER IX.

SHADING.

1. Having given previously the methods for laying flat and graduated tints, let us see how, by their use, we may bring out the true form of an object. The following rules should be carefully studied and followed:

I. *Flat tints should be given to plane surfaces, when in the light, and parallel to the vertical plane; those nearest the eye being lightest.*

II. *Flat tints should be given to plane surfaces, when in the shade, and parallel to the vertical plane; those nearest the eye being darkest.*

III. *Graduated tints should be given to plane surfaces, when in the light and inclined to the vertical plane; increasing the shade as the surfaces recede from the eye; when two such surfaces incline unequally the one on which the light falls most directly should be lightest.*

IV. *Graduated tints should be given to plane surfaces, when in the shade, and inclined to the vertical plane; decreasing the shade as the surfaces recede from the eye.*

2. Applying these rules to the shading of an hexagonal prism (Pl. I**. Fig. 11), we find by I., that the front face should have a flat tint; by III., that the left-hand face should have a graduated tint, darkest at the left-hand edge; by IV., the right-hand face has also a graduated tint, darkest at the left-hand edge.

As the left-hand face receives the light more directly than the front face, the nearest part of it should be lighter than the front of the prism. The darkest part of the left-hand face should have about the same shade as the lightest part of the right-hand face.

3. The preceding rules also apply to the shading of curved surfaces, as the cylinder (Pl. I**. Fig. 12). The element of shade $a'—b'$ separates the light from the dark part of the cylinder.

The surface *a*—*n* by IV. should be darkest at *a* and grow lighter as it approaches *n*.

The part *a*—*p* of the illuminated surface, by III. should grow lighter as it approaches *p*; the part *m*—*p* by III. should be darkest at *m* and lightest at *p*; but by the second part of III. that part of the surface which receives the light most directly should be the lightest, which would make *c* the brightest point; if then we take a point, *e*, half way between *c* and *p*, it will give, approximately, the point which will appear the brightest.

The surface *c*—*e* is brighter than *e*—*p* as it receives the light more directly; it is also lighter than a corresponding space to the left of *c*, as it is nearer the eye; so that it is the lightest part of the cylinder.

4. Upon Figs. 13 and 14, Pl. I**. are shown in dotted lines the positions of the darkest and lightest parts of the cone and sphere. The method of finding the lines of shade upon each has been given in the chapter on shadows. As it is not necessary in practice to locate these lines exactly, the eye being a sufficient guide, it will be well to notice that the dark line *va* of the cone is a little nearer the right-hand edge than the dark line of the cylinder; while the lightest part, between *vc* and *vb*, has the same position as that of the cylinder, and is determined in the same way.

On the sphere, the point *n* of the line of shade *snp*, is a little nearer *a* than the centre of the sphere; the line of shade is symmetrical respecting the line *ba*, the direction of light. The lightest point *m* is a little nearer the centre than it is to *b*; it is also on the line *ba*.

In shading these solids, commence at the dark line and shade both ways, using lighter tints for the lighter shades. The dark line of the sphere should be widest at *n* and taper both ways to *p* and *s*; on the cone it tapers from the base to the vertex.

CHAPTER X.

ISOMETRICAL DRAWING.

If we take a cube situated as in Fig. 6, Pl. XXII., and tip it up to the left about the point a,e', until it takes the position shown in Fig. 7, the diagonal $a'h'$ being horizontal, and then turn the cube horizontally, without changing its position with respect to H, until it takes the position shown in Fig. 8, we shall have in the vertical projection of Fig. 8, what is called an isometrical projection.

In the case of the cube it is the projection made upon a plane perpendicular to a diagonal of the cube.

The relative position of the eye, the cube, and the vertical plane is shown in Fig. 7, where I, upon $a'h'$ produced, represents the eye (at an infinite distance); xy is the position of the vertical plane; the cube is placed, as shown by the projections, so that the diagonal ah—$a'h'$ is parallel to H and perpendicular to xy or V.

Looking at this isometrical projection of the cube we see that the three visible faces of the cube appear equal, and that all the sides of these faces are equal; this shows that these faces are similarly situated respecting V, and that their sides, or the edges of the cube, are equally inclined to V. It will also be noticed that the isometrical projection of the cube can be inscribed in a circle, as the outer edges form a regular hexagon.

The three angles formed by the edges meeting at the centre are equal, each being 120°.

The point a' is called the *isometric centre;* the three lines passing through the centre being called *isometric axes.*

Any line parallel to one of these axes is called an *isometric line,* while any line not parallel is called a *non-isometric line.*

The plane of any two of the axes, or any parallel plane, is called an *isometric plane.*

The two axes $a'b'$ and $a'd'$ (Fig. 8, Pl. XXII.) and all parallel lines make angles of 30° with a horizontal line.

It has been seen that the isometrical projection of a cube can be inscribed in a circle; this renders it easy to construct an isometrical drawing of a cube, by inscribing a regular hexagon in a circle, whose radius is equal to an edge of the cube, and then drawing radii to the alternate angles. While this would give an isometrical projection of a cube, it would not be the true projection of the cube whose edge was taken as a radius, because the edges of the cube are inclined to the plane of projection, consequently their projections cannot be equal to the edges themselves, but would be less.

Let us see how the true isometrical projection of a cube may be obtained without making it necessary to construct the different projections shown in Figs. 6, 7, 8, Pl. XXII.

The only lines of the cube that are projected in their true size are the diagonals $d'b'$, $d'e'$, $b'e'$ (Fig. 8, Pl. XXII.), of the three visible faces. It is evident that the diagonal db—$d'b'$ (Fig. 8) is parallel to V; by looking at Fig. 7, where the relative position of the eye, the plane of projection, and the cube is shown, it will also be evident that $b'e'$ (corresponding to $b'e'$, Fig. 8) is parallel to the plane xy (V).

If now we draw a line ab (Fig. 9, Pl. XXII.), making an angle of 45° with db at the point b, and note its intersection a with the vertical through c, ab will be the side of a square whose diagonal is db. and would therefore be the true length of the edge of a cube, the diagonal of any face of which is equal to db; but cb is the isometrical projection of this edge, so that we have the means of comparing the two and forming a scale.

Divide ab into any number of equal parts and project the points of division upon cb, by lines parallel to ac, and it will give the isometrical projection of these distances. To construct then an isometric scale draw a horizontal line bc (Fig. 10, Pl. XXII.); draw ba at an angle of 15° with it; divide ba into any number of equal parts and project the points of division upon bc by lines making an angle of 45° with ba

[these projecting lines make an angle of 60° with *bc*]. The distances on *bc* will be the isometric length of the corresponding distances on *ba*.

This scale is only good for isometric lines.

The diagonals *db*, *dm*, *bm* (Fig. 9) are projected in their true lengths; this would also be true of all lines parallel to them.

As *ch* is the projection of a line equal to *db*, a scale may be constructed by projecting any distances, 1, 2, 3, etc., from *db* to *ch*; this scale will be good for all lines parallel to *ch*, *ho*, or *hn*.

Although it is well to understand the construction of these scales, they are seldom used in practice, as it is more convenient to use a common scale, if necessary, making the isometric lines equal to their true length. This method, as already shown, would make the drawing larger than the true projection of the object, but there is no objection to this. When made in this way it is called an *isometrical drawing*, to distinguish from the *isometrical projection*.

The advantage of isometrical drawing is that it offers a simple means of showing in one drawing several faces of an object, thus obviating the necessity of a plan and one or more elevations. It is particularly adapted to the representation of small objects, in which the principal lines are at right angles to each other.

Direction of Light. In isometrical projection the light is supposed to have the same direction as the line *bc* (Fig. 16, Pl. XXIII.), the diagonal of the cube, that is, it makes an angle of 30° with a horizontal line.

Lines of shade. According to a previous definition these are the lines which separate the light from the dark part. In the isometrical projection of the cube (Fig. 16, Pl. XXIII.) the two right-hand faces (front and back) and the bottom are in the dark, while the two left-hand faces (front and back) and the top are in the light; consequently the heavy lines shown in the figure are the visible lines of shade.

***Prob.* 1.** (Fig. 1, Pl. XXIII.) *To construct the isometrical drawing of a cube, with a block upon one face and a recess in another.* Let the edges of the cube be 4″; the block

2″ square and 1½″ thick; the recess 2″ square and 1″ deep; both the block and the recess to be in the centre of the face. The drawing of the cube might be made, as previously described, by using a circle with a radius of 4″, but a more convenient way is to draw the isometric axes, *ca*, *cb*, and *cd*, making each equal to 4″, then isometric lines through the extremities will complete the cube.

After completing the cube, divide the axes into four equal parts. To locate the block, draw isometric lines through 1 and 3, upon *cb* and *cd*, their intersections will give the base of the block; through the points of intersection draw isometric lines parallel to *ca*, make them 1½″ in length, and connect their extremities. The recess is similarly located, the depth of 1″ can be obtained by projecting from 2 on either *ca* or *cb*.

Make the isometrical drawing of a cube with a square hole in each face, running through the cube.

Prob. 2. (Fig. 2, Pl. XXIII.) *To construct the isometrical drawing of three pieces of timber bolted together.* Draw the axes *ca*, *cb*, *cd;* make *cb* equal to 6″; *ce* 3″; *eo* 2″; *on* 4″; *do* equals *ec;* the vertical timber is 5″×8″; the side timbers are each let into the vertical timber the same distance.

The method of constructing the nut and washer is given in *Prob.* 9.

Make a drawing with the front side timber removed.

Prob. 3. (Fig. 3, Pl. XXIII.) *To construct the isometrical drawing of a portion of framing.* The necessary dimensions of the parts are given in Fig. 10, Pl. XXI. The edges of the brace being non-isometric lines, it is necessary to locate the extremities, which are in isometric planes, and then join; *cd* and *ca* are each equal to 28″; the other edges are parallel to *ad; de* is equal to *d′e′* (Fig. 10, Pl. XXI.).

Prob. 4. (Figs. 4, 5, Pl. XXIII.) *To make the isometrical drawing of a circle.* In Fig. 4 is shown a circle with an inscribed and circumscribed square. If we make an isometrical drawing of these squares in their relative positions, we shall have at once eight points through which the isometric circle must pass; these are the points common to the circle and squares; this is shown in Fig. 5, the two figures being lettered the same. To locate any point, as *v* (Fig. 4), draw *on* perpendicular to *ac*, make *on* and *oa* (Fig. 5) equal to the same distances in Fig. 4. In this way any point of the circle, or any point within the square, can be located. This method gives an exact drawing of the circle, the curve being an ellipse.

Prob. 5. (Fig. 6, Pl. XXIII.) *To make an approximate construction of the isometrical drawing of a circle.* Construct the isometric square *abcd*; let *b* be the centre and *ba* the radius of the arc *ac*; *d* is the centre of the arc *pq*, the radius being the same as before; *e* and *f* are the centres of the arcs *cp* and *qa*; the points *n*, *p*, *q*, *s* are the centres of the sides.

The curve, as thus constructed, approximates near enough to the true curve to answer most purposes.

Make an isometrical drawing of a cube with a circle inscribed in each face.

Prob. 6. (Fig. 7, Pl. XXIII.) *To divide the isometrical drawing of a circle into equal parts.*

1st method. At *a*, the centre of *so*, erect the perpendicular *ar*, and make it equal to *as*; from *r* as a centre describe the arc *mp* and divide it into any number of equal parts; draw lines through these points from *r* and produce them until they meet *so*; join the points on *so* with *a*, and the lines drawn will divide the isometric arc into the same number of parts that *mp* contains.

2d method. Describe the semicircle *de'h* upon *dh* as a diameter: this is the semicircle of which *deh* is the isometrical drawing and is in the position *deh* would take when revolved about *dh*, as an axis, until parallel to V. Divide *de'h* into equal parts and project to *deh* by vertical lines; these will divide the isometric curve into a corresponding number of parts.

Prob. 7. (Fig. 8, Pl. XXIII.) *To make the isometrical drawing of a cube, cylinder, and sphere.* Suppose the sphere to rest upon the top of the cylinder, and the cylinder upon the cube.

The diameter of the sphere and cylinder is equal to an edge of the cube; the height of the cylinder is equal to its diameter.

First construct a cube and then inscribe a circle in the top face; this is the lower base of the cylinder; to obtain the upper base, construct a second cube resting upon the first, and of the same size; this is shown in the figure by dotted lines. Inscribe a circle in the top of this second cube and it will be the upper base of the cylinder; *ab* and *cd* tangent to each of these curves are the extreme elements of the cylinder. The sphere rests upon the centre of the upper base; erect a perpendicular at *e*, and make it equal to half the edge of the cube; from *h* as a centre, with a radius equal to *de*, describe the sphere.

Prob. 8. (Figs. 9, 10, 11, Pl. XXIII.) *Isometrical drawing of brackets supporting a shelf.* No. 1 of the brackets has all of its edges right lines, while No. 2 is made up partly of arcs of circles, whose centres are at *h* and *m* (Fig. 11). Figs. 10 and 11 give side elevations of the two brackets, with dimensions.

The shelf is 28″ wide and 6″ thick; make the projection so as to show the under side.

There will be no difficulty in making the drawing of No. 1.

To construct No. 2, after drawing *bc*, *ca*, *ae*, *ed*, *dg*, *ew*, locate *h*, this is the centre of the isometric squares which contain the curves *en* and *ou*; therefore, draw the isometric line *hs* and make it equal to *ho* or *he*; *s* is the centre of the curve *en*; *st* is equal to the thickness of the bracket, and *t* is the centre of the curve through *w*. Make *ht* equal to *hv* and *t* is the centre of the curve *ou*; *p* is the centre of the curve *bn*, and *tz* the centre of *gu* and also of the curve through *x*.

Prob. 9. (Fig. 12, Pl. XXIII.) *The isometrical drawing of a nut and washer.* The washer is 3½″ in diameter and ½″ thick; the nut 2″ square and 1″ thick; the bolt 1″ in diameter.

To construct the washer, make two isometric squares, *ab*, *cd*, ½″ apart and 3½″ on a side; inscribe in each of these a circle and connect by isometric lines at *e* and *h*, tangent to each circle.

Find the centre of the washer and construct the square for the base of the nut.

After completing the nut, construct in the centre of its

face an isometric square 1″ on a side; inscribe in this a circle, which will represent the curve of intersection of the bolt with the nut. In the figure the bolt is supposed to project 1″ from the nut; the rest of the construction will be apparent from the figure.

In Fig. 12, the nut is placed so that its edges are isometric lines; to make a drawing when the nut is turned so that its edges would not be isometric lines, make a plan of the nut and washer as in Fig. 13, Pl. XXIII., and draw through the corners of the nut a square, *abcd*, with its sides parallel to the sides of the square which circumscribes the washer. After constructing the washer as before, make in the centre of the washer an isometrical drawing of the square, *abcd*, and locate on it the points *ehon*; the method of completing will be the same as before.

Make a drawing when the nut is oblique.

Prob. 10. (Figs. 14 and 15, Pl. XXIII.) *The isometrical drawing of letters.* In these letters the position of the isometric axes is changed, one being placed in a horizontal position. The construction of these letters is apparent from the figures; in the letter *S*, the curves not being isometric circles, will have to be sketched in or drawn with an irregular curve.

Try other letters of the alphabet, as *d*, *w*, *x*, *o*.

Shadows. In isometrical drawing the shadow of a point on any plane surface is at the intersection of the ray through the point, and the projection of the ray on the surface.

We have seen that in isometrical projection rays of light make an angle of 30° with a horizontal line.

Turning to Fig. 16, Pl. XXIII., let *be*, the diagonal of the cube, represent a ray of light; *bd* is the projection of this ray on the top of the cube, and *bm* the projection on the face *bmx*. Thus we see that the position of the projection of a ray of light upon a horizontal plane, as *bnds*, is horizontal, while the projection of a ray of light upon a vertical plane, as *bmx*, makes an angle of 60° with a horizontal line.

Suppose the edge *bo* produced to *a* and it is required to find the shadow of *a*: draw the ray *ag* at 30°; through *h*, the projection of *a* upon the plane of the top, draw the horizontal line *bg;* this is the projection of the ray, and the intersection of this with *ag* is the shadow of *a* upon the top of the cube.

Produce the edge *bn* to *c;* the shadow of *c* is at *h*, the intersection of the ray *ch* with *bh*, its projection upon the vertical face.

Prob. 11. (Fig. 16, Pl. XXIII.) *The isometrical drawing of a cube with its shadow on the horizontal plane.* The shadow of *s* is at *t; tm* is the shadow of *sm; w* is the shadow of *d*, and *tw* the shadow of *sd; vw* is the shadow of *nd*, and *vs* the shadow of *ns*, the back edge.

Prob. 12. (Fig. 2, Pl. XXIV.) *The isometrical drawing of an hexagonal prism with the shadow.* The prism is represented standing on H at a distance *xy* from V. The edges which cast shadows are *ia, ab, bc, cd, de.* Since *ia* is perpendicular to H, its shadow upon that plane will have the same direction as the projection of light upon H; the shadow of *ia* falls partly on V, as at *ok*, which is parallel to *ia; k*, the shadow of *a*, is at the intersection of the ray through *a*, and the vertical through *o*. In the same way *l, m, n*, the shadows of *b, c, d*, are found.

In finding the shadow of the prism upon V. the vertical projection of the rays of light have not been used, as they were not necessary.

Prob. 13. (Fig. 3, Pl. XXIV.) *The isometrical drawing of a beam, projecting from a vertical wall, with the shadow.* The construction of the drawing is evident from the figure. The edges which cast shadows are *ca, ab, bd, dn.* Only the projections of the rays are used to find the shadow. To find the shadow of *a*, draw through *c*, the vertical projection of *a*, the line *ce* at an angle of 60°; through *h*, the horizontal projection of *a*, draw the horizontal line *hi;* these two lines *ce* and *hi* are the projections of the ray through *a*, and they determine *e*, the shadow of *a*. The accuracy of this construction can be tested by drawing a ray through *a*. In the same way the points *i* and *k* are found.

Prob. 14. (Fig. 5, Pl. XXIV.) *The isometrical drawing of a four-armed cross, with the shadows.* It is required to find the shadow of the cross on H, and also upon itself; *a*—1 is the shadow of *ae*; 1—2 the shadow of *gf*; 2—3 of *fh*; 3—4 of *li*; 4—5 of *lm*; 5—6 of *bc*; 6—7 of *cn*; 7—8 of *cq*; the rest of the shadow is cast by edges upon the back, which are not seen.

The shadows upon the cross are *si* the shadow of *sh*; *sm* of *bs*; *he* of *hg*; *bq* of *bn*.

Keeping the same thickness of the cross make the arms longer, and then find the shadows.

Prob. 15. (Fig. 1, Pl. XXIV.) *The isometrical drawing of a vertical cylinder passing through an hexagonal block, with the shadows.* A plan of the cylinder and block is shown in Fig. 4; the diameter of the cylinder is $\frac{8}{10}''$; any edge of the block, as *bc*, is $\frac{7}{10}''$ in length; the block is $\frac{2\frac{1}{2}}{10}''$ thick. First make an isometrical drawing of this plan; this is shown in Fig. 1, with the points numbered and lettered the same. At any assumed distance above the plan construct a similar figure; this gives the top of the block, which can readily be completed. The method of completing the cylinder will be evident from what has preceded.

Shadows. Find first the shadow which the block casts upon the cylinder. Assume any vertical plane of rays as the one whose horizontal trace is *vx*; this cuts the point *v'* from the lower edge of the block, and the element *xx'* from the cylinder; the ray through *v'* intersects the element at *x'* one point of the required shadow. In the same way other points can be found; *ky* is the element of shade found by passing the plane of rays *wy* tangent to the cylinder. At *z* the shadow passes to the back part of the cylinder.

The method of finding the shadow which the cylinder casts upon the block will be evident from the figure, with what has just been shown.

Show how the shadows given on Fig 3, Pl. XXIII., are found.

Determine whether the brace would cast a shadow on the top of the horizontal timber or not.

Find the shadow of the framing upon H.

CHAPTER XI.

OBLIQUE PROJECTION.

This method of projection is similar to isometrical projection in showing three faces of the object, but unlike isometrical it gives the exact form of one of these. It is called *oblique*, because the projecting lines are oblique to V instead of being perpendicular, as they have been previously.

It is sometimes called Parallel Perspective; it does not however give a true perspective of the object, but offers a substitute, simple in construction, and one as well adapted for representing small objects.

An oblique projection of a cube is given in Fig. 11, Pl. XXIV.; the face *abcd* has its true form, while the other two faces are shown equally, but not in their true shape. The edges *ce*, *bh*, *ai*, make an angle of 45° with a horizontal line, and are equal to the other edges of the cube.

Since the face *abcd* is projected in its true form, it must be parallel to V; if then we suppose the cube placed with one face parallel to V, it is evident that this projection (Fig 11) could not be obtained, when the projecting lines are perpendicular to V; the square, *abcd*, would be the projection in that case. In order then to obtain this projection, the projecting lines cannot be perpendicular to V, but must be oblique.

Now when a line is perpendicular to a plane, in order that the projection of the line, upon that plane, should be equal to the line itself, the projecting lines must make an angle of 45° with the plane. In the case of a line parallel to a plane, its projection would be equal to the line, whatever the direction of the projecting lines, provided they were parallel.

Thus we see that if the projecting lines make an angle of 45° with *V*, we shall obtain, in the case of the cube, the projection shown in Fig. 11.

Since an infinite number of projecting lines could be passed through a point, all making the required angle of 45°, it follows that the projection of a line might have an infinite number of positions. Thus the edges *ce*, *bh*, *etc.* (Fig. 11), could be drawn at any angle, and still give an oblique projection of the cube. Fig. 8, Pl. XXIV., gives an oblique projection of the cube, with the edges *ce*, *bh*, *etc.*, drawn at an angle of 30°; other angles might be used, but these two (45° and 30°) are most convenient, as they are found on the triangles.

Only those lines that are parallel or perpendicular to *V* are projected in their true size.

Prob. 1. (Fig. 12, Pl. XXIV.) *To make the oblique projection of a circle.* Let *abcd* be the circumscribed, and *hken* the inscribed squares of the circle *mpoq*. Construct *a'b'c'd'*, and *h'k'e'n'*, the oblique projection of these squares, and we shall have eight points (*m'n'p'e'o'k'q'h'*) of the oblique projection of the circle. The method of finding other points will readily suggest itself, but the points already found will be sufficient to enable us to trace the curve quite accurately. The curve thus found would be an ellipse; for an approximate construction of it by arcs of circles, draw the lines *m's* and *q's* perpendicular to the sides of the square, their intersection, *s*, will give a centre for the curve *q'h'm'*; in the same way the curve *p'e'o'* can be drawn as an arc; for the ends use *v* and *w* as centres.

This figure (12) represents the projection of the circle when horizontal, as upon the top of the cube. When the circle is parallel to *V*, or upon the front face of the cube, its projection would be an equal circle; this is shown in Fig. 9, Pl. XXIV., which is the oblique projection of three-fourths of a hollow cylinder, whose axis is perpendicular to *V*, the ends being projected as circles.

Fig. 6, Pl. XXIV., gives an example of the oblique projection of the circle when perpendicular to both *H* and *V*, as upon the right-hand face of the cube.

Construct an oblique projection of a cube with a circle upon each of the three visible faces.

Direction of light. The light is assumed, as in isometrical projection, to have the same direction as the diagonal of the cube. The arrow in Fig. 11, Pl. XXIV., indicates the direction of light, corresponding to the direction of the diagonal *ae*; *ah* is the projection of this ray (*ae*) upon the top of the cube, and *ac* the projection upon the front face. The method of finding shadows is similar to that in isometrical projection. The shadow of the cube upon *H* is shown in Fig. 11; if the shadow of the cube (Fig. 8, Pl. XXIV.) was to be found, the direction of light would correspond with the direction of its diagonal *ae*.

Only a few examples of this method of projection are given, sufficient, however, to show its application. Fig. 7, Pl. XXIV., represents an irregular block; it is 4″ long and 1″ square on the ends, the short lines are ½″ in length. Fig. 10, Pl. XXIV., is the oblique projection of a mortise and tenon; the under side of the tenon is shown; notice the position of the shade lines on the upper piece.

CHAPTER XII.

LINEAR PERSPECTIVE.

Linear perspective is the representation of the form of an object upon any plane surface, just as it appears to the eye when viewing it from any given point. To use a common illustration: if we should close one eye, and, keeping the other at a fixed distance from the window, should trace upon the glass the outlines of what could be seen through it, we should have a true perspective of the objects seen.

Supposing then, the perspective plane to be transparent, and always placed between the eye and the object, we see that *the perspective of a point is where a visual ray* (a line drawn from the point to the eye) *pierces the perspectie plane.* To illustrate, let A (Fig. 1, Pl. XXV.) be a point in space, behind the vertical plane which is used as the perspective plane; C is the position of the eye, or point of sight; the the visual ray CA pierces V at a'', which is the perspective of A.

It is impossible in practice to draw the visual ray itself, as in Fig. 1; the point of sight and the point in space are given by their projections only, so that it is necessary to use the projections of the visual ray to find the perspective. To do this, join the horizontal projection of the point of sight with the horizontal projection of the point, join also the vertical projections; the two lines thus drawn are the projections of the visual ray, and the point in which it pierces V is the required perspective. In Figs. 1 and 2, Pl. XXV., the visual ray $ca—c'a'$ pierces V at a''. Fig. 2 has the same letters and measurements as Fig. 1, and represents the same thing, with the customary position of the planes of projection.

It will be noticed in Fig. 2, that both projections of the point A are above the ground line; as this has not happened before, a word or two in explanation. Looking at Fig. 1 we see that the two intersecting planes of projection form four dihedral angles; the one above H and in front of V, is called the 1st; the 2d is behind V and above H; the 3d is below the 2d, and the 4th below the 1st. The point of sight is in the first angle. Now, all the objects that we have previously considered have been placed in the first angle, and, as we have seen, the horizontal projections are always below the ground line, and the vertical above; but if an object is placed in the second angle (as it is in perspective) when the vertical plane is revolved back, both projections will appear above the ground line, as in Fig. 1, where a' revolves to a' The same rules that we have had for determining the position of a point in space from its projections, hold good when both projections are above the ground line; the distance ah (Figs. 1 and 2) is the distance of *A* from V, and the distance a'h is the distance of A from H.

Prob. 1. (Figs. 3, 4, 5, Pl. XXV.) *To find the perspective of right lines in different positions by means of visual rays.*

1st, *when perpendicular to H:* let *a—a'b'* (Fig. 3) be a line perpendicular to H, and at the distance *ab'* behind V; cc' is the point of sight. Draw the ray *ac—a'c';* this pierces V at *e*, the perspective of the point *aa'; f* is the perspective of the point *ab'; fe* is the perspective of the line *a—a'b';* in the same way is found hg, the perspective of the line *d—a'b'*, which is parallel to *a—a'b'*.

2d, *when parallel to H and V:* let *ab—a'b'* (Fig. 4) be the given line, situated in H and at the distance *bb'* behind V; the perspective of the point *aa'* is at *e; f* is the perspective of the point *bb'*, whence *ef* is the perspective of *ab—a'b';* hg is the perspective of the line *dm—a'b'*, which is parallel to *ab—a'b'*.

3d, *when perpendicular to V: ab—b'* (Fig. 5) is the given line, situated in H, and at the distance *bb'* from V; *ef* is its perspective; *in—n'* is a line parallel to *ab—b'; hb* is its perspective.

Prob. 2. (Fig. 7, Pl. XXV.) *To find the perspective of a cube when placed with a face parallel to V.* Let *abid*, and *a'd'f'e'* be the projections of the cube, and *cc'* the point of sight. Find first the perspective of the point *df'*, by drawing the ray *cd—c'f'*; this gives *o* as the perspective; the ray *ca—c'e'* gives *r*, the perspective of the point *ae'*; *t* is the perspective of *aa'*, and *s* of *dd'*; in the same way are found the points *p*, *q*, *v*, *z*.

Prob. 3. (Fig. 6, Pl. XXV.) *To find the perspective of a cube when placed with its faces oblique to V.* Let *abid*, and *a'i'h'e'* be the projections of the cube; *s* is the perspective of the point *dd'*; *o* of the point *df'*; *r* of *ae'*; *t* of *aa'*, etc.

By an examination of Figs. 3, 4, 6, 7, Pl. XXV., it will be seen that *the perspective of any right line is parallel to that line when the line is parallel to the perspective plane.*

It will also be noticed that the edges *op*, *sq*, *tv*, &c., (Figs. 6 and 7), when produced, meet at a point; this is called the *vanishing point* of these lines, and since the lines *op*, *sq*, *tv*, etc., are the perspectives of parallel lines, we have the principle that *the perspectives of all parallel lines have a common vanishing point.*

To find then the vanishing point of any line, draw a line through the point of sight parallel to the given line, and where it pierces the perspective plane will be the vanishing point of this line, and all parallel lines. In Fig. 6, *cw—c'w'* is parallel to *di—d'i'*; it pierces V at *w'*, which is the vanishing point of *di—d'i'*, and the edges parallel to it. The vanishing point of *ro*, *ts*, *vq*, etc., could be found in the same way.

The vanishing point of parallel lines, parallel to the perspective plane, is situated at an infinite distance; hence the perspectives will be parallel.

In Figs. 5 and 7, Pl. XXV., the lines which are perpendicular to V vanish at *c'*; whence the principle that *all lines perpendicular to the perspective plane vanish in the vertical projection of the point of sight*; this is called the *centre of the picture.*

The horizontal line through the centre of the picture is called the *horizon.*

The vanishing points of all horizontal lines are situated somewhere on the horizon.

The point in which a line pierces a plane is called its *trace;* the trace of a line on the perspective plane is one point of its perspective; the vanishing point of the line is another point of its perspective; whence, *the perspective of a right line joins its vanishing point with its trace.*

It is customary to use the vertical plane as the perspective plane, the object being placed in the second angle; this brings the two projections of the object and the perspective together, as in Fig. 6, Pl. XXV., which is objectionable. Different methods may be used to prevent this, but the most convenient is by supposing the horizontal plane revolved 180°, so as to bring the plan of the object in front of V, and then instead of using visual rays, to make use of auxiliary lines called *perpendiculars* and *diagonals,* by which method the vertical projection of the object is not necessary.

It is evident that *if two lines intersect at a point in space, their perspectives will intersect in the perspective of the point;* so that if we pass any two lines through a point and find their perspectives, their intersection will be the perspective of the point.

The two lines most convenient to use are a perpendicular and a diagonal.

A *perpendicular* is a line perpendicular to the perspective plane, and vanishes, as we have seen, in the centre of the picture.

A *diagonal* is a horizontal line, making an angle of 45° with the perspective plane.

A diagonal being a horizontal line its vanishing point is on the horizon, and since it makes an angle of 45° with V, *the distance of the vanishing point from the centre of the picture is equal to the distance of the point of sight in front of V.* This is shown in Fig 2, Pl. XXVI., *cc'* being the point of sight, and *c'd* the horizon; to find the vanishing point of diagonals draw through *cc'* the line *ch—c'd,* parallel to H, and making an angle of 45° with V; it pierces V at *d,* the vanishing point of all diagonals parallel to *ch—c'd.* It is evident that $c'd=wh=cw$. As diagonals may be drawn either to the right or left, there are two vanishing points of diagonals, as at d and d_1 (Fig. 2).

Prob. 4. (Fig. 8, Pl. XXV.) *To construct the perspective of a regular hexagon, by means of diagonals and perpendiculars.* The hexagon is situated in H, at the distance *nn'* behind V. The horizontal plane has been revolved 180°, so that the plan of the hexagon comes in front of V, while the horizontal projection of the point of sight at the same time revolves to *c*, behind V; *c'* is the centre of the picture, *d* and d_1 the vanishing points of diagonals, found by making *c'd* and $c'd_1$ equal to *cw*.

To find the perspective of the point *e*, draw through it the perpendicular *ee'*, *e'c'* is its perspective; also draw through *e* the diagonal *ez*, zd_1 is its perspective; the point *o* in which these intersect is the perspective of *e*; *g'* and *r* are the traces of the perpendicular and diagonal through *g*; *g'c'* and rd_1 are their perspectives, and *l* is the perspective of *g*; *p* is the perspective of *f*; *s* of *b*; *h* of *a*; and *m* of *n*.

Remark. In Fig. 8 diagonals are drawn in both directions, and it is seen that either diagonal with the perpendicular gives the perspective, or that two diagonals without the perpendicular are sufficient.

Those diagonals which in plan are drawn to the right, vanish to the left of the centre of the picture, while those drawn to the left in plan, vanish to the right of the centre; this comes from having revolved the plan 180°.

Prob. 5. (Fig. 9, Pl. XXV.) *To construct the perspective of a pavement made up of squares.* Let *abef* represent the plan of the pavement, the squares being set with their sides diagonally to V; *c'* is the centre of the picture, *d* and d_1 the vanishing points of diagonals.

As the sides of the squares are diagonal lines, their perspectives will join their traces and the vanishing points of diagonals; produce *mn* to *o*, od_1 is the perspective of *mo*; *ad* is the perspective of *ae*; the perspectives of the other edges are similarly found, and their intersections will give the perspectives of the squares; *af* and *be*, being perpendiculars, vanish at *c'*.

Prob. 6. (Fig. 1, Pl. XXVI.) *To find the perspective of a cube.* Let *abih*, *a'h'f'e'* be the projections of the cube, which is placed with its face parallel to V, and at the distance *ae'* behind V.

The lines $e'c'$ and $f'c'$ are the indefinite perspectives of the lower edges of the cube, which are horizontally projected in ab and hi; draw the diagonals gd_1, nd_1, md_1, and we shall obtain the points r, o, p, z; at these points erect perpendiculars and limit them by the lines $a'c'$ and $h'c'$.

Remark. In this figure the vertical projection of the cube is given, but it evidently is not necessary in order to construct the perspective; it is sufficient to know the height of the cube, since perpendiculars and diagonals passed through points in the upper base of the cube would pierce V somewhere in the vertical trace of the plane of the top, as they are horizontal lines, and are in that plane.

Prob. 7. (Fig. 8, Pl. XXVI.) *To find the perspective of a vertical hexagonal prism.* The prism is placed with one face in V; the line $n'g'$ is the vertical trace of the plane of the top of the prism. First, construct the perspective of the lower base according to *Prob.* 4; then construct the perspective of the upper base, remembering that the traces of the perpendiculars and diagonals passed through points in the upper base, will be in the line $n'g'$. Connect the two bases by vertical lines to complete the prism.

Prob. 8. (Fig. 6, Pl. XXVI.) *To find the perspective of a square pillar resting upon a pedestal.* Let $abhe$, $a'e'ea$ be the projections of the pedestal, placed with its face in V; $kipl$ is the horizontal projection of the pillar; $k'l'$ is the vertical trace of the plane of the top of the pillar.

First, construct the perspective of the pedestal in the same way that the perspective of the cube was found in *Prob.* 6. The face $aa'e'e$ is its own perspective, as it is in V.

To find the perspective of the pillar, construct first the perspective of the lower base; draw a perpendicular and diagonal through the point ln', n' and e' are the traces of these lines, and $n'c'$ and $e'd_1$ their perspectives; their intersection is the perspective of the point ln'; g' is the trace of the diagonal through p, and $g'd_1$ its perspective; the point o in which this intersects $n'c'$ is the perspective of the point pn'; in the same way the remaining points of the base can be found.

The perspective of the upper base of the pillar might be found in the same way, or by erecting perpendiculars at the four points already found, and limiting them by the lines *k'd'* and *l'c*.

Prob. 9. (Fig. 3, Pl. XXVI.) *To find the perspective of a square pyramid.* Let *abde* be the plan of the pyramid; *hv'* is the height of the vertex above the base. Find first the perspective of the base; *e* is its own perspective, as it is in V; *m* is the perspective of *a*; *em* the perspective of *ea*; *ep* the perspective of *ed*, etc.

To obtain the perspective of the vertex, find *o*, the perspective of its horizontal projection; at *o* erect a perpendicular until it meets *v'c'*, this gives *n*, the perspective of the vertex; joining *n* with the corners of the base completes the perspective.

Prob. 10. (Fig. 5, Pl. XXVI.) *To find the perspective of a square pyramid resting upon a pedestal.* Let *abeh* be the plan of the pedestal; *r'w'* is the vertical trace of the upper base; the edge *aa'* is in V and is part of the perspective; *z* is the perspective of the point *bb'*; *x* of *hh'*, etc.

After completing the perspective of the pedestal, find the perspective of the base of the pyramid; *n'c'* and *p'd* are the perspectives of a perpendicular and diagonal through *n*, and *o* is the perspective of *n*; in the same way the other corners of the base can be found.

To find the perspective of the vertex, draw through *v* a perpendicular and diagonal; their traces are *v'* and *p'* and their perspectives *v'c'* and *p'd*; *s* is the perspective of the vertex.

Prob. 11. (Fig. 7, Pl. XXVI.) *To find the perspective of an hexagonal prism, whose axis is parallel to H and inclined to V.*

The prism rests with one face in H; *aekl* is the plan; *m'p'* is the trace upon V of the plane of the upper face of the prism; *t'n'* is the trace upon V of the horizontal plane which contains the edges projected in *al* and *ek*; *cc'* is the point of sight.

As the edges *al*, *bh*, etc., of the prism are parallel lines, and are so situated that they pierce V within the drawing, the most convenient way to find their perspectives is by joining their traces with their vanishing point. To find the vanishing point, draw *ow*—*o'w'* parallel to *al*, *bh*, etc.; this pierces V at *w'*, the vanishing point of the edges of the prism.

The edge *al* pierces V at *a'*, and *a'w'* is its indefinite perspective; this is limited at *s* by the diagonal *t'd*; *q'* is the trace of *bh*, when an edge of the upper face, and *q'w'* is its indefinite perspective; this is limited by the diagonals *m'd* and *o'd*; *qw'* is the indefinite perspective of *bh*, when an edge of the lower face, and is limited by the diagonals *md* and *od*; in the same way the perspective of the other edges can be found. The method of completing the perspective of the prism will be apparent.

Construct the perspective when the axis of the prism is parallel to both planes of projection.

Prob. 12. (Fig. 1, Pl. XXVII.) *To find the perspective of a circle.* Let *aebk* be the circle situated in the horizontal plane. Find the perspectives of the squares *aebk* and *hmno*; this will give eight points of the perspective of the circle; the curve should be tangent to the sides of the circumscribed square at the points *xzyv*.

Prob. 13. (Fig. 2, Pl. XXVII.) *To find the perspective of a circle when it is perpendicular to both H and V.* Let *ek* and *a'b'* be the projections of the circle; *ad''a''e''* represents the circle with inscribed and circumscribed squares when revolved about the point *ab'* into H.

To find the perspective of the circumscribed square, draw *a'c'* and *b'c'*; these are the indefinite perspectives of the upper and lower edges; draw the diagonals *kp* and *eq*, and find their perspectives; at *r* and *l* erect perpendiculars, and they will be the perspectives of the vertical edges of the square.

The perspective of the inscribed square can be found in the same way; *b'o'* is equal to *oo''* and *b'h'* to *oh*.

Prob. 14. (Fig. 5, Pl. XXVII.) *To find the perspective of a vertical cylinder.* The cylinder is tangent to V; *xy* is the vertical trace of the plane of the top. Construct the perspectives of the two bases by *Prob.* 12. Vertical lines tangent to the two curves will be the extreme elements of the cylinder.

Remark. In this problem, and some of the others, the perspectives appear somewhat unnatural; this is owing to the point of sight being taken too near the object; with more room this can be remedied.

Prob. 15. (Fig. 4, Pl. XXVIII.) ***To find the perspective of a cylinder whose axis is perpendicular to V.*** Let *abef* be the cylinder resting upon H. As the ends of the cylinder are parallel to V, their perspectives will be circles, and it will only be necessary to locate their centres and determine the length of their radii: *o'e'* is the indefinite perspective of the axis of the cylinder; *o'x* being equal to *ob*; *x* d_1 is the perspective of the diagonal through *s*; hence *r* is the perspective of the centre of the front end, and *rn*, the perspective of *o'z*, is the radius; *w* is the centre of the back end and *wa* the radius; lines drawn from *e'* tangent to these two circles will be the extreme elements of the cylinder.

The cylinder is represented with a square hole running through it; the perspective of the hole is left for the student to construct.

Construct the perspective of a cylinder with a circular hole running through it.

Prob. 16. (Fig. 3, Pl. XXVII.) ***To find the perspective of a rectangular block with a semicircular top.*** The lower part of the block is square, with a square opening in it; the top is semicircular with a triangular opening; *bea* represents the projection of the top when revolved about the horizontal diameter *be* of the semicircle until parallel to H; *c* is the centre of the picture; *d* and d_1 the vanishing points of diagonals, and also the vanishing points of the edges of the block, as it is placed diagonally to V.

The edge [illegible]*p* is equal to *qf*, and since it is in V, it is its own perspective; *p*d_1 and *q*d_1 are the indefinite perspectives of the upper and lower edges of the block; using the diagonal [illegible]*d* we obtain [illegible] as the perspective of the vertical edge, which is horizontally projected in *f*.

To obtain the perspective of the opening, make [illegible] and *pq* each equal to [illegible]; draw the lines *q*d_1 and *l*d_1; these are the indefinite perspectives of the top and bottom edges of the hole; the sides are obtained by erecting perpendiculars through the points *t* and *s*.

The completion of the rest of the perspective of the lower part of the block is evident from the figure.

To construct the perspective of the upper part, make $pk' = yk$; $ph' = mh$; $pv' = yv$; draw the lines $k'd_1$, $h'd_1$, $v'd_1$, where these meet perpendiculars, erected through t, g, r, will be points of the perspective; in the same way other points may be found if necessary. The completion of the perspective is left for the student.

Construct the perspective when the block is placed so that its edges will not vanish at d and d_1.

[illegible]

[illegible] and horizontally, termed *purlins* [illegible] the inclined beams, [illegible] termed *long rafters* [illegible] boards, slate, metal, etc., of the roof covering are attached. The top purlin [illegible] resting on the top of the main rafters, is termed the ridge beam; the bottom one, *O*, on which the ends of the long rafters rest, the *pole-plate.*

Drawing of a roof truss. We commence the drawing of the truss by constructing the triangle *abc* formed by the top line of the tie-beam and the inner lines of the main rafters. Next draw the centre lines *d—e* and *g—h* of the king and queen-posts; next the top line, *m—n*, of the straining beam.

Having thus made an outline sketch of the general form, proceed by putting in the other lines of the different beams in their order.

To show the connection of the queen-posts with the tie-beam, etc., a longitudinal section (Pl. VIII. Fig. 101) is given, which may be drawn on a larger scale, if requisite. Also a drawing to a larger scale is sometimes made, to show the connection between the bottom of the rafters and the tie-beam.

Remarks. As it is usual in drawings of simple frames like the above to give but one projection, showing only the cross dimensions of the beams in one direction, the dimensions in the other are witten either above, or alongside of the former. When above, a short line is drawn between them; when alongside, the sign × of multiplication is placed between them. The better plan is to write the number of the cross dimension that is projected in the usual way, and to place the other above it with a short line between, as in Pl. XI. Fig. *c*, that is, 8 inches by 9 inches.

Columns and Entablatures. In making drawings of these elements, it is usual to take the diameter of the column at the base, and divide it into sixty equal parts, termed *minutes*; the radius of the base containing thirty of those parts, and termed a *module*, being taken as the unit of measure, the fractional parts of which are minutes. For building purposes the actual dimensions of the various parts would be expressed in feet and fractional parts of a foot.

To commence the drawing, three parallel lines (Pl. IX. Fig. 102) are drawn on the left-hand side of the sheet of paper. The middle space, headed *S*, is designed to express the *heights*, or distances apart vertically of the main divisions;

that on the left, headed *R*, is for the heights of the subdivisions of the main portions; and that on the right, headed *T*, is for what are termed the *projections*, that is, the distances measured horizontally between the centre line, or *axis* of the column, and the parts which project beyond the axis.

At a suitable distance on the right of these lines another parallel, *X—Y*, is drawn for the axis of the column. At some suitable point, towards the bottom of the sheet, a perpendicular is drawn to the axis, and prolonged to cut the parallels to it. This last line is taken as the bottom line of the base of the column. From this line set off upwards—1st, the height of the base; 2d, that of the shaft of the column; 3d, that of the capital of the column; 4th, the three divisions of the entablature; and through these points draw parallels to the bottom line.

Commencing now at the top horizontal line set off along it from the axis to the right, the distance *a—b*, equal to the projection of the point *b*; in the same way the projections of the successive points, in their order below, as *d*, *f*, etc. Having marked these points distinctly, to guide the eye in drawing the other lines for projections, commence by setting off accurately, from the top downwards, the heights of the respective subdivisions along the space headed *R*. These being set off draw parallels, through the points set off, to the horizontals, commencing at the top, and guiding the eye and hand by the points *b*, *d*, etc., in order not to extend the lines unnecessarily beyond the axis.

Having drawn the horizontals, proceed to set off upon them their corresponding projections; which done, connect the horizontal lines by right lines, or arcs of circles, as shown in the figure.

Mouldings. The mouldings in architecture are the portions formed of curved surfaces. The outlines, or profiles of those in most common use in the Roman style, are shown in (Pl. IX. Fig. 108), they consist of either a single arc of a circle, which form what are termed *simple* mouldings; or of two or more arcs, termed *compound* mouldings. The arcs in the Plate are either semicircles, as in the *torus*, etc., or quadrants of a circle, as in the *ovolo*, *scotia*, etc. The manner of constructing these curves is explained (Pl. III. Figs. 39, 40, etc.).

The entire outline to the right of the axis is termed a *profile* of the column and entablature.

Remarks. In setting off projections, those of the parts above the shaft are sometimes estimated from the outer point of the radius of the top circle of the shaft; and those below it from the outer point of the lower radius; but the method above explained is considered the best, as more uniform.

Where the scale of the drawing is too large to admit of the entire column being represented, it is usual to make the drawing, as shown in the figure, a part of the shaft being supposed to be removed.

The outline of the sides of the shaft are usually curve lines, and constructed as follows:—Having drawn a line *o—p* (Pl. IX. Fig. 104) equal to the axis, and the lines of the top and bottom diameters being prolonged, set off on the latter their respective radii *o—b*, and *p—a*. From *a* set off a distance to the axis *a—c*, equal to *o—b*, the lower radius; and prolong *a—c*, to meet the lower diameter prolonged at *Z*. From the point *Z* draw lines cutting the axis at several points, as *d*, *e*, *f*, etc. From these points set off along the lines *Z—d*, etc., the lengths *d—m*, *e—n*, &c., respectively equal to *a—c*, or the lower radius; the points *m*, *n*, etc., joined, will be the outline of the side of the column.

Arches. (Pl. VIII. Fig. 105.) The arch of simplest form, and most usual application in structures, is the *cylindrical*, that is, one of which the cross section is the same throughout, and upon the interior surface of which, termed the *soffit* of the arch, right lines can be drawn between the two ends of it. The cross sections of most usual form are the semicircle, an arc of a circle, oval curves, and curves of four centres

Right arch. The example selected for this drawing is the one with a semicircular cross section, the elements of the cylinder being perpendicular to the ends, and which is termed the *full centre right arch.*

We commence this drawing by constructing, in the first place, the elevation of the *face*, or the front view of the end of the arch. Having drawn a ground line *G—L*, set off from any point, as C, a distance a—l, equal to the diameter of the extrados of the cross-section; erecting perpendiculars at a and l, set off on them the equal distances a—A and l—L, for the height of the lower lines of the arch above the horizontal base of projection; join A and L, and on it describe the semicircle A l L. And from the same centre O another semicircle, with an assumed radius OD. Divide the semicircle A l L into an odd number of equal parts, as five, for example; and from the centre draw the radii Om, On, through the points of division m, n, etc., and prolong them to m', n', etc., on the outer semicircle. From the points D, m', n', etc., draw the vertical lines D—d, m'—c, n'—e, etc., to intersect the horizontal lines drawn through m, n, etc. The pentagonal figures D[illegible], II, etc., thus formed will be the form of the arch stones or the faces of the arch. The top stone, as at I, is termed the key-stone; its vertical side [illegible]—g is known as [illegible].

Having obtained the shapes of the face stones, we next proceed to draw those of the face of the wall contiguous to them. The manner of combining the stones of these two parts is purely arbitrary. The only rule is so to combine the horizontal lines of the two as to present a pleasing architectural effect to the eye. The usual method for obtaining this result is to bring the horizontal lines of the face of the wall on each side of the arch to be the prolongations of those D—d, m—c, etc., of the arch; and so to divide the vertical distances d—c, n—e, etc., that the distances between the intermediate horizontal lines be as nearly equal as practicable. The distances between the horizontals of the face of the wall below the arch are usually the same, and equal to those just above.

If the walls on which the arch rests are built for the sole purpose of supporting it they are termed *abutments*. The portions of these, here shown in front view, are termed the *ends*, or *heads* of the abutments; the portions projected in A—a, and B—b, and lying below the soffit of the arch, are termed the *sides* or *faces*.

The lines projected in A, and B, along which the soffit joins the faces of the abutments, are termed the *springing lines* of the arch. The right line projected in O, and parallel to the springing lines, is termed the *axis* of the arch. The right lines of the soffit projected in m, n, etc., are termed the *soffit edges* of the *coursing joints* of the arch; the lines $m—m'$, $n—n'$, etc., the *face edges* of the same.

To construct a longitudinal section of the arch by a vertical plane through the axis of which the trace on the face is the line $M—N$, commence by drawing a line $b''—B''$ parallel to $b—B$, and at any convenient distance from the front elevation; from b'' set off along the ground line the distance $b''—b'$, equal to that between the front and back faces, or the length of the arch; from b' draw $b'—B'$ parallel to $b''—B''$, and prolong upwards these two lines. The rectangle $b'B'B''b''$ will be the projection of the face of the abutment on the plane of section; the line $b'—B'$, corresponding to that $b—B$, etc. Drawing the horizontal lines $B''—B'$, $m''—m'''$, etc., at the same height above the ground line as the respective points B, m, etc., they will be the projections of the soffit edges of the coursing joints. The half of the soffit on the right of the plane of section $M—N$, is projected into the rectangle $B'C'C''B''$. The arch stones k, k, etc., forming the key of the arch, are represented in section, the two forming the ends of greater depth than those intermediate, as is very often done. That is, the key-stones at the ends, and the end walls of the abutments, are built up higher than the interior masonry between them; the top of this last being represented by the dotted line $o—p$ in the elevation and the full line $o—p'$ on the cross section.

The arch stones running through from one end to the other, and projected between any two soffit edges, as $B''—B'$, and $m''—m'''$, are termed a *string course*. The contiguous stones running from one springing line to the other, as those projected in k, k', k'', &c., are termed *ring courses*. The lines, of which those $r—s$ are the projections, are the soffit edges of the joints, termed *heading joints*, between the stones of the string courses. These edges in one course alternate with those of the courses on either side of it.

The cross section on $R—S$ requires no particular explanation. From its conventional lines, it will be seen that the

[illegible]

[illegible]

[illegible] conditions. [illegible] VII. Fig. 10.

CHAPTER XIV

MECHANISM.

Prob. 114. (Pl. XIV. Fig. 137.) *To construct the projections of a cylindrical spur wheel.*

The wheel work employed, in mechanism, to transmit the motion of rotation of one shaft to another (the axis of the second being parallel to that of the first), usually consists of a cylindrical disk, or ring, from the exterior surface of which projects a spur shaped combination, termed *teeth*, or *cogs*, so arranged that, the teeth on one wheel interlocking with those of the other, any motion of rotation, received by the one wheel, is communicated to the other by the mutual pressure of the sides of the teeth. There are various methods by which this is effected; but it will be only necessary in this place to describe the one of most usual and simple construction, for the object we have in view.

The thickness of each tooth, and the width of the space between each pair of teeth, are set off upon the circumference of a circle, which is termed the *pitch line* or *pitch circle*. The thickness of the tooth and the width of the space taken together, as measured along the pitch line, is termed the *pitch of the tooth.* The pitch being divided into eleven equal parts, five of these parts are taken for the thickness of the tooth, and six for the width of the space. Having given the radius *o—m* of the pitch circle, and described this circle, it must first be divided into as many parts, each equal to *b—h*, the pitch of the teeth, as the number of teeth. Having made this division, the outline of each tooth may be set out as follows:—From the point *h*, with the distance *h—b* as a radius, describe an arc *b—c*, outwards from the pitch circle; having set off *b—e*, the thickness of the tooth; from the point *k*, with the same radius, describe the arc *e—f*. To obtain the *apex c—f*, of the tooth, which may be either a right line, or an arc described from *o* as a centre; place this arc three-tenths of the pitch *b—h* from the pitch line. The sides of the tooth, within the [illegible] circle, are in the directions of radii drawn from the [illegible] and [illegible] The bottom *d—g* of each space is also an arc, [illegible] from *o*, and at a distance, from and within the [illegible] of four-tenths of the pitch. From the preceding [illegible], the outline of each tooth will be the same as [illegible] of each space *fdgi*. The curved portions [illegible] each tooth are termed the *faces*, the straight [illegible] and *d—e*, the *flanks*. The outline here [illegible] profile of the parts, made by a plane [illegible] axis of the cylindrical surface, to which [illegible] which surface forms the bottom of [illegible] of the teeth is the same as the [illegible] surface to which they are attached.

[illegible] teeth are attached or of which they [illegible] same material as the teeth; [illegible] central *boss*, either by *arms*, like [illegible] or else by a thin plate. The [illegible] large wheels; the latter for [illegible]

[illegible] are let into the rims, by holes [illegible] wheels, the rim and teeth [illegible] the latter material is [illegible] are also cast in one piece [illegible] wheels; but in large sized [illegible] separate portions, which are [illegible] arms, &c.

[illegible] suppose, for simplifica- [illegible] the latter being [illegible] each face of the [illegible] the same as that of [illegible] placed.

[illegible] horizontal and [illegible] position of the [illegible] vertical projec- [illegible] horizontal projec- [illegible] that of the [illegible] and *E—O'*, [illegible]

[illegible] apex, and the

bottom of each space are all portions of cylindrical surfaces, the elements of which are parallel to the axis of the wheel. The horizontal projections of the edges of the teeth $C''-C'$ and $F''-F'$, which correspond to the points projected in c, and f, as well as those of the spaces, which correspond to the points a and d, will be right lines parallel to $O-O'$. Drawing the projections as $C-C'$, and $F-F'$, &c., of these edges, we obtain the complete horizontal projection of the wheel.

Prob. 115. (Pl. XIV. Fig. 138.) *To construct the projections of the same wheel when the axis is still horizontal but oblique to the vertical plane.*

As in the preceding *Probs.*, of like character to this, the horizontal projection of all the parts will, in this position of the axis, be the same as in the preceding case; and the vertical projections will be found as in like cases. The pitch circle and other circles on the faces of the wheel, and the ends of the boss, will be projected in ellipses; the transverse axes of which are the vertical diameters of these circles; and the conjugate axes the vertical projections of the correspond ing horizontal diameters. The vertical projections of the edges of the teeth, which correspond to the horizontal projections $C-C'$, and $F-F'$, &c., will be the lines $c-c'''$, and $f-f'''$, &c., parallel to the projection $o'-o''$, of the axis.

Prob. 116. (Pl. XV. Fig. 139.) *To construct the projections of a mitre, or beveled wheel, the axis of the wheel being horizontal, and perpendicular to the vertical plane.*

The spur wheel, we have seen, is one in which the teeth project beyond a cylindrical rim, attached to a central boss either by arms, or by a thin connecting plate; moreover that portions of the teeth project beyond the pitch line, or circle, whilst other portions lie within this line. *Mitre*, or *beveled wheels*, are those in which the teeth are attached to the surface of a conical rim; the rim being connected with a central boss, either by arms, or a connecting plate. In the beveled wheel the faces of the teeth project beyond an imaginary conical surface, termed the *pitch cone*, whilst the flanks lie within the pitch cone. The faces and flanks are conical surfaces, which have the same vertex as the pitch cone; the apex of each tooth is either a plane, or a conical [illegible] would pass through the vertex [illegible] of the space between each [illegible] cone, or a plane passing through [illegible]

[illegible] be on conical surfaces, [illegible] perpendicular to those of the pitch [illegible]

[illegible] it will be necessary to [illegible] as well as the rim from [illegible] V be the vertex of the [illegible] its generating triangle. [illegible] $V—n$ and $V—m$, let [illegible] prolonged, be the [illegible] the larger ends of the [illegible] distances $m—m'$ and [illegible] respectively parallel to [illegible] of the cone, and $v'm'n'$ [illegible] other end of the teeth [illegible]

[illegible] of which v is [illegible] of the circle of its [illegible] with the radius [illegible] the teeth, together [illegible] as in the preceding [illegible] tooth and space [illegible] to $a—b$, for the [illegible] describe the circle [illegible] we wrap this [illegible] mark out upon its [illegible] teeth; and we [illegible] beyond [illegible] If we next [illegible] the several [illegible] between them. [illegible] drawn will [illegible] and the [illegible] having the [illegible] teeth, will [illegible] ends of the teeth and rim. The length of each tooth, measured along the element $V—n$ of the pitch cone, will be $n—n'$.

To construct the vertical projection of the wheel, we observe, in the first place, that the points n, b, e, &c. (Fig. B), where the faces and flanks join, lie upon the circumference of the circle of which $o—n$ is the radius, and which is the pitch circle for the outline of the ends of the teeth; in like manner that the points e, f, &c., of the apex of each tooth, lie on a circle of which $p—q$ is the radius; the points s, a, d, &c., lie on the circle of which $r—s$ is the radius; and the interior circle of the rim has $t—u$ for its radius. The radii of the corresponding circles, on the smaller ends of the teeth and rim, are $o'—n'$; $p'—q'$; $r'—s'$; and $t—u'$. In the second place all these circles are parallel to the vertical plane of projection, since the axis of the wheel is perpendicular to this plane, and they will therefore be projected on this plane in their true dimensions.

From the point O then, the vertical projection of the axis, describe in the first place the four concentric circles with the radii $O—Q$, $O—N$, $O—S$, and $O—U$ respectively equal to $p—q$, $o—n$, &c.; and, from the same centre, the four others with radii $O—Q'$, &c', respectively equal to $p'—q'$, &c.

On the circle having the radius $O—N$, set off the points N, B, E, &c., corresponding to n, b, e, &c.; on the one $O—Q$, the points C, F, &c., corresponding to c, f, &c.; on the one $O—S$, the points S, A, D, &c., corresponding to s, a, d, &c. From the points C and F, thus set off, draw right lines to the point O; the portions of these lines, intercepted between the circles of which $O—Q$ and $O—Q'$ are respectively the radii, with the portions of the arcs, as $C—F$, $C'—F'$, intercepted between these lines, will form the outline of the vertical projection of the figure of the apex of the tooth. The portions of the lines, drawn from B and E to O, intercepted between the circles described with the radii $O—N$ and $O—N'$, together with the portions of the lines forming the edge of the apex, and the curve lines $B—C$, $E—F$ and the corresponding curves $B'—C'$, $F'—E'$ on the smaller end, will be the projections of the outlines of the faces and flanks of the tooth. The outline of the projection of the bottom of the space will lie between the right lines drawn from S and A to O, and the arcs $S—A$, $S'—A'$, intercepted between these lines, on the circles described with the radii $O—S$, and $O—S'$.

The projection of the cylindrical eye of the boss is the circle described with the radius $O—K$. Having completed the vertical projection, the corresponding points in horizontal projection are found by projecting the points C, F, B, E, A, D, &c., into their respective circumferences (Fig. A) at c, f, b, &c. The portions of the lines drawn from C and F to D, in vertical projection, will, in horizontal projection, be drawn from c' and f' to V; and so for the other elements of the surfaces of the faces, flanks, &c., of the teeth. The horizontal projection of the larger end of each tooth will be a figure like the one $a'b'c'f'e'd'$.

The boss projects beyond the rim at the larger end of the wheel; it is usually a hollow cylinder. Its horizontal projection is the figure $xyzv$, &c.

Prob. 111. (Pl. XV. Fig. 140.) *To construct the projection of the same wheel, when the axis is oblique to the vertical plane, and parallel as before to the horizontal.*

This variation of the problem requires no particular verbal explanation, as from preceding problems of the like character, and the Figs. the manner in which the vertical projections are obtained from the horizontal will be readily made out. The best manner however of commencing the vertical projection will be to draw, in the first place (Fig. D), all the ellipses which are the projections of the circles described with the radii $O—Q$, $O—N$, &c. (Fig. C), and next those of the vertices of the three cones, which will be the points [illegible]. These being drawn the projections of the different lines forming the outline of the projection of any tooth, can be easily determined.

Prob. 112. (Pl. X. Fig. [illegible]) *To construct the projection [illegible].*

[illegible] it will be requisite to show how [illegible] can be so marked out on the surface of a [illegible] that when this surface is developed [illegible] a right line on the development; [illegible] having a right line drawn on the developed surface of a right circular cylinder, to find the projection of this line, when the development is wrapped around the surface.

Let *ABCD* be the horizontal projection of the cylinder: *acc'a'* its vertical projection; *O* and the line *o—o'* the projections of its axis. Let the circle of the base be divided into any number of equal parts, for example eight, and draw the vertical projections *e—e'*, *f—f'*, &c., corresponding to the points of division *E*, *F*, &c. Having found the development of this cylinder, by constructing a rectangle (Pl. X. Fig. 142), of which the base *a—a* is equal to the circumference of the cylinder's base, and the altitude *a—a'* is that of the cylinder; through the points *e*, *b*, *f*, *c*, &c., respectively equal to the equal parts *A—E*, &c., of the circle, draw the lines *e—e'*, *b—b'*, &c., parallel to *a—a'*. These lines will be the developed positions of the elements of the cylinder, projected in *e—e'*, *b—b'*, &c. Now on this development let any inclined line, as *a—m*, be drawn; and from the point *n*, at the same height above the point *a*, on the left, as the point *m* is above *a* on the right, let a second inclined line *n—m'* be drawn parallel to *a—m*; and so on as many more equidistant inclined parallels as may be requisite. Now it will be observed, that the first line, *a—m*, cuts the different elements of the cylinder at the points marked 1, 2, 3, &c.; and therefore when the development of the cylinder is wrapped around it these points will be found on the projections of the same elements, and at the same heights above the projection of the base as they are on the development. Taking, for example, the elements projected in *b—b'*, and *c—c'*, the points 2 and 4 of the projection of the helix will be at the same heights, *b—2*, and *c—4* on the projections, above *a—c*, as they are on the development above *a—a*. It will be further observed, that the helix of which *a—m* is the development will extend entirely around the cylinder; so that the point *m*, on the projection, will coincide with the two *m* and *n* on the development, when the latter is wrapped round; and so on for the other points *m*, *n'*, and *m'*; so that the inclined parallels will, in projection, form a continuous line or helix uniformly wound around the cylinder. Moreover, it will be seen, if through the points 1, 2, 3, &c., on the development, lines are drawn parallel to the base a—a, that these lines will be equidistant, or in other words the point 2 is at the same height above 1, as 1 is above a, &c.; and that, in projection also, these points will be at the same heights above each other; this gives an easy method of constructing any helix on a cylinder when the height between its lowest and highest point for one turn around the cylinder is given. To show this; having divided the base of the cylinder into any number of equal parts (Pl. X. Fig. 141), and drawn the vertical projections of the corresponding elements, set off from the foot of any element, as a, at which the helix commences, the height a—m, at which the helix is to end on the same element; divide a—m into the same number of equal parts as the base; through the points of division draw lines parallel to a—c, the projection of the base; the points in which these parallels cut the projections of the elements will be the required points of the projection of the helix; drawing the curved line a, 1, 2, &c., through these points it will be the required projection.

Having explained the method for obtaining the projections of a helix on a cylinder, that of obtaining the projections of the parts of a screw with a square fillet will be easily understood.

Prob. 119. (Pl. XVI. Fig. 148.) *To construct the projections of a screw with a square fillet.*

Draw as before a circle, with any assumed radius A—B, for the base of the solid cylinder which forms what is termed the newel of the screw, and around which the fillet is wrapped. Construct, as above, the projections of two parallel helices on the newel, the one $a2a$; the other $x2x$: their distance apart [illegible] being the height, or thickness of the fillet, estimated along the element a—a of the cylinder. From O, with a radius [illegible], describe another circle, such that [illegible] shall be the breadth of the fillet as estimated in a direction perpendicular to the axis of the newel: and let the [illegible] be the vertical projection of this cylinder. Having divided the base of the second cylinder into a like number of equal parts corresponding to the first, and drawn the vertical projections of the elements corresponding to these points, as $b—b'$, &c., construct the vertical projection of a helix on this cylinder, which, commencing at the point a'' shall in one turn reach the point m'', at the same height above a'' as the point m is above a. The helix thus found will evidently cut the elements of the outer cylinder at the same heights above the base as the corresponding one on the inner cylinder cuts the corresponding elements to those of the first; the projections of the two will evidently cross each other at the point 2 on the line $b—b'$. In like manner construct a second helix $x''22''$, on the second cylinder and parallel to the first, commencing at a point x'' at the same height above a'' as x is above a. This, in like manner, will cross the projection $x2z$ at the point 2. The four projections of helices thus found will be the projections of the exterior and interior lines of the fillet; the exterior surface of which will coincide with that of the exterior cylinder, and the top and bottom surfaces of which will lie between the corresponding helices at top and bottom. The void space between the fillet which lies between the exterior cylinder and the surface of the newel is termed the *channel;* its dimensions are usually the same as those of the fillet.

Prob. 120. (Pls. XVI. XVII. Figs. 144 to 157.) *To construct the lines showing the usual combination of the working beam, the crank, and the connecting rod of a steam engine.*

In a drawing of the kind of which the principal object is to show the combination of the parts, no other detail is put down but what is requisite to give an idea of the general forms and dimensions of the main pieces, and their relative positions as determined by the motions of which they are susceptible.

As each element of this combination is symmetrically disposed with respect to a central line, or axis, we commence the drawing by setting off, in the first place, these central lines in any assumed position of the parts; these are the lines $o—f$, the distance from the centre of motion of the working beam A to that of its connexion with the connecting rod B, and which is 3 inches and 55 hundredths of an inch actual measurement on the drawing, or 4 feet 48 hundredths of the machine itself, the scale of the drawing being 1 inch to [illegible] foot, or [illegible]; next the line [illegible], the distance of the centre of motion [illegible] to that [illegible] of the connecting rod and crank [illegible]; lastly the line [illegible]—c, from the centre of motion [illegible] to that d of the crank and the working shaft, the actual distance being 1 inch 34 hundredths. These lines being accurately set off, the outlines of the parts which are symmetrically placed with respect to them may be then set off, such dimensions as are not written down being obtained by using the scale of the drawing, or from the more detailed Figs. 145 to 157.

Having completed the outlines we next add a sufficient number of lines, termed *indicating lines*, to show the amplitude of motion of the parts, or the space passed over between the extreme positions of the axes, as well as the direction or *paths* in which the parts move. These are shown by the arc described from [illegible] with the radius [illegible]; the circle described with [illegible]; the lines [illegible], [illegible], and [illegible], the extreme and mean positions of the axis [illegible], with b—i, and b—g the extreme positions of [illegible].

Besides the axes and indicating lines, others which may be termed *axial lines*, being lines drawn across the centre of motion of articulations as through the point of the axis on cross sections, are requisite for the full understanding of the combinations of the parts; such, for example, as the lines x—x and [illegible], on Fig. 147, which is a cross section of the connecting rod made at n—o, n'—o', Figs. 145, 146; those X—Y, X'—Y', &c.; those Z—W, Z—W' on Figs. 148 to 157.

Prob. 121. (Pl. XVIII. Figs. 158 to 170.) *To make the measurements, the sketches, and finished drawing of a machine from the machine itself.*

A very important part of the business of the draftsman and engineer is that of taking the measurements of industrial objects, with a view to making a finished drawing from the rough sketches made at the time of the measurements. For the purposes of this latter, the draftsman requires the usual instruments for measuring distances and determining the horizontal and vertical distances apart of points; as the carpenter's rule, measuring rods, or tape, compasses, chalk line, an ordinary level, and a plumb line. The first three are used for ascertaining the actual distances between points, lines, &c.; the chalk line to mark out on the parts to be measured central lines, or axes; the two last to determine the horizontal and vertical distances between points. For sketching, paper ruled into small squares with blue, or any other colored lines, is most convenient; such as is used, for example, by engineers in plotting sections of ground. With such paper, or lead pencil, and pen and ink, the draftsman needs nothing more to note down the relative positions of the parts with considerable accuracy. Taking for example the side of the small square to represent one or more units of the scale adopted for the sketch, he can judge, by the eye, pretty accurately, the fractional parts to be set off. In making measurements, it should be borne in mind, that it is better to lose the time of making a dozen useless ones, than to omit a single necessary one. The sketch is usually made in lead pencil, but it should be put in ink, by going over the pencil lines with a pen, as soon as possible; otherwise the labor may be lost from the effacing of numbers or lines by wear. The lines running lengthwise and crosswise on the paper, and which divide its surface into squares, will serve, as vertical and horizontal lines on the sketch, to guide the hand and eye where projections are required.

It is important to remember, that in making measurements we must not take it for granted that lines are parallel that seem so to the eye; as, for example, in the sides of a room, house, &c. In all such cases the diagonals should be measured. These are indispensable lines in all rectilineal figures which are either regular or irregular except the square and rectangle.

The mechanism selected for illustrating this *Prob.* is the ordinary machine termed a *crab engine* for raising heavy weights. It consists, 1st (Fig. 158), of a frame work composed of two standards of cast iron *A*, *A*, connected by wrought iron rods *b*, *b* with screws and nuts; the frame being firmly fastened, by bolts passing through holes in the bottoms of the standards, to a solid bed of timber framing; 2d, of the mechanism for raising the weights, a *drum B* to which is fastened a toothed wheel *C* that *gears* or works into a pinion *D* placed on the axle *a;* 3d, two crank arms *E* where the animal power as that of men is applied ; 4th, of a rope wound round the drum, at the end of which the resistance or weight to be raised is attached.

The sketch (Figs. 159 to 168) is commenced by measuring the end view *A′* of the standards and other parts as shown in this view ; next that of the side view, as shown in (Fig. 160). To save room, the middle portion of the drum *B″*, &c., is omitted here, but the distances apart of the different portions laid down. These parts should be placed in the same relative positions on the sketch as they will have in projection on the finished drawing (Figs. 169, 170). The drum being, in the example chosen, of cast iron, sections of a portion of it are given in Figs. 163, 164. The other details speak for themselves.

The chief point in making measurements is a judicious selection of a sufficient number of the best views, and then a selection of the best lines to commence with from which the details are to be laid in. This is an affair of practice. The draftsman will frequently find it well to use the chalk line to mark out some guiding lines on the machine to be copied, before commencing his measurements, so as to obtain central lines of beams, &c. ; and the sides of triangles formed by the meeting of these lines.

CHAPTER XV.

TOPOGRAPHICAL DRAWING.

THE term topographical drawing is applied to the methods adopted for representing by lines, or other processes, both the natural features of the surface of any given locality, and the fixed artificial objects which may be found on the surface.

This is effected, by the means of projections, and profiles, or sections, as in the representation of other bodies, combined with certain conventional signs to designate more clearly either the forms, or the character of the objects of which the projections are given.

As it would be very difficult and, indeed with very few exceptions, impossible to represent, by the ordinary modes of projection, the natural features of a locality of any considerable extent, both on account of the irregularities of the surface, and the smallness of the scale to which drawings of objects of considerable size must necessarily be limited, a method has been resorted to by which the horizontal distances apart of the various points of the surface can be laid down with great accuracy even to very small scales, and also the vertical distances be expressed with equal accuracy either upon the plan, or by profiles.

To explain these methods by a familiar example which any one can readily illustrate practically, let us suppose (Pl. XIX. Fig. 171) a large and somewhat irregularly shaped potato, melon, or other like object selected, and after being carefully cut through its centre lengthwise, so that the section shall coincide as nearly as practicable with a plane surface, let one half of it be cut into slices of equal thickness by sections parallel to the one through the centre. This being done, let the slices be accurately placed on each other, so as to preserve the original shape, and then two pieces of straight stiff wire, *A*, *B*, be run through all the slices, taking care to place the wires as nearly perpendicular as practicable to the surface of the board on which the bottom slice rests, and into which they must be firmly inserted. Having marked out carefully on the surface of the board the outline of the figure of the under side of the bottom slice, take up the slices, being careful not to derange the positions of the wires, and, laying aside the bottom slice, place the one next above it on the two wires, in the position it had before being taken up, and, bringing its under side in contact with the board, mark out also its outline as in the first slice. The second slice being laid aside, proceed in the same manner to mark out the outline on the board of each slice in its order from the bottom; by which means supposing the number of slices to have been five a figure represented by Fig. 171 will be obtained. Now the curve first traced may be regarded as the outline of the base of the solid, on a horizontal plane; whilst the other curves in succession, from the manner in which they have been traced, may be regarded as the horizontal projections of the different curves that bound the lower surfaces of the different slices; but, as these surfaces are all parallel to the plane of the base, the curves themselves will be the horizontal curves traced upon the surface of the solid at the same vertical height above each other. With the projections of these curves therefore, and knowing their respective heights above the base, we are furnished with the means of forming some idea of the shape and dimensions of the surface in question. Finally, if to this projection of the horizontal curves we join one or more profiles, by vertical planes intersecting the surface lengthwise and crosswise, we shall obtain as complete an idea of the surface as can be furnished of an object of this character which cannot be classed under any regular geometrical law.

The projections of the horizontal curves being given as well as the uniform vertical distance between them, it will be very easy to construct a profile of the surface by any vertical plane. Let $X—Y$ be the trace of any such vertical plane, and the points marked x, x', x'', &c., be those in which it cuts the projections of the curves from the base upwards. Let $G—L$ be a ground line, parallel to $X—Y$, above which the points horizontally projected in x, x', x'', &c., are to be vertically projected. Drawing perpendiculars from these points to $G—L$, the point x will be projected into the ground line at y; that marked x' above the ground line at y', at the height of the first curve next to the base above the horizontal plane; the one marked x'', will be vertically projected in y'', at the same vertical height above x' as y' is above y; and so on for the other points. We see therefore that if through the points y, y', y'', &c., we draw lines $y'—y'$, &c., parallel to the ground line these lines will be at equal distances apart, and are the vertical projections of the lines in which the profile plane cuts the different horizontal planes that contain the curves of the surface, and that the curve traced through $yy'y''$, &c., is the one cut from the surface. In like manner any number of profiles that might be deemed requisite to give a complete idea of the surface could be constructed.

In examining the profile in connexion with the horizontal projection of the curves it will be seen that the curve of the profile is more or less steep in proportion as the horizontal projections of the curves are the nearer to or farther from each other. This fact then enables us to form a very good idea of the form of the surface from the horizontal projections *alone* of its curves; as the distance apart of the curves will indicate the greater or less declivity of the surface, and their form as evidently shows where the surface would present a convex, or concave appearance to the eye.

For any small object, like the one which has served for our illustration, the same scale may be used for both the horizontal and vertical projections. But in the delineation of large objects, which require to be drawn on a small scale, to accommodate the drawing to the usual dimensions of the paper used for the purpose, it often becomes impracticable to make the profile on the same scale as the plan, owing to the smallness of the vertical dimensions as compared with the horizontal ones. For example, let us suppose a hill of irre gular shape, like the object of our preceding illustration, and that the horizontal curve of its base is three miles in its longest direction, and two in its narrowest, and that the highest point of the hill above its base is ninety feet; and let us further suppose that we have the projections of the horizontal curves of the hill for every three feet estimated vertically. Now supposing the drawing of the plan made to a scale of one foot to one mile, the curve of the base would require for its delineation a sheet of paper at least 3 feet long and 2 feet broad. Supposing moreover the projection of the summit of the hill to be near the centre of the base and the declivity from this point in all directions sensibly uniform, it will be readily seen that the distance apart of the horizontal curves, estimated along the longest diameter of the curve of the base will be about half an inch, and along the shortest one about one-third of an inch; so that although the linear dimensions of the horizontal projections are only the $\frac{1}{5280}$ of the actual dimensions of the hill yet no difficulty will be found in putting in the horizontal curves. But if it were required to make a profile on the same scale we should at once see that with our ordinary instruments it would be impracticable. For as any linear space on the drawing is only the $\frac{1}{5280}$ part of the corresponding space of the object, it follows that for a vertical height of three feet, the distance between the horizontal curves, will be represented on the drawing [illegible] by the $\frac{1}{1760}$ part of a foot, a distance too small to be laid off by our usual means. Now to meet this kind of difficulty, the method has been devised of drawing profiles by maintaining the same horizontal distances between the points as on the plan, but making the vertical distances on a scale, any multiple whatever greater than that of the plan, which may be found convenient. For example, in the case before us, by preserving the same scale as that of the plan for the horizontal distances, the total length of the profile would be 3 feet; but if we adopt for the vertical distances a scale of $\frac{1}{10}$ of an inch to one foot, then the vertical distance between the horizontal curves would be $\frac{3}{10}$ of an inch, and the summit of the profile would be 9 inches above the base. It will be readily seen that this method will not alter the relative vertical distances of the points from each other; for $\frac{3}{10}$ of an inch, the distance between any two horizontal curves on the profile, is the $\frac{1}{30}$ of 9 inches the height of the projection of the summit, just as 3 feet is the $\frac{1}{30}$ of 90 feet on the actual object. But it will be further seen that the profile otherwise gives us no assistance in forming an idea of the actual shape and slopes of the object, and in fact rather gives a very erroneous and distorted view of them.

Plane of Comparison, or *Reference*. To obviate the trouble of making profiles, and particularly when the scale of the plan is so small that a distorted and therefore erroneous view may be given by the profile made on a larger scale than that of the plan, recourse is had to the projections alone of the horizontal curves, and to numbers written upon them which express their respective heights above some assumed horizontal plane, which is termed the plane of reference, or of comparison. In Fig. 171, for example, the plane of the base may be regarded as the one from which the heights of all objects above it are estimated. If the scale of this drawing was $\frac{1}{4}$ of an inch to $\frac{1}{2}$ an inch, and the actual distance between the planes of the horizontal curves was equal to $\frac{1}{2}$ an inch, then the curves would, in their order from the bottom, be $\frac{1}{2}$ an inch vertically above each other. To express this fact by numbers, let there be written upon the projection of the curve of the base the cypher (0); upon the next this (1); &c. These numbers thus written will indicate that the height of each curve in its order above that of the base is $\frac{1}{2}$, $\frac{2}{2}$, $\frac{3}{2}$, &c., of an inch. The unit of measure of the object in this case being half an inch. The numbers so written are termed the *references* of the curves, as they indicate their heights above the plane to which reference is made in estimating these heights.

The selection of the position of the plane of comparison is at the option of the draftsman; as this position, however chosen, will in no respects change the actual heights of the points with respect to each other; making only the references of each greater or smaller as the plane is assumed at a lower or higher level. Some fixed and well defined point is usually taken for the position of this plane. In the topography of localities near the sea, or where the height of any point of the locality above the lowest level of tide water is known, this level is usually taken as that of the plane of comparison. This presents a convenient starting point when all the curves of the surface that require to be found lie in planes *above* this level. But if there are some below it, as those of the extension of the shores below low water, then it presents a difficulty, as these last curves would require a different mode of reference from the first to distinguish them. This difficulty may be gotten over by numbering them thus (-1), (-2), &c., with the - sign before each, to indicate references belonging to points below the plane of comparison. The better method, however, in such a case, is to assume the plane of comparison at any convenient number of units below the lowest water level, so that the references may all be written with numbers of the same kind.

References. In all cases, to avoid ambiguity and to provide for references expressed in fractional parts of the unit, the references of whole numbers alone are written thus (2.0), that is the integer followed by a decimal point, and a 0; those of mixed or broken numbers, thus (2.30), (3.58), (0.37), &c., that is with the whole number followed by two decimal places to express the fractional part.

Projections of the Horizontal Curves. No invariable rule can be laid down with respect to the vertical distance apart at which the horizontal curves should be taken. This distance must be dependent on the scale of the drawing, and the purpose which the drawing is intended to subserve. In drawings on a large scale, such for example as are to serve for calculating excavations and embankments, horizontal curves may be put in at distances of a foot, or even at less distances apart. In maps on a smaller scale they may be from a yard upwards apart. Taking the scale No. 8, in the Table of Scales farther on, which is one inch to 50 feet, or $\frac{1}{600}$, as that of a detailed drawing, the horizontal curves may be put in even as close as one foot apart vertically. A convenient rule may be adopted as a guide in such cases, which is to divide 600 by the fraction representing the ratio which designates the scale, and to take the resulting quotient to express the number of feet vertically between the horizontal curves. Thus $600 \div \frac{1}{600}$ gives one foot as the required distance; $600 \div \frac{1}{1800}$ gives 3 feet; $600 \div \frac{1}{300}$ gives the half of a foot, &c., &c.

But whatever may be this assumed distance the portion of the surface lying between any two adjacent curves is supposed to be such, that a line drawn from a point on the upper curve, in a direction perpendicular to it and prolonged to meet the lower, is assumed to coincide with the real surface. This hypothesis, although not always strictly in accordance with the facts, approximates near enough to accuracy for all practical purposes; especially in drawings made to a small scale, or in those on a large one where the curves are taken one foot apart or nearer to each other.

Let *d* (Fig. 172) for instance be a point on the curve (3.0), drawing from it a right line perpendicular to the direction of the tangent to the curve (3.0) at the point *d*, and prolonging it to *c* on the curve (2.0), the line *d—c* is regarded as the projection of the line of the surface between the points projected in *d* and *c*. In like manner *a—b* may be regarded as the projection of a line on the portion of the surface between the same curves. It will be observed however that the line *a—b* is quite oblique with respect to the curve (2.0), whereas *d—c* is nearly perpendicular to (2.0) as well as to (3.0), owing to the portions of the curves where these lines are drawn being more nearly parallel to each other in the one case than in the other. This would give for the portion to which *a—b* belongs a less approximation to accuracy than in the other portion referred to. To obtain a nearer degree of approximation in such cases, portions of intermediate horizontal curves as *x—x*, *y—y*, &c., may be put in as follows. Suppose one of the new curves *y—y* is to be midway between (2.0) and (3.0). Having drawn several lines as *a—b*, bisect each of them, and through the points thus obtained draw the curve *y—y*, which will be the one midway required. In like manner other intermediate curves as *x—x*, *y—y* may be drawn. Having put in these curves, the true line of declivity, between the points *e* and *f* for example, will be the curved or broken line, $e—f$ cutting the intermediate curves at right angles to the tangents where it crosses them.

The intermediate curves are usually only marked in pencil, as they serve simply to give the position of the line that shows the direction of greatest declivity of the surface between the two given curves.

Prob. 122. *Having the references of a number of points on a drawing, as determined by an instrumental survey, to construct from these data the approximate projection of the equidistant horizontal curves having whole numbers for references.*

Engineers employ various methods for determining equidistant horizontal curves, either directly by an instrumental process on the ground, or by constructions, based upon the considerations just explained, from data obtained by the ordinary means of leveling, &c.

Let us suppose for example that $ABCD$ (Fig. 173) represents the outline of a portion of ground which has been divided up into squares of 50 feet by the lines $x—x$, $x'—x'$, $y—y$, &c., run parallel to the sides $A—B$ and $A—C$, and that pickets having been driven at the points where these lines cut each other and the parallel sides, it has been determined by the usual methods of leveling that these points have the references respectively written near them. With these data it is required to determine the projections of the equidistant horizontal curves with whole number references which lie one foot apart vertically.

Having set off a line $A—x$ (Fig. 174), equal to $A—x$, on (Fig. 173) draw perpendiculars to it at the points A and x. From these two points set off along the perpendiculars any number of an assumed unit (say half an inch as the one taken), and divide each one into ten equal parts. Through these points of division draw lines parallel to $A—x$.

Cut from a piece of stiff paper a narrow strip like $A—O$ (Fig. 174), making the edge $A—O$ accurately straight. By means of a large pin fasten this strip to the paper and drawing board at the point A.

If we consider that for the distance of 50 feet between any two points on ground, of which the surface is uniform (as is most generally the case), the line of the surface between the two points will not vary very materially from a right line, and that any inconsiderable difference will be still less sensible on a drawing of the usual proportions, we may without any important error then assume the line in question to be a right line. Now as the reference of the point x is (26.20) the difference of level between it and A, or the height of x above A is 1.70 ft., or equal to the difference of the two references. But from what has just been laid down with respect to the line joining the points A and x drawn on the actual surface, it is plain that the point on this line having the whole reference (25.0) lies between A and x, and that as it is 0.50 ft. higher than A its projection will lie between A and x and its distance from A will be to the distance of x from A in the same proportion as its height above A is to the height of x above A, or as 0.50 ft. is to 1.70 ft. By calculating, or by constructing by (*Prob.* 54, Fig. 55) a fourth proportional to $A—x$ = 50 ft.; 1.70 ft. = the height of x above A; and 0.50 ft. = the height of the required point above A; we shall obtain the distance of the projection of this point from A. In like manner by calculation, or construction, we can obtain the distance from A of any other point between A and x of which the reference is given.

But as the calculation of these fourth proportionals would require some labor the Fig. 174 is used to construct them by this simple process. Find on the perpendicular to $A—x$ on the right the division point marked 1.70; turn the strip of paper around its joint at A until the edge $A—O$ is brought on this point, and confine it in this position. The portions of the parallels intercepted between $A—O$ and the perpendiculars at A will be the fourth proportionals required. For example, the vertical height between the point (24.50) and the one (25.0) being equal to the difference of the two references, or 0.50 foot, the horizontal distance which corresponds to this is at once obtained by taking off in the dividers the distance, on the parallel drawn through the point .5, between the perpendiculars at A and the edge $A—O$. This distance set off along the line $A—B$ (Fig. 174) from A to

(25.0) will give the required point. In like manner the distance from A to (26.0) will be found, by taking off in the dividers the portion of the parallel drawn through the point 1.5 on the perpendicular at A.

To find the points corresponding to the references (24.0), (25.0), and (26.0), on the line x—x parallel to A—D, which lie between the points marked (26.20) and (23.30), the vertical height between these points being (26.20) — (23.30) = 2.90 feet, first bring the edge A—O to the point marked 2.90 on the perpendicular on the right, then, to obtain the distance corresponding to (24.0), take off the portion of the intercepted parallel through the point .7 and set it off from (23.30) towards (26.20), and so on for the other points (25.0) and (26.0).

Having in this manner obtained all the points on the parallels to A—B and A—D, with entire numbers for references, the curves drawn through the points having the same references will be the projections of the corresponding horizontal curves of the surface.

It may happen, owing to an abrupt change in the declivity of the ground between two adjacent angles of one of the squares, as at b between the point A and y, on the line A—D, that it may be necessary to obtain on the ground the level and reference of this point, for greater accuracy in delineating the horizontal curves. Suppose the reference of b thus found to be (21.50), it will be seen that the rise from y to b is only 0.4 foot, whilst from b to A it is 3 feet. To obtain the references with whole numbers between b and A, take off the distance A—b (Fig. 173) and set it off from A to b on (Fig. 174), and through b erect a perpendicular to A—x, marking the point where this perpendicular cuts the parallel drawn through the point 3, and bringing the edge A—O of the strip of paper on this point, we can obtain as before the distances to be set off from b towards A (Fig. 173) to obtain the required references.

CONVENTIONAL METHODS OF REPRESENTING THE NATURAL AND ARTIFICIAL FEATURES OF A LOCALITY.

For the purposes of an engineer, or for the information of a person acquainted with the method, that of representing the surface of the ground by the projections of equidistant horizontal curves is nearly all that is requisite; but to aid persons in general to distinguish clearly and readily the various features of a locality, certain conventional means are employed to express natural features as well as artificial objects, which are termed *topographical signs.*

Slopes of ground. The line of the slope, o declivity of the surface at any given point between any two equidistant horizontal curves, it has been shown is measured along a right line drawn from the upper to the lower curve, and perpendicular to the tangent to the upper curve at the given point. This slope may be estimated either by the number of degrees in the angle contained between the line of declivity and a horizontal line, in the usual way of measuring such angles; or it may be expressed by the ratio between the perpendicular and base of a right angle triangle, the vertical distance between the equidistant horizontal curves being the perpendicular, and the projection of the line of declivity the base. If for example the line of declivity of which a—b (Fig. 172) is the projection makes an angle of 45° with the horizontal plane, then the vertical distance between the points a and b on the two curves will be equal to a— b, and the ratio between the perpendicular and base of the righ. angle triangle, by which the declivity in this case is estimated, is $\frac{1}{ab} = \frac{1}{1}$, since the equidistant curves are taken one unit apart.

As a general rule all slopes greater than 45° or $\frac{1}{1}$ are regarded as too precipitous to be expressed by horizontal equidistant curves, the most that is done to represent them is to draw when practicable the top and bottom lines of the surface. In like manner all slopes less than 0°..53′..43″ or $\frac{1}{64}$ are regarded as if the surface were horizontal; stiL upon such slopes the horizontal curves may when requisite be put in; but nothing further is added to express the declivity of the surface.

Lines of declivity, &c. The lines used in topographical drawing to picture to the eye the undulations of the ground, and which are drawn in the direction of the lines of declivity of the surface, serve a double purpose, that of a popular representation of the object expressed, and with which most intelligent persons are conversant, and that of giving the means, when they are drawn in accordance to some system agreed upon, of estimating the declivities which they figure, with all the accuracy required in many practical purposes for which accurate maps are consulted by the engineer or others.

As the horizontal curves when accompanied by their references to some plane of comparison are of themselves amply sufficient to give an accurate configuration of the surface represented, it is not necessary to place on such drawings the lines used on general maps, and which to a certain extent replace the horizontal curves. The lines of declivity in question will therefore be confined to maps on a somewhat small scale, in which horizontal curves are not resorted to with any great precision, although they may have been used to some extent as a general guide in constructing the outlines of the map, such for example as from one inch to 100 feet, or $\frac{1}{1200}$, and upwards as far as such lines can serve any purpose of accuracy, say one inch to half a mile, or $\frac{1}{31680}$.

To represent therefore the form and declivities of all slopes, from $\frac{1}{4}$ to $\frac{1}{64}$ inclusive, in maps on these and intermediate scales, the following rules may be followed for proportioning the breadth and the length of the lines of declivity, and the blank spaces between them.

1st. *The distance between the centre lines of the lines of declivity shall be 2 hundredths of an inch added to the $\frac{1}{4}$ of the denominator of the fraction denoting the declivity expressed in hundredths of an inch.*

Thus for example in the declivity denoted $\frac{1}{64}$ the rule gives $(2 + \frac{64}{4}) = 18$ hundredths of an inch for the distance apart of the lines. In the declivity of $\frac{1}{4}$ we obtain $(2 + \frac{1}{4}) = 2\frac{1}{4}$ hundredths of an inch.

2d. The lines should be the heavier as they are nearer to each other, or as the declivity expressed by them is the steeper. For the most gentle slope so expressed, that of $\frac{1}{64}$, the lines should be fine, for those of $\frac{1}{4}$, or steeper, their breadth should be $1\frac{1}{2}$ hundredths of an inch.

This rule will make the blank space between the heavy strokes equal to half the breadth of the stroke.

3d. No absolute rules can be laid down with respect to the lengths of the strokes, these will depend upon the scale of the drawing, the skill of the draftsman, and the form of the surface to be defined by them. If we take for example the scale of $\frac{1}{600}$ or one inch to 50 feet, and suppose the horizontal curves to be put in at one foot apart vertically, which on the drawing corresponds to $\frac{1}{50}$ or 2 hundredths of an inch, the distance between these curves on slopes of $\frac{1}{1}$ would be 2 hundredths of an inch, whilst on a slope of $\frac{1}{64}$, the curves would be $2 \times 64 = 128$ hundredths, or 1.28 in., nearly an inch and one third apart. In the first case therefore if the strokes were limited between the two curves of each zone they would be only 2 hundredths of an inch long, whilst in the second, if a like limit were prescribed, they would be an inch and a third in length; both of which would be inconvenient to the draftsman, and would present an awkward appearance, particularly the latter, on the drawing. To obviate this difficulty then it has been found well, on gentle slopes, to limit the length of the stroke to about 6 tenths of an inch, and in steep slopes to adopt strokes of the length from 8 to 16 hundredths of an inch.

These limits will require on steep slopes to certain scales that the strokes shall embrace the zones comprised between three or more horizontal curves, whilst on gentle slopes to some scales it will be necessary to divide up the zone comprised by two curves into two or more by intermediate curves in pencil, so as to obtain auxiliary zones of convenient breadth for the draftsman between which the strokes are put in, according to the 1st and 2d rules, the strokes of one auxiliary zone not running into those of the other.

Practical applications. Suppose on a zone between the curves (2.0) and (3.0) that the distance between the points *e* and *f* is 1.2 in., or 120 hundredths of an inch, it would be necessary according to the 3d rule to divide this zone into at least two by one auxiliary curve. Let us suppose it to be divided into four parts by three auxiliary curves *x—x*, *y—y*, *z—z* put in according to what has been already laid down. Having done this calculate by rule 1st the distance occupied along this curve by 5 strokes or lines of declivity. Supposing the slope to be $\frac{1}{8}$, the rule would give $(2 + \frac{120}{8}) = 17$ hundredths of an inch for the distance apart of two strokes; and for five it would give $4 \times 17 = 68$ hundredths. Take now a strip of paper and set off on its edge 68 hundredths of an inch, which divide into four equal parts; then apply this edge to the curve *z—z* and set off from *o* to *p* the dots for the five strokes; do the same for the curves *y—y*, and *x—x*, and through the points thus set off draw the strokes normal to the curve along which they are set off.

Where the curves approach nearer to each other, and are less than 6 tenths of an inch apart and over 4 tenths, as at *d—c*, it will be well to draw an intermediate line as *m—n* along which the strokes will be set off, and to which they will be drawn perpendicularly.

Lines of declivity put in accurately in this manner, in groups of five, from distance to distance between the horizontal curves, will serve to guide the hand, in judging by the eye the positions of the intermediate lines between the groups; the spaces gradually contracting, or widening, as the slope, as shown by the positions of the horizontal curves, becomes steeper, or more gentle.

Scale of spaces. When the spaces between the lines of declivity have been carefully put in according to the preceding system, they will serve to determine the declivity at any point; and a scale of spaces, corresponding to the declivities, ought to be put down on the drawing, in like manner as we put down a scale for ascertaining horizontal distances. The following method may be taken to construct this scale. On a right line estimating from the point *A* (Pl. XIX. Fig. 175) set off 64 equal parts to *B*, each part being equal say to $\frac{1}{16}$, or $\frac{1}{32}$ of an inch. Number the points of division from *o* at *A*, to 64 at *B*. Construct perpendiculars to the right line at *A* and *B*, and on the one at *A* set off a distance to *C* corresponding to four spaces of the lines of declivity for the slope of $\frac{1}{4}$, and at *B* for spaces to *D* for the slope of $\frac{1}{64}$. Draw a right line *C—D* through the points thus set off. Through each of the equal divisions on *A—B*, or through every fifth one, draw lines parallel to the two perpendiculars; each of these lines, intercepted between *A—B* and *C—D*, will represent four spaces, corresponding to the slope marked at the points on *A—B*.

To find the declivity of a zone between two horizontal curves, at any point, from the scale, we take off in the dividers the distance of four spaces of the lines of declivity at the point, then place the points of the dividers on the lines *A—B* and *C—D* so that the line drawn between the points will be perpendicular to *A—B*, the corresponding number on *A—B* will give the slope. Suppose for example the points of the dividers when placed embrace the points *m* and *n*, the corresponding number on *A—B* being about 34 gives $\frac{1}{34}$ for the required slope.

Surfaces of water. (Pl. XX. Fig. 176.) To represent water a series of wavy lines *A*, *A* are drawn parallel to the shores. The lines near the shores are heavier and nearer together than those towards the middle of the surface. No definite rule can be laid down further than to make the lines finer and to increase the distance between them as they recede from the shore. When the banks are steep the slope is represented by heavy lines of declivity. The water line is a tolerably heavy line.

If islands *B* occur in the water course, some pains must be taken in uniting the water lines around its shores with the others.

Shores. Sandy shelving shores *C* are represented by fine dots uniformly spread over the part they occupy on the drawing. The dots are strewn the more thickly as the shore is steeper.

Gravelly shores are represented by a mixture of fine and coarse dots

Meadows. These are represented *E* by systems of very short fine lines placed in fan shape, so as to give the idea of tufts of grass. The tufts should be put in uniformly, parallel to the lower border of the drawing, so as to produce a uniform tint.

Marshy ground. This feature *F*, *F* is represented by a combination of water and grass, as in the last case. The lines for the water surfaces are made straight, and varied in depth of tint, giving the idea of still water with reflections from its surface.

Trees. Single trees *I*, *I* are represented either by a tuft resembling the foliage of a bush, with its shadow, a small circle, or a black dot, according to the scale of the drawing Evergreens may be distinguished from other trees by tufts of fine short lines disposed in star shape. Forests *G* are represented by a collection of tufts, small circles, and points, so disposed as to cover the part uniformly. Brushwood *H* and clearings with undergrowth standing, with smaller and more sparse tufts, &c. Orchards as in *O*.

Rivulets, ravines, &c. Small water-courses of this kind *K*, *K* and their banks are represented by the shore lines or bank slopes, when the scale of the drawing is large enough to give the breadth of the stream. The lines gradually diverging, or else made farther apart below the junction of each affluent. On small scales a single line is used, which is gradually increased in heaviness below each affluent.

Rocks. This feature *L* is expressed by lines of more or less irregularity of shape, so disposed as to give an idea of rocky fragments interspersed over the surface, and connected by lines with the other portions intended to represent the mass of whole rock.

Artificial objects. The above are the chief natural features represented conventionally. The principal conventional signs for artificial objects will be best gathered from Plates XIX. and XX.

In most works for elementary instruction, and in the systems of topographical signs adopted in public services, almost every natural and artificial feature has its representa tive sign. The copying of these is good practice for the pupil, but for actual service those signs alone which designate objects of a somewhat permanent character are strictly requisite; as in culture, for example, rice fields may be expressed by a sign, as they, for the most part, retain for a long time this destination; whereas the ploughed field of the Spring is in grain in Summer and barren in Winter; and the field of Indian corn of this year is in wheat the next, &c., &c.

Practical methods. Finished topographical drawings form a part of the office work of the civil engineer, that require great time, skill, and care. For field duties he is obliged to resort to methods more expeditious in their results than those of the pen, and the use of the lead pencil furnishes one of the best. The draftsman should therefore accustom himself to sketch in ground by the eye, and endeavor to give to his sketch at once, without repeated erasures and interlineation, the final finish that it should receive to subserve his purposes. Hill slopes, horizontal curves, water, &c., &c., may be sketched in either by lines, according to rules already laid down, or else by uniform tints obtained by rubbing the pencil over the paper until a tint is obtained of such intensity as to represent the general effect of lines of declivity of varying grade, water lines, &c. The pencil used for this purpose should be very black and moderately hard, so as to obtain tints of any depth, from deep black to the lightest shade which will not be easily effaced. The effects that may be produced in this manner are very good, and considerable durability may be given to the drawing by pasting the paper on a coarse cotton cloth, and then wetting the surface of the drawing with a mixture of milk and water half and half. Every draftsman will do well to exercise himself at this work in the office until he finds he can imitate any given ground by tints.

Colored Topography. The use of colors in topography is an effective and rapid method of indicating the features of land, and one largely employed.

The colors used are indigo, Hooker's green, No. 2, yellow ochre, burnt sienna, carmine, gamboge, and sepia.

Water (*a* Pl. XXVIII.) is indicated by a flat tint of *indigo*, it is shaded out from the shore-line, when there is one.

Grass-land (*b* Pl. XXVIII.) is indicated by a flat tint of *green*.

Sand, roads, and streets (*c* Pl. XXVIII.) are indicated by a flat tint of *yellow ochre*.

Buildings, bridges, and all structures (*d*. Pl. XXVIII.) are indicated by a tint of *carmine*.

Railroads (*e*. Pl. XXVIII.) are indicated by a dark line of *carmine* without cross lines.

Cultivated land (*f*. Pl. XXVIII.) is indicated by a flat tint of *burnt sienna;* sometimes parallel lines (*g*. Pl. XXVIII.) are ruled over the flat tint, using for the purpose either a darker tint of *burnt sienna*, *green*, or, more commonly, *sepia*.

Uncultivated land (*h*. Pl. XXVIII.) is indicated by a double tint of *burnt sienna* and *green*. To lay a double tint, prepare the two tints in separate saucers, then using a brush for each tint, carry one color for a short distance upon the surface, and then change for the other color and brush, letting the colors join and blend of themselves; alternate the tints in this way until the whole surface is covered. Avoid any regularity in the mottled tint obtained.

Hills (*i*. Pl. XXVIII.) are indicated by a tint of *sepia*, the depth of the tint corresponding to the slope of the land, being darkest where the slope is greatest, and becoming lighter as the slope decreases. The sepia is laid over the land tints.

Trees (*k*. Pl. XXVIII.). There are a number of steps to be followed in indicating trees. 1st, lay the land tint; 2d, pencil in fine lines the outlines of the trees; 3d, tint them with *green*, making the lower right-hand part the darkest; 4th, touch up the trees with *gamboge* upon the light side (the upper left-hand); 5th, add the shadows of the trees with *sepia*.

Marshy ground (*l*. Pl. XXVIII.) is indicated by water and grass land so arranged that the position of the patches of land shall be horizontal; draw a shade line of *sepia* along the lower edges of the land.

Light is supposed to come from the upper left-hand corner of the drawing; hills are shaded without any reference to the direction of light; only the shadows of such objects as houses, trees, etc., are represented; sepia is used for shadows.

For the method of preparing and using tints, see the chapter on tinting.

When making a colored plate, first pencil everything, then lay the flat tints, then touch up the trees, then the hills and shadows.

The division lines between fields and all outlines are ruled with *sepia*.

For pen drawings the draftsman should always have at hand a good supply of pens made of the best quills, with nebs of various sizes to suit lines of various grades, for slopes, &c. His ink should be of the best, and of a decided tint when laid on; deep black, red, green, &c.

The breadth of lines adopted for different objects must depend upon the importance of the object, and the magnitude of the scale to which the drawing is made. In drawings to small scales lines of not more than two breadths can be used, as the fine and medium. For those to larger scales, three sizes of lines may be introduced, the fine, medium, and heavy.

Similar remarks may be made on lettering and the size, &c., of borders. To letter well requires much practice from good models. The draftsman should be able to sketch in by the eye letters of every character and size without resorting to rulers or dividers; until he can do this, whatever pains he may take, his lettering will be stiff and ungainly. The size of the lettering will be dependent upon that of the drawing and the importance of the object. The character is an affair of good taste, and is best left to the skill and fancy of the draftsman; for arbitrary rules cannot alone suffice, even were they ever rigorously attended to.

As it is of some importance to obtain the best effects in drawings which demand so much time and labor as topographical maps, it may be well to observe that, in pen or line drawings, it is best to put in the letters before the lines of declivity, water lines, &c.; as it is less difficult to put in the lines without disfiguring the letters than to make clean and well defined letters over the lines.

The border of the drawing, like the lettering, is frequently a fancy composition of the draftsman. It most generally consists of a light line on the interior and a heavy one on the exterior; the heavy line having the same breadth as that of the blank space between it and the light line. As the border is generally a rectangle in shape, the rule usually followed for proportioning its breadth—which includes the light line, the blank space, and the heavy line—is to make it the one hundredth part of the length of the shorter side of the rectangle.

The title of the drawing is placed without the border at top when it takes up but one line; when it requires several it is usually placed within it. The greatest height of the letters of the title should be three hundredths of the length of the shorter side of the border; and when the title is without the border the blank space between it and the border should be from two to four hundredths of the shorter side.

In every kind of topographical drawing there should be two scales, one to express the horizontal distances between the points laid down, the other a scale to express the slopes as in Fig. [illegible]. The scales should be at the bottom of the drawing, either within or without the border, according to the space unoccupied by the drawing.

Finally every drawing should receive the signature of the draftsman, the date of the drawing; and state from what authorities or sources compiled; and under whose direction, or supervision executed. If emanating from any recognized public office, it ought also to be stamped with the seal of the office.

Scales of distances. In our corps of military engineers, for the purposes of preserving uniformity and attaining accuracy in the execution of maps and plans for official action, a system of regulations is adopted, to the requirements of which strict conformity is enjoined on all in any way connected with those corps, prescribing the manner in which all objects are to be represented, and the scales to which the drawings of them shall be made. As the last point is the result of much experience, and may save the young draftsman much time in the selection of a suitable scale for any given object, it has been thought well to add in this place the following Table of Scales, adopted for the guidance of

TABLE OF SCALES.

No.	Proportion of the Scale	Application of the Scale.
1	1 inch to $\frac{1}{2}$ an inch, $\frac{2}{1}$.	Details of surveying instruments, &c, when great accuracy is required.
2	1 inch to 1 inch, $\frac{1}{1}$.	All models for masons, carpenters, &c.; and for the drawings of small objects requiring the details accurately.
3	1 inch to 6 inches, $\frac{1}{6}$.	Machines and tools of small dimensions, as the jack, axes, saws, &c.; hangings of gates, &c., &c.
4	1 inch to 1 foot, $\frac{1}{12}$.	Machines of mean size, as capstans, windlasses, vehicles of transportation, &c.
5	1 inch to 2 feet, $\frac{1}{24}$.	Large machines, as pile engines, pumps, &c.; details of arrangement of stone masonry, of carpentry, &c.
6	1 inch to 5 feet, $\frac{1}{60}$.	Canal lock, scaffoldings, separate drawings of light-houses, buildings of various kinds.
7	1 inch to 10 feet, $\frac{1}{120}$.	General plans of buildings where minute details are not put down.
8	1 inch to 50 feet, 12 inches to 200 yards, $\frac{1}{600}$.	Sections and profiles of roads, canals, &c. Maps of ground with horizontal curves one foot apart.
9	1 inch to 220 feet, 24 inches to 1 mile, $\frac{1}{2640}$.	Topographical maps comprising one mile and a half square, as important parts of anchorages, harbors, &c.
10	1 inch to 440 feet, 12 inches to 1 mile. $\frac{1}{5280}$.	Topographical maps embracing three miles square.
11	1 inch to 880 feet, 6 inches to 1 mile. $\frac{1}{10560}$.	Topographical maps exceeding four and within eight miles square.
12	1 inch to 1320 feet, 4 inches to 1 mile, $\frac{1}{15840}$.	Topographical maps embracing nine miles square.
13	1 inch to 2640 feet, 2 inches to 1 mile, $\frac{1}{31680}$.	Maps not exceeding 24 miles square.
14	1 inch to 5280 feet, 1 inch to 1 mile, $\frac{1}{63360}$.	Maps comprising 50 miles square.
15	1 inch to 10560 feet. $\frac{1}{2}$ an inch to 1 mile, $\frac{1}{126720}$.	Maps comprising 100 miles square.

the Corps of Engineers. The first column of this table gives the unit of the drawing which corresponds to the number of units of the object itself; and under this the vulgar fraction which shows the ratio of the linear dimensions of the drawing to the corresponding linear dimensions of the object. For example, at No. 3 of the Table we find for the designation of the scale "*one inch to 50 feet, or 12 inches to 200 yards*," and below this the fraction $\frac{1}{600}$; this then is understood to express that the distance between any two points on the drawing being one inch the actual horizontal distance between the same points on the object is 50 feet; or, if the distance between two points on the drawing is 12 inches then the corresponding horizontal distance on the object is 200 yards. In like manner that every linear inch or foot on the drawing is the $\frac{1}{600}$ part of the corresponding horizontal distance on the object.

Copying maps, &c. As the topographical sketches taken on the ground are to serve as models from which the finished drawings are to be made, either on the same scale as the sketch, or on one greater or smaller than it, the draftsman must have some accurate and at the same time speedy method of copying from an original, either on the same, or a different scale. The most simple, and at the same time the most accurate and speedy in skilful hands, is to divide the original into squares, by pencil lines drawn on it lengthwise and crosswise; the side of the square being of any convenient length that will subserve the purposes of accuracy. Having prepared the original in this manner, the sheet on which the copy is to be made is divided into squares in like manner; the side of each being the same as that of the original when the copy is to be of the same size: or in any proportion shorter or longer than those of the original when the linear dimensions of the copy are to be in any given proportion shorter or longer than those of the original. Having prepared the blank sheet in this way, we have only to judge by the eye, when it is well trained, how the different objects on the original lie with respect to the sides of the squares on it; to be enabled, by the hand, to put them in pencil on the blank sheet. After roughly putting in the outline work is this way, the corrections of inaccuracies can be afterwards readily effected. All the outline having been completed in pencil, the labor of the pen is commenced, and the details, as lines of declivity, conventional signs, &c., are put in by it alone.

SHORT-TITLE CATALOGUE

OF THE

PUBLICATIONS

OF

JOHN WILEY & SONS, Inc.

NEW YORK

London: CHAPMAN & HALL, Limited

Montreal, Can.: RENOUF PUB. CO.

ARRANGED UNDER SUBJECTS

Descriptive circulars sent on application. Books marked with an asterisk (*) are sold at *net* prices only. All books are bound in cloth unless otherwise stated.

AGRICULTURE—HORTICULTURE—FORESTRY.

Armsby—Principles of Animal Nutrition....8vo, $4 00
Bowman—Forest Physiography....8vo, *5 00
Bryant—Hand Book of Logging.... (*Ready*, Fall 1913)
Budd and Hansen—American Horticultural Manual:
  Part I. Propagation, Culture, and Improvement....12mo, 1 50
  Part II. Systematic Pomology....12mo, 1 50
Elliott—Engineering for Land Drainage....12mo, 2 00
  Practical Farm Drainage. (Second Edition, Rewritten)....12mo, 1 50
Fuller—Domestic Water Supplies for the Farm....8vo, *1 50
Graham—Text-book on Poultry....(*In Preparation.*)
  Manual on Poultry (Loose Leaf Lab. Manual)....(*In Preparation.*)
Graves—Forest Mensuration....8vo, 4 00
  Principles of Handling Woodlands....Small 8vo, *1 50
Green—Principles of American Forestry....12mo, 1 50
Grotenfelt—Principles of Modern Dairy Practice. (Woll.)....12mo, 2 00
Hawley and Hawes—Forestry in New England....8vo, *3 50
Herrick—Denatured or Industrial Alcohol....8vo, *4 00
Howe—Agricultural Drafting....oblong quarto, *1 25
  Reference and Problem Sheets to accompany Agricultural Drafting, each *0 20
Keitt—Agricultural Chemistry Text-book....(*In Preparation.*)
  Laboratory and Field Exercises in Agricultural Chemistry (*In Preparation.*)
Kemp and Waugh—Landscape Gardening. (New Edition, Rewritten)..12mo, *1 50
Larsen—Exercises in Dairying (Loose Leaf Field Manual)....4to, paper, *1 00
  Single Exercises each.... *0 02
  and White—Dairy Technology....Small 8vo, *1 50
Levison—Studies of Trees, Loose Leaf Field Manual, 4to, pamphlet form, Price from 5–10 cents net, each, according to number of pages.
McCall—Crops and Soils (Loose Leaf Field Manual)....(*In Preparation.*)
  Soils (Text-book)....(*In Preparation.*)
McKay and Larsen—Principles and Practice of Butter-making....8vo, *1 50
Maynard—Landscape Gardening as Applied to Home Decoration....12mo, 1 50
Moon and Brown—Elements of Forestry....(*In Preparation.*)
Record—Identification of the Economic Woods of the United States..8vo, *1 25
Recknagel—Theory and Practice of Working Plans (Forest Organization)....8vo, *2 00

[illegible]

ARCHITECTURE.

[illegible]

... Paper Hanging and Whitewashing ..12mo. [illegible]

... Stone-cutting and Masonry ....8vo. [illegible]

... Wood 8vo. 3 50

WAIT Engineering and Architectural Jurisprudence 8vo. 6 00

Sheep, 6 50

Law of Contracts 8vo. 3 00

Law of Operations Preliminary to Construction in Engineering and Architecture 8vo. 5 00

Sheep, 5 50

WILSON—Air Conditioning 12mo, $1 50
WORCESTER and ATKINSON—Small Hospitals, Establishment and Maintenance, Suggestions for Hospital Architecture, with Plans for a Small Hospital.......................................12mo, 1 25

ASSAYING.

BETTS—Lead Refining by Electrolysis.......................................8vo, 4 00
FLETCHER—Practical Instructions in Quantitative Assaying with the Blowpipe.......................................16mo, mor., 1 50
FURMAN and PARDOE—Manual of Practical Assaying.......................................8vo, 3 00
LODGE—Notes on Assaying and Metallurgical Laboratory Experiments 8vo, 3 00
LOW—Technical Methods of Ore Analysis.......................................8vo, 3 00
MILLER—Cyanide Process.......................................12mo, 1 00
Manual of Assaying.......................................12mo, 1 00
MINET—Production of Aluminum and its Industrial Use. (WALDO)..12mo, 2 50
PRICE and MEADE—The Technical Analysis of Brass and the Non-Ferrous Alloys.......................................12mo, *2 00
RICKETTS and MILLER—Notes on Assaying.......................................8vo, 3 00
ROBINE and LENGLEN—Cyanide Industry. (LE CLERC.).............8vo, 4 00
SEAMON—Manual for Assayers and Chemists..................Small 8vo, *2 50
ULKE—Modern Electrolytic Copper Refining.......................................8vo, 3 00
WILSON—Cyanide Processes.......................................12mo, 1 50

ASTRONOMY.

COMSTOCK—Field Astronomy for Engineers.......................................8vo, 2 50
CRAIG—Azimuth.......................................4to, 3 50
CRANDALL—Text-book on Geodesy and Least Squares.......................................8vo, 3 00
DOOLITTLE—Treatise on Practical Astronomy.......................................8vo, 4 00
HAYFORD—Text-book of Geodetic Astronomy.......................................8vo, 3 00
HOSMER—Azimuth.......................................16mo, mor., 1 00
Text-book on Practical Astronomy.......................................8vo, *2 00
MERRIMAN—Elements of Precise Surveying and Geodesy 8vo, 2 50
MICHIE and HARLOW—Practical Astronomy.......................................8vo, *3 00
RUST—Ex-meridian Altitude, Azimuth and Star-Finding Tables.......8vo, 5 00
WHITE—Elements of Theoretical and Descriptive Astronomy........12mo, *2 00

BIOLOGY.

COHNHEIM—Enzymes.......................................12mo, *1 50
DAVENPORT—Statistical Methods with Special Reference to Biological Variation.......................................16mo, mor., 1 50
EFFRONT and PRESCOTT—Enzymes and Their Applications............8vo, 3 00
EULER and POPE—General Chemistry of the Enzymes..............8vo, *3 00
MAST—Light and Behavior of Organisms 8vo, *2 50
PRESCOTT and WINSLOW—Elements of Water Bacteriology, with Special Reference to Sanitary Water Analysis. Third Edition, Rewritten. Small 8vo, *1 75
WARD and WHIPPLE—Freshwater Biology ....(*In Press.*)
WHIPPLE—The Microscopy of Drinking Water.......................................8vo, 3 50
WINSLOW—The Systematic Relationship of the Coccaceæ......Small 8vo, 2 50

CHEMISTRY.

ABDERHALDEN—Physiological Chemistry in Thirty Lectures. (HALL and DEFREN).......................................8vo, *5 00
ABEGG—Theory of Electrolytic Dissociation. (VON ENDE.)..........12mo, *1 25
ALEXEYEFF—General Principles of Organic Syntheses. (MATTHEWS.)..8vo, 3 00

—Text-book of Organic Chemi
nalysis of Paint and Varnish P
and Zinc Pigments. . . . .
—Oil-chemists' Handbook.. ...
—Directions for Laboratory Worl
—Rapid Methods for the Chemic
making Alloys and Graphite. . . .
gricultural Chemistry . . . . . .
—Spectrum Analysis. (TINGLI
OHN—Application of Some Gen
Organic Chemistry. (TINGLE.).
INTON—Food Inspection and An
by Dr. Andrew L. Winton. . . .
ctrochemistry of Organic Comp
Notes on Assaying and Metallurg
chnical Method of Ore Analysis.
Paint for Steel Structures. . . . .
—Techno-chemical Analysis. (Co
and LARSEN—Principles and Pra
—Modern Pigments and their Vehi
—Laboratory Guide to Qualitat

—Examination of Water. (Chemi
er-supply. (Considered Principa

SON—First Principles of Chemica
WS—Laboratory Manual of Dyei
tile Fibres. Third Edition. Rev
—Determination of Radicles in
Third Edition. . . . .
—Cyanide Process . . . . . .
anual of Assaying. . . . .
—Production of Aluminum and its I
STAEDT—Technical Calculations

—Elementary Text-book of Chemi
N—Elements of Physical Chemistr
Physical Chemistry for Electrical En
—Experiments in Organic Chemist
Outlines of Organic Chemistry. . . .
—Calculations used in Cane-sugar
—History of Chemical Theories and
LIKEN—General Method for the Ide
pounds. Vol. I. Compounds
Oxygen . . . .
Vol. II. Nitrogenous Compounds. .
Vol. III. The Commercial Dyestuffs
SON—Analysis of Drugs and Medicine
WALD—Conversations on Chemistry.

Introduction to Chemistry. (HALL a
EN and STANDAGE—Dyeing and Cleani
—Practical Test Book of Chemis
—Physical Chemistry in the Service
—Alkaloids and their Chemical Co
COTT and WINSLOW—Elements of
Reference to Sanitary Water Ana

—Guide to Piece-Dyeing. . . . .
CHARDS and WOODMAN—Air, Water a
point . . . .
ETTS and MILLER—Notes on Assayin
AL—Disinfection and the Preservatio
—Elementary Manual for the Chem
and LENGLEN—Cyanide Industry
GERS—Exercises in Industrial Chemistr

RUDDIMAN—Incompatibilities in Prescriptions. 8vo, $2 00
Whys in Pharmacy 12mo, 1 00
RUER—Elements of Metallography. (MATHEWSON.) 8vo, *3 00
SABIN—Industrial and Artistic Technology of Paint and Varnish. 8vo, 3 00
SALKOWSKI—Physiological and Pathological Chemistry. (Orndorff.) . . 8vo, 2 50
SCHIMPF—Essentials of Volumetric Analysis . . . . Small 8vo, *1 50
Manual of Volumetric Analysis. 8vo, 5 00
Qualitative Chemical Analysis. 8vo, *1 25
SEAMON—Manual for Assayers and Chemists. . . . . Small 8vo, *2 50
SMITH—Lecture Notes on Chemistry for Dental Students. 8vo, *2 50
SPENCER—Handbook for Cane Sugar Manufacturers . . . . 16mo, mor., 3 00
Handbook for Chemists of Beet-sugar Houses. . . . . 16mo, mor., 3 00
STOCKBRIDGE—Rocks and Soils. 8vo, 2 50
STONE—Practical Testing of Gas and Gas Meters. 8vo, 3 50
TILLMAN—Descriptive General Chemistry 8vo, *3 00
Elementary Lessons in Heat 8vo, *1 50
TREADWELL—Qualitative Analysis. (HALL.) 8vo, 3 00
Quantitative Analysis. (HALL.) 8vo, 4 00
TURNEAURE and RUSSELL—Public Water-supplies. 8vo, 5 00
VENABLE—Methods and Devices for Bacterial Treatment of Sewage . . . 8vo, 3 00
WARD and WHIPPLE—Freshwater Biology. . . . . (*In Press.*)
WARE—Beet-sugar Manufacture and Refining. Vol. I 8vo, 4 00
Vol. II 8vo, 5 00
WASHINGTON—Manual of the Chemical Analysis of Rocks 8vo, 2 00
WEAVER—Military Explosives 8vo, *3 00
WELLS—Laboratory Guide in Qualitative Chemical Analysis. 8vo, 1 50
Short Course in Inorganic Qualitative Chemical Analysis for Engineering Students. 12mo, 1 50
Text-book of Chemical Arithmetic 12mo, 1 25
WHIPPLE—Microscopy of Drinking-water 8vo, 3 50
WILSON—Cyanide Processes 12mo, 1 50
WINTON—Microscopy of Vegetable Foods 8vo, 7 50
ZSIGMONDY—Colloids and the Ultramicroscope. (ALEXANDER.) Small 8vo, 3 00

CIVIL ENGINEERING.

BRIDGES AND ROOFS. HYDRAULICS. MATERIALS OF ENGINEERING. RAILWAY ENGINEERING.

AMERICAN CIVIL ENGINEERS' POCKET BOOK. (MANSFIELD MERRIMAN, Editor-in-chief.) . . . . 16mo, mor., *5 00
BAKER—Engineers' Surveying Instruments 12mo, 3 00
BIXBY—Graphical Computing Table . . . . Paper 19½×24¼ inches, 0 25
BREED and HOSMER—Principles and Practice of Surveying.
Vol. I. Elementary Surveying 8vo, 3 00
Vol. II. Higher Surveying 8vo, 2 50
BURR—Ancient and Modern Engineering and the Isthmian Canal. 8vo, *3 50
COMSTOCK—Field Astronomy for Engineers. 8vo, 2 50
CORTHELL—Allowable Pressure on Deep Foundations 12mo, *1 25
CRANDALL—Text-book on Geodesy and Least Squares. 8vo, 3 00
DAVIS—Elevation and Stadia Tables 8vo, 1 00
ELLIOTT—Engineering for Land Drainage 12mo, 2 00
FIEBEGER—Treatise on Civil Engineering 8vo, *5 00
FLEMER—Phototopographic Methods and Instruments 8vo, 5 00
FOLWELL—Sewerage. (Designing and Maintenance.) 8vo, 3 00
FREITAG—Architectural Engineering 8vo, 3 50
HAUCH and RICE—Tables of Quantities for Preliminary Estimates . . . 12mo, *1 25
HAYFORD—Text-book of Geodetic Astronomy 8vo, 3 00
HERING—Ready Reference Tables (Conversion Factors.) . . . . . 16mo, mor., 2 50
HESS—Graphics and Structural Design. 8vo, *3 00
HOSMER—Azimuth . . . . 16mo, mor., 1 00
Text-book on Practical Astronomy 8vo, *2 00
HOWE—Retaining Walls for Earth 12mo, 1 25

IVES—Adjustments of the Engineer's Transit and Level ......,16mo, bds.,*$0 25
and HILTS—Problems in Surveying, Railroad Surveying and Geodesy.................16mo, mor., 1 50
JOHNSON (J. B.) and SMITH—Theory and Practice of Surveying. Small 8vo, *3 50
(L. J.)—Statics by Algebraic and Graphic Methods..............8vo, 2 00
KINNICUTT, WINSLOW and PRATT—Sewage Disposal..................8vo, *3 00
KIRBY—Elements of Specification Writing 8vo, *1 25
MAHAN—Descriptive Geometry 8vo, *1 50
MERRIMAN—Elements of Precise Surveying and Geodesy.............8vo, 2 50
and BROOKS—Handbook for Surveyors.....................16mo, mor., 2 00
NUGENT—Plane Surveying.....................................8vo, 3 50
OGDEN—Sewer Construction.....................................8vo, 3 00
Sewer Design...12mo, 2 00
and CLEVELAND—Practical Methods of Sewage Disposal for Residences, Hotels, and Institutions...........................8vo, *1 50
PARSONS—Disposal of Municipal Refuse..........................8vo, 2 00
PATTON—Treatise on Civil Engineering..............8vo, half leather, 7 50
REED—Topographical Drawing and Sketching.......................4to, 5 00
RIEMER—Shaft-sinking under Difficult Conditions. (CORNING and PEELE.) 8vo, 3 00
SIEBERT and BIGGIN—Modern Stone-cutting and Masonry...........8vo, 1 50
SMITH—Manual of Topographical Drawing. (McMILLAN.)...........8vo, 2 50
SOPER—Air and Ventilation of Subways..........................12mo, 2 50
TRACY—Exercises in Surveying.............................12mo, mor., *1 00
Plane Surveying.....................................16mo, mor., 3 00
VENABLE—Garbage Crematories in America.........................8vo, 2 00
Methods and Devices for Bacterial Treatment of Sewage..........8vo, 3 00
WAIT—Engineering and Architectural Jurisprudence.................8vo, 6 00
Sheep, 6 50
Law of Contracts 8vo, 3 00
Law of Operations Preliminary to Construction in Engineering and Architecture...8vo, 5 00
Sheep, 5 50
WARREN—Stereotomy—Problems in Stone-cutting...................8vo, 2 50
WATERBURY—Vest-Pocket Hand-book of Mathematics for Engineers. 2⅞×5⅜ inches, mor., *1 00
Enlarged Edition, Including Tables ....mor., *1 50
WEBB—Problems in the Use and Adjustment of Engineering Instruments. 16mo, mor., 1 20
WILSON—Topographic, Trigonometric and Geodetic Surveying 8vo, 3 50

BRIDGES AND ROOFS.

BISHOP—Drafting Forms. Loose Leaf Sheets, each *0 02
Structural Details of Hip and Valley Rafters.........Oblong large 8vo, *1 75
Structural Drafting.................................(*In Press.*)
BOLLER—Practical Treatise on the Construction of Iron Highway Bridges 8vo, 2 00
Thames River Bridge................................Oblong paper, *5 00
BURR—Suspension Bridges ....(*Ready*, Fall 1913)
and FALK—Design and Construction of Metallic Bridges..........8vo, 5 00
Influence Lines for Bridge and Roof Computations..............8vo, 3 00
DU BOIS—Mechanics of Engineering. Vol. II ....Small 4to, 10 00
FOSTER—Treatise on Wooden Trestle Bridges. Fourth Edition.......4to, *5 00
FOWLER—Ordinary Foundations.................................8vo, 3 50
GREENE—Arches in Wood, Iron, and Stone 8vo, 2 50
Bridge Trusses...8vo, 2 50
Roof Trusses...8vo, 1 25
GRIMM—Secondary Stresses in Bridge Trusses 8vo, 2 50
HELLER—Stresses in Structures and the Accompanying Deformations, 8vo, 3 00
HOWE—Design of Simple Roof-trusses in Wood and Steel 8vo, 2 00
Symmetrical Masonry Arches 8vo, 2 50
Treatise on Arches 8vo, 4 00

HUDSON—Deflections and Statically Indeterminate Stresses.....Small 4to, *3 50

Plate Girder Design.........................8vo, *1 50

JACOBY—Structural Details, or Elements of Design in Heavy Framing, 8vo, *2 25

JOHNSON, BRYAN and TURNEAURE—Theory and Practice in the Designing of Modern Framed Structures. New Edition.

Part I. Stresses in Simple Structures.........................8vo, *3 00

Part II. Statically Indeterminate Structures and Secondary Stresses 8vo, *4 00

MERRIMAN and JACOBY—Text-book on Roofs and Bridges:

Part I. Stresses in Simple Trusses.........................8vo, 2 50

Part II. Graphic Statics.........................8vo, 2 50

Part III. Bridge Design.........................8vo, 2 50

Part IV. Higher Structures.........................8vo, 2 50

RICKER—Design and Construction of Roofs.........................8vo, 5 00

SONDERICKER—Graphic Statics, with Applications to Trusses, Beams, and Arches.........................8vo, *2 00

WADDELL—De Pontibus, Pocket-book for Bridge Engineers....16mo, mor., 2 00

Specifications for Steel Bridges.........................12mo, *0 50

HYDRAULICS.

BARNES—Ice Formation.........................8vo, 3 00

BAZIN—Experiments upon the Contraction of the Liquid Vein Issuing from an Orifice. (TRAUTWINE.).........................8vo, 2 00

BOVEY—Treatise on Hydraulics.........................8vo, 5 00

CHURCH—Diagrams of Mean Velocity of Water in Open Channels. Oblong 4to, paper, 1 50

Hydraulic Motors.........................8vo, 2 00

Mechanics of Fluids (Being Part IV of Mechanics of Engineering). 8vo, 3 00

COFFIN—Graphical Solution of Hydraulic Problems.........16mo, mor., 2 50

FLATHER—Dynamometers, and the Measurement of Power.........12mo, 3 00

FOLWELL—Water-supply Engineering.........................8vo, 4 00

FRIZELL—Water-power.........................8vo, 5 00

FUERTES—Water and Public Health.........................12mo, 1 50

FULLER—Domestic Water Supplies for the Farm.........................8vo, *1 50

GANGUILLET and KUTTER—General Formula for the Uniform Flow of Water in Rivers and Other Channels. (HERING and TRAUTWINE.).. 8vo, 4 00

HAZEN—Clean Water and How to Get It.........................Small 8vo, 1 50

Filtration of Public Water-supplies.........................8vo, 3 00

HAZELHURST—Towers and Tanks for Water-works.........................8vo, 2 50

HERSCHEL—115 Experiments on the Carrying Capacity of Large, Riveted, Metal Conduits.........................8vo, 2 00

HOYT and GROVER—River Discharge.........................8vo, 2 00

HUBBARD and KIERSTED—Water-works Management and Maintenance, 8vo, 4 00

LYNDON—Development and Electrical Distribution of Water Power 8vo, *3 00

MASON—Water-supply. (Considered Principally from a Sanitary Standpoint.).........................8vo, 4 00

MERRIMAN—Elements of Hydraulics.........................12mo, *1 00

Treatise on Hydraulics. 9th Edition, Rewritten.........................8vo, *4 00

MOLITOR—Hydraulics of Rivers, Weirs and Sluices.........................8vo, *2 00

MORRISON and BRODIE—High Masonry Dam Design.........................8vo, *1 50

RECTOR—Underground Waters for Commercial Purposes.........................12mo, *1 00

SCHUYLER—Reservoirs for Irrigation, Water-power, and Domestic Water supply. Second Edition, Revised and Enlarged.......Large 8vo, 6 00

THOMAS and WATT—Improvement of Rivers. Second Edition, 2 Vols. 4to, *7 50

TURNEAURE and RUSSELL—Public Water-supplies.........................8vo, 5 00

WEGMANN—Design and Construction of Dams. 6th Ed., enlarged.....4to, *6 00

Water Supply of the City of New York from 1658 to 1895.........4to, 10 00

WHIPPLE—Value of Pure Water.........................Small 8vo, 1 00

WHITE—Catskill Water Supply of New York City.........................8vo, *6 00

WILLIAMS and HAZEN—Hydraulic Tables.........................8vo, 1 50

WILSON—Irrigation Engineering.........................8vo, 4 00

WOOD—Turbines.........................8vo, 2 50

Baker—Roads and Pavements . . . 8vo, $5 00
Treatise on Masonry Construction . . . 8vo, 5 00
Black—United States Public Works . . . Oblong 4to, 5 00
Blanchard and Drowne—Highway Engineering, as Presented at the Second International Road Congress, Brussels, 1910 . . . 8vo, *2 00
Text-book on Highway Engineering . . . 8vo, *4 50
Bottler—German and American Varnish Making. (Sabin.) . . . Small 8vo, *3 50
Burr—Elasticity and Resistance of the Materials of Engineering . . . 8vo, 7 50
Byrne—Highway Construction . . . 8vo, 5 00
Inspection of the Materials and Workmanship Employed in Construction. 16mo, 3 00
Church—Mechanics of Engineering . . . 8vo, 6 00
Mechanics of Solids (Being Parts I, II, III of Mechanics of Engineering) . . . 8vo, 4 50
Mechanics of Fluids (Being Part IV of Mechanics of Engineering) 8vo, 3 00
Du Bois—Mechanics of Engineering:
Vol. I. Kinematics, Statics, Kinetics . . . Small 4to, 7 50
Vol. II. The Stresses in Framed Structures, Strength of Materials and Theory of Flexures . . . Small 4to, 10 00
Eckel—Building Stones and Clays . . . 8vo, *3 00
Cements, Limes, and Plasters . . . 8vo, *6 00
Fowler—Ordinary Foundations . . . 8vo, 3 50
Fuller and Johnston—Applied Mechanics:
Vol. I. Theory of Statics and Kinetics . . . (*Ready*, Fall 1913)
Vol. II. Strength of Materials . . . (*In Preparation.*)
Greene—Structural Mechanics . . . 8vo, *2 50
Holley—Analysis of Paint and Varnish Products . . . Small 8vo, *2 50
Lead and Zinc Pigments . . . Small 8vo, *3 00
Hubbard—Dust Preventives and Road Binders . . . 8vo, *3 00
Johnson—Materials of Construction . . . Large 8vo, 6 00
Keep—Cast Iron . . . 8vo, 2 50
King—Elements of the Mechanics of Materials and of Power of Transmission . . . 8vo, *2 50
Lanza—Applied Mechanics . . . 8vo, 7 50
Lowe—Paints for Steel Structures . . . 12mo, 1 00
Maire—Modern Pigments and their Vehicles . . . 12mo, 2 00
Maurer—Technical Mechanics . . . 8vo, 4 00
Merrill—Stones for Building and Decoration . . . 8vo, 5 00
Merriman—Mechanics of Materials . . . 8vo, 5 00
Strength of Materials . . . 12mo, *1 00
Metcalf—Steel. A Manual for Steel-users . . . 12mo, 2 00
Mills—Materials for Construction . . . (*In Press.*)
Morrison—Highway Engineering . . . 8vo, 2 50
Murdock—Strength of Materials . . . 12mo, *2 00
Patton—Practical Treatise on Foundations . . . 8vo, 5 00
Rice—Concrete Block Manufacture . . . 8vo, 2 00
Richardson—Modern Asphalt Pavement . . . 8vo, 3 00
Richey—Building Foreman's Pocket Book and Ready Reference. 16mo, mor., 5 00
Cement Workers' and Plasterers' Edition (Building Mechanics' Ready Reference Series) . . . 16mo, mor., *1 50
Handbook for Superintendents of Construction . . . 16mo, mor., 4 00
Stone and Brick Masons' Edition (Building Mechanics' Ready Reference Series) . . . 16mo, mor., *1 50
Ries—Building Stones and Clay Products . . . 8vo, *3 00
Clays. Their Occurrence, Properties, and Uses . . . 8vo, *5 00
and Leighton—History of the Clay-working Industry of the United States . . . 8vo, *2 50
and Watson—Engineering Geology . . . (*In Press.*)
Sabin—Industrial and Artistic Technology of Paint and Varnish . . . 8vo, 3 00
Smith—Strength of Material . . . 12mo, *1 25
Snow—Principal Species of Wood . . . 8vo, 3 50
Spalding—Hydraulic Cement . . . 12mo, 2 00
Text-book on Road and Pavements . . . 12mo, *2 00

TAYLOR and THOMPSON—Concrete Costs. . . . . Small 8vo,*$5 00
Extracts on Reinforced Concrete Design. 8vo, *2 00
Treatise on Concrete, Plain and Reinforced. 8vo, 5 00
THURSTON—Materials of Engineering. In Three Parts. 8vo, 8 00
Part I. Non-metallic Materials of Engineering and Metallurgy. . . 8vo, 2 00
Part II. Iron and Steel. 8vo, 3 50
Part III. A Treatise on Brasses, Bronzes, and Other Alloys and their Constituents 8vo, 2 50
TILLSON—Street Pavements and Paving Materials 8vo, *4 00
TURNEAURE and MAURER—Principles of Reinforced Concrete Construction. 8vo, 3 50
WATERBURY—Cement Laboratory Manual. 12mo, 1 00
Laboratory Manual for Testing Materials of Construction. 12mo, *1 50
WOOD (DE V.) Treatise on the Resistance of Materials, and an Appendix on the Preservation of Timber. 8vo, 2 00
(M. P.)—Rustless Coatings: Corrosion and Electrolysis of Iron and Steel. 8vo, 4 00

RAILWAY ENGINEERING.

BERG—Buildings and Structures of American Railroads. 4to, 5 00
BROOKS—Handbook of Street Railroad Location. . . . . 16mo, mor., 1 50
BURT—Railway Station Service 12mo, *2 00
BUTTS—Civil Engineer's Field-book. 16mo, mor., 2 50
CRANDALL—Railway and Other Earthwork Tables. 8vo, 1 50
and BARNES—Railroad Surveying. 16mo, mor., 2 00
CROCKETT—Methods for Earthwork Computations. 8vo, *1 50
DREDGE—History of the Pennsylvania Railroad. (1879). . . . . Paper, 5 00
FISH—Earthwork Haul and Overhaul. 8vo, *1 50
FISHER—Table of Cubic Yards. . . . . Cardboard, 0 25
GILBERT, WIGHTMAN and SAUNDERS—Subways and Tunnels of New York. 8vo, *4 00
GODWIN—Railroad Engineers' Field-book and Explorers' Guide. . 16mo, mor., 2 50
HUDSON—Tables for Calculating the Cubic Contents of Excavations and Embankments. 8vo, 1 00
IVES and HILTS—Problems in Surveying, Railroad Surveying and Geodesy. 16mo, mor., 1 50
MOLITOR and BEARD—Manual for Resident Engineers. 16mo, 1 00
NAGLE—Field Manual for Railroad Engineers. . . . . 16mo, mor., 3 00
ORROCK—Railroad Structures and Estimates. 8vo, *3 00
PHILBRICK—Field Manual for Engineers. . . . . 16mo, mor., 3 00
RAYMOND—Elements of Railroad Engineering. 8vo, 3 50
Railroad Engineer's Field Book. (*In Preparation.*)
Railroad Field Geometry. . . . . 16mo, mor., 2 00
ROBERTS—Track Formulæ and Tables. . . . . 16mo, mor., 3 00
SEARLES—Field Engineering. . . . . 16mo, mor., 3 00
Railroad Spiral. . . . . 16mo, mor., 1 50
TAYLOR—Prismoidal Formulæ and Earthwork. 8vo, 1 50
WEBB—Economics of Railroad Construction . . . . Small 8vo, 2 50
Railroad Construction. . . . . 16mo, mor., 5 00
WELLINGTON—Economic Theory of the Location of Railways. . . Small 8vo, 5 00
WILSON—Elements of Railroad-Track and Construction. 12mo, 2 00

DRAWING.

BARR and WOOD—Kinematics of Machinery. 8vo, 2 50
BARTLETT—Mechanical Drawing. Third Edition. 8vo, *3 00
" " Abridgment of the Second Edition. . . . 8vo, *1 50
and JOHNSON—Engineering Descriptive Geometry. 8vo, *1 50
BISHOP—Drafting Forms Loose Leaf Sheets, each. *0 02
Structural Details of Hip and Valley Rafters. . . . . . Oblong large 8vo, *1 75
Structural Drafting. . . . . (*In Press.*)
BLESSING and DARLING—Descriptive Geometry 8vo, *1 50
Elements of Drawing. 8vo, *1 50

Coolidge—Manual of Drawing............................8vo, paper, $1 00
and Freeman—Elements of General Drafting for Mechanical Engineers
Oblong 4to, 2 50
Durley—Kinematics of Machines.......................8vo, 4 00
Emch—Introduction to Projective Geometry and its Application...... 8vo, 2 50
French and Ives—Stereotomy.................. 8vo, 2 50
Hess—Graphics and Structural Design...........................8vo, *3 00
Hill—Text-book on Shades and Shadows, and Perspective...........8vo, 2 00
Howe—Agricultural Drafting.....................oblong quarto, *1 25
Reference and Problem Sheets to accompany Agricultural Drafting.
each, *0 02
Howe-Greenberg—Architectural Drafting..................Oblong 4to, *1 50
James and Mackenzie—Working Drawings of Machinery. (*Ready Fall*, 1913.)
Jamison—Advanced Mechanical Drawing..........................8vo, 2 00
Elements of Mechanical Drawing.............................8vo, 2 50
Jones—Machine Design:
Part I. Kinematics of Machinery............................8vo, 1 50
Part II. Form, Strength, and Proportions of Parts.............8vo, 3 00
Kimball and Barr—Machine Design.................. 8vo, *3 00
MacCord—Elements of Descriptive Geometry.................. 8vo, 3 00
Kinematics; or, Practical Mechanism..................8vo, 5 00
Mechanical Drawing........................4to, 4 00
Velocity Diagrams..................8vo, 1 50
McLeod—Descriptive Geometry...................Small 8vo, 1 50
Mahan—Descriptive Geometry and Stone-cutting..............8vo, *1 50
Industrial Drawing. (Thompson.)..........................8vo, 3 50
Moyer—Descriptive Geometry....................................8vo, 2 00
Reed—Topographical Drawing and Sketching.....................4to, 5 00
Reid—Mechanical Drawing. (Elementary and Advanced.)...........8vo, *2 00
Text-book of Mechanical Drawing and Elementary Machine Design. 8vo, 3 00
Robinson—Principles of Mechanism..............................8vo, 3 00
Schwamb and Merrill—Elements of Mechanism..................8vo, 3 00
Smith (A. W.) and Marx—Machine Design..................8vo, 3 00
(R. S.)—Manual of Topographical Drawing. (McMillan.).......8vo, 2 50
Titsworth—Elements of Mechanical Drawing......... Oblong large 8vo, *1 25
Tracy and North—Descriptive Geometry..............(*In Press.*)
Warren—Elements of Descriptive Geometry, Shadows, and Perspective. 8vo, 3 50
Elements of Machine Construction and Drawing...........8vo, 7 50
Elements of Plane and Solid Free-hand Geometrical Drawing... 12mo, 1 00
General Problems of Shades and Shadows................8vo, 3 00
Manual of Elementary Problems in the Linear Perspective of Forms and
Shadows...............................12mo, 1 00
Manual of Elementary Projection Drawing....................12mo, 1 50
Plane Problems in Elementary Geometry.....................12mo, 1 25
Weisbach—Kinematics and Power of Transmission. (Herrmann and
Klein.)...8vo, 5 00
Wilson (H. M.)—Topographic, Trigonometric and Geodetic Surveying. 8vo, 3 50
(V. T.) Descriptive Geometry.................................8vo, *1 50
Free-hand Lettering......................................8vo, 1 00
Free-hand Perspective.................................. 8vo, 2 50
Woolf—Elementary Course in Descriptive Geometry..........Large 8vo, 3 00

ELECTRICITY AND PHYSICS.

Abegg—Theory of Electrolytic Dissociation. (von Ende.).........12mo, *1 25
Anthony and Ball—Lecture-notes on the Theory of Electrical Measurements...12mo, 1 00
and Brackett—Text-book of Physics. (Magie.).........Small 8vo, 3 00
Benjamin—History of Electricity.................................8vo, 3 00
Betts—Lead Refining and Electrolysis.................8vo, 4 00
Burgess and Le Chatelier—Measurement of High Temperatures. Third
Edition.......................................8vo, *4 00
Calderwood—Wiring Exercises (Loose Leaf Lab. Manual). (*In Preparation.*)
Classen—Quantitative Analysis by Electrolysis. (Hall)..........8vo, *2 50

Collins—Manual of Wireless Telegraphy and Telephony...........12mo, *$1 50
Crehore and Squier—Polarizing Photo-chronograph...............8vo, 3 00
Danneel—Electrochemistry. (Merriam.) 12mo, *1 25
Dawson—"Engineering" and Electric Traction Pocket-book .16mo, mor., 5 00
Dolezalek—Theory of the Lead Accumulator (Storage Battery). (von Ende.) 12mo, 2 50
Duhem—Thermodynamics and Chemistry. (Burgess.)..............8vo, 4 00
Flather—Dynamometers, and the Measurement of Power..........12mo, 3 00
Getman—Introduction to Physical Science...................12mo, *1 50
Gilbert—De Magnete. (Mottelay.)............................8vo, 2 50
Hanchett—Alternating Currents..............................12mo, *1 00
Hering—Ready Reference Tables (Conversion Factors).......16mo, mor., 2 50
Higbie—Electric Lighting and Distribution..........(*In Preparation.*)
Hobart and Ellis—High-speed Dynamo Electric Machinery........ 8vo, *6 00
Holman—Precision of Measurements. 8vo, 2 00
Telescope-Mirror-scale Method, Adjustments, and Tests... Large 8vo, 0 75
Hutchinson—High-Efficiency Electrical Illuminants and Illumination. Small 8vo, *2 50
Jones—Electric Ignition for Combustion Motors.................8vo, *4 00
Karapetoff—Elementary Electrical Testing (Loose Leaf Lab. Manual) 4to, Paper, *0 50
Single Exercises, each *0 02
Experimental Electrical Engineering:
Vol. I...8vo, *3 50
Vol. II..8vo, *2 50
Kinzbrunner—Testing of Continuous-current Machines..............8vo, 2 00
Koch—Mathematics of Applied Electricity ....Small 8vo, *3 00
Landauer—Spectrum Analysis. (Tingle.)........................ 8vo, 3 00
Lauffer—Electrical Injuries.................................16mo, *0 50
Resuscitation, from Electric and Traumatic Shock, etc. 16mo, *0 40
In lots of 100 Copies or more.................................. *0 30
Löb—Electrochemistry of Organic Compounds. (Lorenz.)...........8vo, 3 00
Lyndon—Development and Electrical Distribution of Water Power....8vo, *3 00
Lyons—Treatise on Electromagnetic Phenomena. Vols. I and II, 8vo, each, *6 00
Martin—Measurement of Induction Shocks 12mo, *1 25
Michie—Elements of Wave Motion Relating to Sound and Light. 8vo, *4 00
Morecroft—Electrical Machinery. Text-book .... Small 8vo, *1 50
Morgan—Physical Chemistry for Electrical Engineers.............12mo, *1 50
Norris—Introduction to the Study of Electrical Engineering........8vo, *2 50
Parshall and Hobart—Electric Machine Design .... 4to, half mor., *12 50
Reagan—Locomotives: Simple, Compound, and Electric ......Small 8vo, 3 50
Rodenhauser and Schoenawa—Electric Furnaces in the Iron and Steel Industry (Vom Baur.).. 8vo, *3 50
Rosenberg—Electrical Engineering. (Haldane Gee—Kinzbrunner.).8vo, *2 00
Ryan—Design of Electrical Machinery.
Vol. I. Direct Current Dynamos 8vo, *1 50
Vol. II. Alternating Current Transformers 8vo, *1 50
Vol. III. Alternators, Synchronous Motors, and Rotary Converters.8vo, *1 50
Schapper—Laboratory Guide for Students in Physical Chemistry .12mo, 1 00
Tillman—Elementary Lessons in Heat.............................. 8vo, *1 50
Timbie—Answers to Problems in Elements of Electricity.... 12mo, Paper, *0 25
Electrical Measurements, A. C. and D. C. (Loose Leaf Lab. Manual). 4to, Paper, *0 85
Single Exercises, each *0 02
Elements of Electricity...............................Small 8vo, *2 00
Essentials of Electricity.....................................12mo, *1 25
Introduction to Industrial Electricity.............(*In Preparation.*)
and Higbie—Alternating Currents...................(*In Preparation.*)
Tory and Pitcher—Manual of Laboratory Physics ....Small 8vo, 2 00
Ulke—Modern Electrolytic Copper Refining 8vo, 3 00
Waters—Commercial Dynamo Design................................ 8vo, *2 00

LAW.

Brennan—Hand-book of Useful Legal Information for Business Men. 16mo, mor., *5 00
Davis—Elements of Law...8vo, *2 50

DAVIS—Treatise on the Military Law of United States..............8vo, *$7 00
DUDLEY—Military Law and the Procedure of Courts-martial...Small 8vo, *2 50
MANUAL FOR COURTS MARTIAL..............................16mo, mor., 1 50
WAIT—Engineering and Architectural Jurisprudence.................8vo, 6 00
Sheep, 6 50
Law of Contracts..8vo, 3 00
Law of Operations Preliminary to Construction in Engineering and Architecture..8vo, 5 00
Sheep, 5 50

MATHEMATICS.

BAKER—Elliptic Functions..8vo, 1 50
BRIGGS—Elements of Plane Analytic Geometry. (BÔCHER.)..........12mo, 1 00
BUCHANAN—Plane and Spherical Trigonometry..........................8vo, *1 00
BURNHAM—Mechanics for Machinists.......................(*In Preparation.*)
Shop Mathematics for Machinists........................(*In Preparation.*)
BYERLY—Harmonic Functions..8vo, 1 00
CARMICHAEL—Relativity..8vo, 1 00
CHANDLER—Elements of the Infinitesimal Calculus...................12mo, 2 00
COFFIN—Vector Analysis..12mo, *2 50
COMPTON—Manual of Logarithmic Computations........................12mo, 1 50
DICKSON—College Algebra.....................................Small 8vo, *1 50
Elementary Theory of Equations.........................(*In Preparation.*)
Introduction to the Theory of Algebraic Equations............Small 8vo, *1 25
EMCH—Introduction to Projective Geometry and its Application.......8vo, 2 50
FISKE—Functions of a Complex Variable...............................8vo, 1 00
HALSTED—Elementary Synthetic Geometry...............................8vo, 1 50
Elements of Geometry..8vo, 1 75
Rational Geometry..12mo, *1 50
Synthetic Projective Geometry.......................................8vo, 1 00
HANCOCK—Lectures on the Theory of Elliptic Functions................8vo, *5 00
HYDE—Grassmann's Space Analysis.....................................8vo, 1 00
JOHNSON (J. B.) Three-place Logarithmic Tables: Vest-pocket size, paper, *0 15
100 copies, *5 00
Mounted on heavy cardboard, 8×10 inches, *0 25
10 copies, *2 00
(W. W.) Abridged Editions of Differential and Integral Calculus. Small 8vo, 1 vol., 2 50
Curve Tracing in Cartesian Co-ordinates.............................12mo, 1 00
Differential Equations...8vo, 1 00
Elementary Treatise on Differential Calculus.................Small 8vo, 1 50
Elementary Treatise on the Integral Calculus.................Small 8vo, 1 50
Theoretical Mechanics...12mo, *3 00
Theory of Errors and the Method of Least Squares....................12mo, 1 50
Treatise on Differential Calculus............................Small 8vo, 3 00
Treatise on the Integral Calculus............................Small 8vo, 3 00
Treatise on Ordinary and Partial Differential Equations......Small 8vo, 3 50
KARAPETOFF—Engineering Applications of Higher Mathematics:
Part I. Problems on Machine Design...........................Small 8vo, *0 75
KOCH—Mathematics of Applied Electricity......................Small 8vo, *3 00
LAPLACE—Philosophical Essay on Probabilities. (TRUSCOTT and EMORY.) 12mo, 2 00
LE MESSURIER—Key to Professor W. W. Johnson's Differential Equations. Small 8vo, *1 75
LUDLOW—Logarithmic and Trigonometric Tables..........................8vo, *1 00
and BASS—Elements of Trigonometry and Logarithmic and Other Tables..8vo, *3 00
Trigonometry and Tables published separately....................Each, *2 00
MACFARLANE—Vector Analysis and Quaternions...........................8vo, 1 00
McMAHON—Hyperbolic Functions...8vo, 1 00
MANNING—Irrational Numbers and their Representation by Sequences and Series...12mo, 1 25
MARSH—Industrial Mathematics.................................Small 8vo, *2 00
Technical Algebra. Part I...........................(*Ready*, Fall 1913)

MATERIALS OF ENGINEERING.

Bottler—German and American Varnish Making. (Sabin.) Small 8vo, *$3 50

Burr—Elasticity and Resistance of the Materials of Engineering. 8vo, 7 50

Church—Mechanics of Engineering. 8vo, 6 00

Mechanics of Solids (Being Parts I, II, III of Mechanics of Engineering). 8vo, 4 50

Fuller and Johnston—Applied Mechanics:

Vol. I. Theory of Statics and Kinetics. (Ready Fall 1913)

Vol. II. Strength of Materials. (In Preparation.)

Greene—Structural Mechanics. 8vo, *2 50

Holley—Analysis of Paint and Varnish Products. Small 8vo, *2 50

Lead and Zinc Pigments. Small 8vo, *3 00

Johnson (C. M.)—Rapid Methods for the Chemical Analysis of Special Steels, Steel-making Alloys and Graphite. Small 8vo, 3 00

(J. B.) Materials of Construction. 8vo, 6 00

Keep—Cast Iron. 8vo, 2 50

King—Elements of the Mechanics of Materials and of Power of Transmission. 8vo, *2 50

Lanza—Applied Mechanics. 8vo, 7 50

Lowe—Paints for Steel Structures. 12mo, 1 00

Maire—Modern Pigments and their Vehicles. 12mo, 2 00

Martin—Text-Book of Mechanics:

Vol. I. Statics. 12mo, *1 25

Vol. II. Kinematics and Kinetics. 12mo, *1 50

Vol. III. Mechanics of Materials. 12mo, *1 50

Vol. IV. Applied Statics. 12mo, *1 50

Maurer—Technical Mechanics. 8vo, 4 00

Merriman—Mechanics of Materials. 8vo, 5 00

Strength of Materials. 12mo, *1 00

Metcalf—Steel. A Manual for Steel-users. 12mo, 2 00

Mills—Materials of Construction. (In Press.)

Murdock—Strength of Materials. 12mo, *2 00

Sabin—Industrial and Artistic Technology of Paint and Varnish. 8vo, 3 00

Smith (A. W.)—Materials of Machines. 12mo, 1 00

(H. E.)—Strength of Material. 12mo, *1 25

Thurston—Materials of Engineering. 3 vols., 8vo, 8 00

Part I. Non-metallic Materials of Engineering. 8vo, 2 00

Part II. Iron and Steel. 8vo, 3 50

Part III. A Treatise on Brasses, Bronzes, and Other Alloys and their Constituents. 8vo, 2 50

Waterbury—Laboratory Manual for Testing Materials of Construction. 12mo, *1 50

Wood (De V.)—Elements of Analytical Mechanics. 8vo, 3 00

Treatise on the Resistance of Materials and an Appendix on the Preservation of Timber. 8vo, 2 00

(M. P.) Rustless Coatings. Corrosion and Electrolysis of Iron and Steel. 8vo, 4 00

STEAM-ENGINES AND BOILERS.

Abraham—Steam Economy in the Sugar Factory. (Bayle.) 12mo, *1 50

Berry—Temperature-entropy Diagram. Third Edition Revised and Enlarged. 12mo, 2 50

Carnot—Reflections on the Motive Power of Heat. (Thurston.) 12mo, 1 50

Chase—Art of Pattern Making. 12mo, 2 50

Creighton—Steam-engine and other Heat Motors. 8vo, 5 00

Dawson—"Engineering" and Electric Traction Pocket-book. 16mo, mor. 5 00

Gebhardt—Steam Power Plant Engineering. Fourth Edition. 8vo, *4 00

Goss—Locomotive Performance. 8vo, 5 00

Hemenway—Indicator Practice and Steam-engine Economy. 12mo, 2 00

Hirshfeld and Barnard—Heat Power Engineering. 8vo, *5 00

Hutton—Heat and Heat-engines. 8vo, 5 00

Mechanical Engineering of Power Plants. 8vo, 5 00

KENT—Steam Boiler Economy ... 8vo, $4 00
KING—Steam Engineering ... 8vo, *4 00
KNEASS—Practice and Theory of the Injector ... 8vo, 1 50
MACCORD—Slide-valves ... 8vo, 2 00
MEYER—Modern Locomotive Construction ... 4to, 10 00
MILLER, BERRY, and RILEY—Problems in Thermodynamics ... 8vo, paper, 0 75
MOYER—Steam Turbines ... 8vo, 4 00
PEABODY—Manual of the Steam-engine Indicator ... 12mo, 1 50
  Tables of the Properties of Steam and Other Vapors and Temperature-Entropy Table ... 8vo, 1 00
  Thermodynamics of the Steam-engine and Other Heat-engines ... 8vo, 5 00
  Thermodynamics of the Steam Turbine ... 8vo, *3 00
  Valve-gears for Steam-engines ... 8vo, 2 50
  and MILLER—Steam-boilers ... 8vo, 4 00
PERKINS—Introduction to General Thermodynamics ... 12mo, *1 50
PUPIN—Thermodynamics of Reversible Cycles in Gases and Saturated Vapors. (OSTERBERG.) ... 12mo, 1 25
RANDALL—Heat. A Manual for Technical and Industrial Students. Small, 8vo, *1 50
  Exercises in Heat (Loose Leaf Lab. Manual). Single Exercises, each. *0 02
REAGAN—Locomotives: Simple, Compound, and Electric. New Edition. Small 8vo, 3 50
SINCLAIR—Locomotive Engine Running and Management ... 12mo, 2 00
SMART—Handbook of Engineering Laboratory Practice ... 12mo, 2 50
SNOW—Steam-boiler Practice ... 8vo, 3 00
SPANGLER—Notes on Thermodynamics ... 12mo, 1 00
  Valve-gears ... 8vo, 2 50
  GREENE, and MARSHALL—Elements of Steam-engineering ... 8vo, 3 00
THOMAS—Steam-turbines ... 8vo, 4 00
THURSTON—Manual of Steam-boilers, their Designs, Construction, and Operation ... 8vo, 5 00
  Manual of the Steam-engine ... 2 vols., 8vo, 10 00
    Part I. History, Structure, and Theory ... 8vo, 6 00
    Part II. Design, Construction, and Operation ... 8vo, 6 00
WEHRENFENNIG—Analysis and Softening of Boiler Feed-water. (PATTERSON.) ... 8vo, 4 00
WEISBACH—Heat, Steam, and Steam-engines. (DU BOIS.) ... 8vo, 5 00
WHITMAN—Heat for Students of Household Science. ... (*In Preparation.*)
WOOD—Thermodynamics, Heat Motors, and Refrigerating Machines. 8vo, 4 00

MECHANICS PURE AND APPLIED.

BURNHAM—Mechanics for Machinists ... (*In Preparation.*)
CHURCH—Mechanics of Engineering ... 8vo, 6 00
  Mechanics of Solids (Being Parts I, II, III of Mechanics of Engineering). 8vo, 4 50
  Mechanics of Fluids (Being Part IV of Mechanics of Engineering). 8vo, 3 00
  Mechanics of Internal Work ... 8vo, *1 50
  Notes and Examples in Mechanics ... 8vo, 2 00
DANA—Text-book of Elementary Mechanics for Colleges and Schools ... 12mo, 1 50
DU BOIS—Elementary Principles of Mechanics:
  Vol. I. Kinematics ... 8vo, 3 50
  Vol. II. Statics ... 8vo, 4 00
  Mechanics of Engineering. Vol. I ... Small 4to, 7 50
    Vol. II ... Small 4to, 10 00
FULLER and JOHNSTON—Applied Mechanics:
  Vol. I. Theory of Statics and Kinetics ... (*Ready*, Fall 1913)
  Vol. II. Strength of Materials ... (*In Preparation.*)
GREENE—Structural Mechanics ... 8vo, *2 50
HARTMANN—Elementary Mechanics for Engineering Students ... 12mo, *1 25
JAMES—Kinematics of a Point and the Rational Mechanics of a Particle. Small 8vo, 2 00
JAMESON—Elementary Practical Mechanics ... 12mo, *1 50
JOHNSON—Theoretical Mechanics ... 12mo, *3 00
KING—Elements of the Mechanics of Materials and of Power of Transmission ... 8vo, *2 50

KOTTCAMP—Exercises for the Applied Mechanics Laboratory, Loose Leaf Laboratory Manual . . . . Oblong 4to, paper, *$1 0
LANZA—Applied Mechanics 8vo, 7 50
MARTIN—Text Book of Mechanics:
Vol. I. Statics 12mo, *1 25
Vol. II. Kinematics and Kinetics 12mo, *1 50
Vol. III. Mechanics of Materials 12mo, *1 50
Vol. IV. Applied Statics 12mo, *1 50
MAURER—Technical Mechanics 8vo, 4 00
MERRIMAN—Elements of Mechanics 12mo, *1 00
Mechanics of Materials 8vo, 5 00
MICHIE—Elements of Analytical Mechanics 8vo, *4 00
ROBINSON—Principles of Mechanism 8vo, *3 00
SANBORN—Mechanics Problems . . . . Small 8vo, *1 50
SCHWAMB and MERRILL—Elements of Mechanism 8vo, 3 00
WOOD—Elements of Analytical Mechanics 8vo, 3 00
Principles of Elementary Mechanics 12mo, 1 25

MEDICAL.

ABDERHALDEN—Physiological Chemistry in Thirty Lectures. (HALL and DEFREN.) 8vo, *5 00
VON BEHRING—Suppression of Tuberculosis. (Bolduan.) 12mo, 1 00
BOLDUAN—Immune Sera 12mo, *1 50
BORDET—Studies in Immunity. (GAY.) 8vo, 6 00
CHAPIN—The Sources and Modes of Infection . . . . Small 8vo, *3 00
COHNHEIM—Enzymes 12mo, *1 50
DAVENPORT—Statistical Methods with Special Reference to Biological Variations . . . . 16mo, mor., 1 50
DE FURSAC—Manual of Psychiatry. (ROSANOFF and COLLINS.) . Small 8vo, *2 50
EFFRONT—Enzymes and Their Applications. (PRESCOTT.) 8vo, 3 00
EHRLICH—Studies on Immunity. (BOLDUAN.) 8vo, 6 00
EULER—General Chemistry of the Enzymes. (POPE.) 8vo, *3 00
FISCHER—Nephritis . . . . Small 8vo, *2 50
Oedema 8vo, *2 00
Physiology of Alimentation . . . . Small 8vo, *2 00
FULLER—Qualitative Analysis of Medicinal Preparations 12mo, *1 50
HAMMARSTEN—Text-book on Physiological Chemistry. (MANDEL.) 8vo, *4 00
JACKSON—Directions for Laboratory Work in Physiological Chemistry . 8vo, 1 25
LASSAR-COHN—Praxis of Urinary Analysis. (LORENZ.) 12mo, 1 00
LAUFFER—Electrical Injuries 16mo, *0 50
MANDEL—Hand-book for the Bio-Chemical Laboratory 12mo, 1 50
MARTIN—Measurement of Induction Shocks 12mo, *1 25
NELSON—Analysis of Drugs and Medicines 12mo, *3 00
PAULI—Physical Chemistry in the Service of Medicine. (FISCHER.) . . 12mo, *1 25
POZZI-ESCOT—Toxins and Venoms and their Antibodies. (COHN.) . . 12mo, *1 00
ROSTOSKI—Serum Diagnosis. (BOLDUAN.) 12mo, 1 00
RUDDIMAN—Incompatibilities in Prescriptions 8vo, 2 00
Whys in Pharmacy 12mo, 1 00
SALKOWSKI—Physiological and Pathological Chemistry. (ORNDORFF.) . 8vo, 2 50
SATTERLEE—Outlines of Human Embryology 12mo, *1 25
SMITH—Lecture Notes on Chemistry for Dental Students 8vo, *2 50
WHIPPLE—Typhoid Fever . . . . Small 8vo, *3 00
WOODHULL—Military Hygiene for Officers of the Line . . . . . Small 8vo, *1 50
Personal Hygiene 12mo, *1 00
WORCESTER and ATKINSON—Small Hospitals Establishment and Maintenance, and Suggestions for Hospital Architecture, with Plans for a Small Hospital 12mo, 1 25

METALLURGY.

BETTS—Lead Refining by Electrolysis 8vo, 4 00
BOLLAND—Encyclopedia of Founding and Dictionary of Foundry Terms used in the Practice of Moulding 12mo, 3 00
Iron Founder 12mo, 2 50

BORCHERS—Metallurgy. (HALL and HAYWARD.) 8vo, *$3 00
BURGESS and LE CHATELIER—Measurement of High Temperatures. Third Edition 8vo, *4 00
DOUGLAS—Untechnical Addresses on Technical Subjects 12mo, 1 00
GOESEL—Minerals and Metals: A Reference Book . . . . 16mo, mor., 3 00
ILES—Lead-smelting 12mo, *2 50
JOHNSON—Rapid Methods for the Chemical Analysis of Special Steels, Steel-making Alloys and Graphite . . . . Small 8vo, 3 00
KEEP—Cast Iron 8vo, 2 50
METCALF—Steel. A Manual for Steel-users 12mo, 2 00
MINET—Production of Aluminum and its Industrial Use. (WALDO.) . . 12mo, 2 50
PALMER—Foundry Practice . . . . Small 8vo, *2 00
PRICE and MEADE—Technical Analysis of Brass 12mo, *2 00
RODENHAUSER and SCHOENAWA—Electric Furnaces in the Iron and Steel Industry. (VOM BAUR.) 8vo, *3 50
RUER—Elements of Metallography. (MATHEWSON.) 8vo, *3 00
SMITH—Materials of Machines 12mo, 1 00
TATE and STONE—Foundry Practice 12mo, 2 00
THURSTON—Materials of Engineering. In Three Parts 8vo, 8 00
Part I. Non-metallic Materials of Engineering, see Civil Engineering, page 9.
Part II. Iron and Steel 8vo, 3 50
Part III. A Treatise on Brasses, Bronzes, and Other Alloys and Their Constituents 8vo, 2 50
ULKE—Modern Electrolytic Copper Refining 8vo, 3 00
WEST—American Foundry Practice 12mo, 2 50
Moulders' Text Book 12mo, 2 50

MILITARY AND MARINE ENGINEERING.

ARMY AND NAVY.

BERNADOU—Smokeless Powder, Nitro-cellulose, and the Theory of the Cellulose Molecule 12mo, 2 50
CHASE—Art of Pattern Making 12mo, 2 50
Screw Propellers and Marine Propulsion 8vo, 3 00
CLOKE—Enlisted Specialists' Examiner 8vo, *2 00
Gunner's Examiner 8vo, *1 50
CRAIG—Azimuth 4to, 3 50
CREHORE and SQUIER—Polarizing Photo-chronograph 8vo, 3 00
DAVIS—Elements of Law 8vo, *2 50
Treatise on the Military Law of United States 8vo, *7 00
DUDLEY—Military Law and the Procedure of Courts-martial . . . . Small 8vo, *2 50
DURAND—Resistance and Propulsion of Ships 8vo, 5 00
DYER—Handbook of Light Artillery 12mo, *3 00
DYSON—Screw Propellers and Estimation of Power . . . . (*In Press.*)
EISSLER—Modern High Explosives 8vo, 4 00
FIEBEGER—Text-book on Field Fortification . . . . Small 8vo, *2 00
HAMILTON and BOND—The Gunner's Catechism 18mo, 1 00
HOFF—Elementary Naval Tactics 8vo, *1 50
INGALLS—Handbook of Problems in Direct Fire 8vo, 4 00
Interior Ballistics 8vo, *3 00
LISSAK—Ordnance and Gunnery 8vo, *6 00
LUDLOW—Logarithmic and Trigonometric Tables 8vo, *1 00
LYONS—Treatise on Electromagnetic Phenomena. Vols. I. and II., 8vo, each, *6 00
MAHAN—Permanent Fortifications. (MERCUR) . . . . 8vo, half mor., *7 50
MANUAL FOR COURTS-MARTIAL . . . . 16mo, mor., 1 50
MERCUR—Attack of Fortified Places 12mo, *2 00
Elements of the Art of War 8vo, *4 00
NIXON—Adjutants' Manual 24mo, 1 00
PEABODY—Computations for Marine Engine 8vo, *2 50
Naval Architecture 8vo, 7 50
Propellers 8vo, 1 25
PHELPS—Practical Marine Surveying 8vo, *2 50
PUTNAM—Nautical Charts 8vo, 2 00
RUST—Ex-meridian Altitude, Azimuth and Star-Finding Tables 8vo, 5 00

Selkirk—Catechism of Manual of Guard Duty..................24mo, *$0 50
Sharpe—Art of Subsisting Armies in War..................18mo, mor., 1 50
Taylor—Speed and Power of Ships. 2 vols. Text 8vo, plates oblong 4to, *7 50
Tupes and Poole—Manual of Bayonet Exercise and Musketry Fencing. 24mo, leather, *0 50
Weaver—Military Explosives..................8vo, *3 00
Woodhull—Military Hygiene for Officers of the Line..........Small 8vo, *1 50

MINERALOGY.

Browning—Introduction to Rarer Elements..................8vo, *1 50
Brush—Manual of Determinative Mineralogy. (Penfield.)..........8vo, 4 00
Butler—Pocket Hand-book of Blowpipe Analysis..................16mo, *0 75
Pocket Hand-book of Minerals..................16mo, mor., 3 00
Chester—Catalogue of Minerals..................8vo, paper, 1 00
Cloth, 1 25
Crane—Gold and Silver..................8vo, *5 00
Dana—First Appendix to Dana's New "System of Mineralogy.". Large 8vo, 1 00
Manual of Mineralogy. (Ford.)..................12mo, *2 00
Minerals, and How to Study Them..................12mo, 1 50
System of Mineralogy..................Large 8vo, half leather, 12 50
Text-book of Mineralogy..................8vo, 4 00
Douglas—Untechnical Addresses on Technical Subjects..................12mo, 1 00
Eakle—Mineral Tables..................8vo, 1 25
Eckel—Building Stones and Clays..................8vo, *3 00
Goesel—Minerals and Metals: A Reference Book..................16mo, mor., 3 00
Groth—The Optical Properties of Crystals. (Jackson.)..................8vo, *3 50
Introduction to Chemical Crystallography. (Marshall.)..................12mo, 1 25
Hayes—Handbook for Field Geologists..................16mo, mor., *1 50
Iddings—Igneous Rocks..................8vo, 5 00
Rock Minerals..................8vo, 5 00
Johannsen—Determination of Rock-forming Minerals in Thin Sections, 8vo, With Thumb Index, 5 00
Lewis—Determinative Mineralogy..................Small 8vo, *1 50
McLeod—The A. B. C. of the Useful Minerals..........(*Ready, Fall 1913*)
Martin—Laboratory Guide to Qualitative Analysis with the Blowpipe. 12mo, *0 60
Merrill—Non-metallic Minerals: Their Occurrence and Uses..........8vo, 4 00
Stones for Building and Decoration..................8vo, 5 00
Penfield—Notes on Determinative Mineralogy and Record of Mineral Tests..................8vo, paper, *0 50
Tables of Minerals, Including the Use of Minerals and Statistics of Domestic Production..................8vo, 1 00
Pirsson—Rocks and Rock Minerals..................12mo, *2 50
Richards—Synopsis of Mineral Characters..................12mo, mor., *1 25
Ries—Building Stones and Clay Products..................8vo, *3 00
Clays: Their Occurrence, Properties and Uses..................8vo, *5 00
and Leighton—History of the Clay-working Industry of the United States..................8vo, *2 50
Rowe—Practical Mineralogy Simplified..................12mo, *1 25
Tillman—Text-book of Important Minerals and Rocks..................8vo, *2 00
Washington—Manual of the Chemical Analysis of Rocks..........8vo, 2 00

MINING.

Beard—Mine Gases and Explosions..................Small 8vo, *3 00
Brunswig—Explosives. (Munroe and Kibler.)..........Ready Fall, 1912
Brunton and Davis—Modern Practice in Tunneling.......(*In Preparation.*)
Crane—Gold and Silver..................8vo, *5 00
Index of Mining Engineering Literature, Vol. I..................8vo, *4 00
8vo, mor., *5 00
Vol. II..................8vo, *3 00
8vo, mor., *4 00
Ore Mining Methods..................8vo, *3 00
Dana and Saunders—Rock Drilling..................8vo, *4 00
Douglas—Untechnical Addresses on Technical Subjects..........12mo, $1 00

Eissler—Modern High Explosives.......................................8vo, 4 00
Gilbert, Wightman and Saunders—Subways and Tunnels of New York. 8vo, *4 00
Goesel—Minerals and Metals: A Reference Book.............16mo, mor., 3 00
Ihlseng—Manual of Mining.......................................8vo, 5 00
Iles—Lead Smelting...12mo, *2 50
Peele—Compressed Air Plant.....................................8vo, *3 50
Riemer—Shaft Sinking under Difficult Conditions. (Corning and Peele.) 8vo, 3 00
Weaver—Military Explosives.....................................8vo, *3 00
Wilson—Cyanide Processes.......................................12mo, 1 50
Hydraulic and Placer Mining....................................12mo, 2 50

SANITARY SCIENCE.

Bashore—Outlines of Practical Sanitation.......................12mo, *1 25
Sanitation of a Country House..................................12mo, 1 00
Sanitation of Recreation Camps and Parks.......................12mo, 1 00
Folwell—Sewerage. (Designing, Construction, and Maintenance.)...8vo, 3 00
Water-supply Engineering.......................................8vo, 4 00
Fowler—Sewage Works Analyses...................................12mo, 2 00
Fuertes—Water-filtration Works.................................12mo, 2 50
Gerhard—Guide to Sanitary Inspections..........................12mo, 1 50
Modern Baths and Bath Houses...................................8vo, *3 00
Sanitation of Public Buildings.................................12mo, 1 50
Gerhard—The Water Supply, Sewerage, and Plumbing of Modern City Buildings.......................................8vo, *4 00
Hazen—Clean Water and How to Get It......................Small 8vo, 1 50
Filtration of Public Water-supplies............................8vo, 3 00
Hooker—Chloride of Lime in Sanitation..........................8vo, 3 00
Kinnicutt, Winslow and Pratt—Sewage Disposal...................8vo, *3 00
Leach-Winton—Inspection and Analysis of Food. Third Edition, Revised and Enlarged by Dr. Andrew L. Winton......................8vo, 7 50
Mason—Examination of Water. (Chemical and Bacteriological.)....12mo, 1 25
Water-supply. (Considered principally from a Sanitary Standpoint.) 8vo, 4 00
Merriman—Elements of Sanitary Engineering......................8vo, *2 00
Ogden—Sewer Construction.......................................8vo, 3 00
Sewer Design...12mo, 2 00
and Cleveland—Practical Methods of Sewage Disposal for Residences, Hotels and Institutions..............................8vo, *1 50
Parsons—Disposal of Municipal Refuse...........................8vo, 2 00
Prescott and Winslow—Elements of Water Bacteriology, with Special Reference to Sanitary Water Analysis. Third Edition Rewritten. Small 8vo, *1 75
Price—Factory Sanitation.............................(*In Preparation.*)
Handbook on Sanitation...12mo, *1 50
Richards—Conservation by Sanitation............................8vo, 2 50
Cost of Cleanness..12mo, 1 00
Cost of Food. A Study in Dietaries.............................12mo, 1 00
Cost of Living as Modified by Sanitary Science.................12mo, 1 00
Cost of Shelter..12mo, 1 00
Laboratory Notes on Industrial Water Analysis..................8vo, *0 50
Richards and Woodman—Air, Water, and Food from a Sanitary Standpoint..8vo 2 00
Richey—Plumbers', Steam-fitters', and Tinners' Edition (Building Mechanics' Ready Reference Series)..........................16mo, mor., *1 50
Rideal—Disinfection and the Preservation of Food................8vo, 4 00
Soper—Air and Ventilation of Subways...........................12mo, 2 50
Turneaure and Russell—Public Water-supplies....................8vo, $5 00
Venable—Garbage Crematories in America.........................8vo, 2 00
Method and Devices for Bacterial Treatment of Sewage............8vo, 3 00
Ward and Whipple—Freshwater Biology..........................(*In Press.*)
Whipple—Microscopy of Drinking-water...........................8vo, 3 50
Typhoid Fever...Small 8vo, *3 00
Value of Pure Water.......................................Small 8vo, 1 00

MISCELLANEOUS.

BURT—Railway Station Service..12mo, *2 00
CHAPIN—How to Enamel..12mo, *1 00
FERREL—Popular Treatise on the Winds..8vo, 4 00
FITZGERALD—Boston Machinist..18mo, 1 00
FRITZ—Autobiography of John..8vo, *2 00
GANNETT—Statistical Abstract of the World..24mo, 0 75
GREEN—Elementary Hebrew Grammar..12mo, 1 25
HAINES—American Railway Management..12mo, 2 50
HANAUSEK—The Microscopy of Technical Products. (WINTON.)........8vo, 5 00
JACOBS—Betterment Briefs. A Collection of Published Papers on Organized Industrial Efficiency..8vo, 3 50
METCALFE—Cost of Manufactures, and the Administration of Workshops. 8vo, 5 00
PARKHURST—Applied Methods of Scientific Management........................8vo, *2 00
PUTNAM—Nautical Charts..8vo, 2 00
RICKETTS—History of Rensselaer Polytechnic Institute, 1824–1894. Small 8vo, 3 00
ROTCH and PALMER—Charts of the Atmosphere for Aeronauts and Aviators. Oblong 4to, *2 00
ROTHERHAM—Emphasised New Testament........................Large 8vo, 2 00
RUST—Ex-Meridian Altitude, Azimuth and Star-finding Tables........8vo, 5 00
STANDAGE—Decoration of Wood, Glass, Metal, etc........................12mo, 2 00
WESTERMAIER—Compendium of General Botany. (SCHNEIDER.)........8vo, 2 00
WINSLOW—Elements of Applied Microscopy..12mo, 1 50

[redacted]

www.ingramcontent.com/pod-product-compliance
Lightning Source LLC
LaVergne TN
LVHW012205040326
832903LV00003B/135
* 9 7 8 1 3 5 7 6 4 3 2 5 6 *